DISABILITY INCOME

THE SALE
THE PRODUCT
THE MARKET

2nd Edition

by
Jeff Sadler

NATIONAL
UNDERWRITER

The National Underwriter Company/505 Gest Street/Cincinnati, Ohio 45203

ISBN: 0-87218-146-4

Printed in U. S. A.

DEDICATION

This book is dedicated to the memory of my father, Raymond A. Sadler, RHU, the finest disability income specialist I'll ever know.

ACKNOWLEDGEMENT

A book often appears with only one author listed, but there are many individuals who contribute in some way to its successful completion. The author wishes to acknowledge the assistance of my wife Eileen, Billy Wells, Bob Parr, Tim Murray, Keith Hickerson, Maureen Geyer-Yelton, RHU, and the editors of this volume, Jaclyn Meder Ruzsa and Darlene K. Chandler, J.D., CLU, ChFC. To all, my heartfelt thanks. To the readers of this book, I hope these words spur you on to higher levels of achievement in the disability income market.

Jeff Sadler began his insurance career with Paul Revere Life Insurance Company in 1975 as an underwriter in the disability income brokerage division. He moved on to the sales department in 1977 working in disability income product development and marketing. In 1979, he transferred to the Fort Lauderdale-Miami brokerage field office where he was named national representative of the month in July, 1980.

In March, 1981, Jeff joined Monarch Life to further develop its national brokerage system and eventually to write its new disability income portfolio, "Advantage," introduced to the field in the spring of 1982. After the initial national training phase of this product introduction, he established a new brokerage sales office for Monarch in Orlando, Florida and quickly built it into the company's third largest office in 1983.

In April, 1984, Jeff teamed up with Financial Security Corporation of America to conduct national training and marketing seminars in the sale of disability income. In addition, in 1986, he wrote another complete disability income portfolio for 20th Century Life Insurance Company of Durham, North Carolina.

In June, 1989, he co-founded, with his father, Sadler Disability Services, Inc., specializing in agent training, joint field work and product development in both the disability income and long term care markets. In November, 1990, he also co-founded Continuing Education Corporation of America, teaching seminars to agents to help them obtain their state-required continuing education credits.

Jeff has won the 1987 Distinguished Service Award from the National Association of Health Underwriters and the 1990 Stanley Greenspun Memorial Health Insurance Person of the Year Award from the Gold Coast Association of Health Underwriters. He is a past president of the Florida Association of Health Underwriters, the Central Florida Association of Health Underwriters, and the Central Florida General Agents and Managers Association.

TABLE OF CONTENTS

A SHORT HISTORY OF DISABILITY INCOME

In the beginning, there were the Chinese, who developed a method for insuring losses on a river voyage. Nine hundred years before the birth of Christ, the Rhodian Sea Law took this insuring idea to the high seas. The Romans liked the Rhodian Sea Law so much they adopted it themselves. The Greeks insured their warriors against sickness and later the Dutch insured their soldiers against catastrophic loss of sight or limbs. The English, a step ahead of the Dutch, provided the first accident and sickness protection along with their customary casualty coverage standards. England then brought the idea to the colonies in America where the Massachusetts Health Insurance Company offered the first disability income policy and the Franklin Health Insurance Company offered the first accident policy. Fraternal organizations offered the first American accident and sickness policy with the first noncancelable policy being offered in 1907. "Own occupation" protection grew after World War II and residual disability was introduced in the mid 1970's.

For those who wish to know a few more details about the evolution of the disability income policy, the following paragraphs flesh out the previous one.

The law of large numbers is the governing principle behind any insurance venture. If you spread the risk among many people, this cooperative effort of sharing a loss means a slight financial setback for many rather than an economic disaster for one.

The Chinese are said to have started the custom of spreading the risk as a result of the calamitous river rapids that had to be negotiated by their merchants. Rather than loading all of the cargo onto one boat, merchandise for each merchant was spread out over several boats. If one boat was lost, the losses were minimal to each merchant.

The same nation that produced Confucius also first mastered the simple concept of spreading the risk.

This type of marine insurance laid the groundwork for the later development of insurance against other types of loss such as the accident and sickness of a breadwinner.

Rhodes, a tiny isle in the Aegean Sea, adopted a similar concept and brought the idea to Europe (and, eventually, to America). Heavy storms forced many of its ships to lighten their load and valuable goods were thrown over the side in an attempt to save the vessel. The Rhodian Sea Law, put into effect around 900 B.C., called for merchants to "come into contribution together with the value of the ship and the goods that are saved."

PROLOGUE

The Romans, long a dominant force in Europe, and parts of Asia and North Africa, saw the Rhodian Sea Law as a practical method of sharing the risk of losses and made it part of their own Justinian Code in 583 A. D. It is from the Italian word "polizza," a promise to pay, that the word "policy" derives.

The Romans started a system whereby all members of the artisan guild contributed to a fund that was used to provide cash payments to families of members who were injured or ill. Sound familiar?

The Greeks, never ones to take a back seat to the Romans, established a program whereby a mariner who came down with an illness during a voyage, was sent ashore and given lodging, candlelight and a ship boy to attend him until he recovered. This was disability insurance that paid off in the form of actual provision of necessities rather than monetary payment.

The practice of disability insurance traveled throughout Europe with these voyagers. In 1663, the Dutch, frequent travelers themselves, provided coverage for soldiers at war in the form of the first known "loss of use" benefit prevalent in noncancelable policies today. These soldiers were insured against the loss of sight in either or both eyes, or loss of both hands, or both feet, or both arms or both legs.

Where there is insurance coverage being provided, can an underwriter be far behind? Lloyd's of London had its start in 17th century England, where private investors signed their names as guarantors of a risk — for a fee, of course. Lloyd's marked its 300th anniversary in 1989 and, though its underwriters have taken some losses in recent years, they still provide individual underwriting for almost any type of risk.

In England in 1757, the British Parliament passed a law making sickness coverage available for stevedores. England also formed the first fire insurance company in response to a major fire in London which destroyed some 14,000 buildings and left 200,000 people homeless. It was a fire insurance company that was started by Benjamin Franklin in Philadelphia in 1752, known as the Philadelphia Contributionship for the Insurance of Houses from Loss by Fire (also called the "Hand In Hand Association"). It remains the oldest insurance company in the United States.

The shift from an agricultural society to an industrial one paved the way for the modern disability income insurance policy. Employees in the industrial sector needed protection for earnings against the hazards of illness and injury. The industrial revolution began in England and moved initially to the northern portions of the United States.

In the 1800's as the Industrial Revolution seized America and led it inexorably towards Civil War, disability income began to thrive. "Establishment funds," the precursor of disability policies, furnished small cash payments to employees who were sick or hurt. In 1847, the Massachusetts Health Insurance Company was formed and sold the first disability income policy.

The Franklin Health Insurance Company, also of Massachusetts, sold the first accident-only plan in 1850. In this same decade, the first travel accident policy was sold by the Railway Passengers Assurance Company. The Travelers Insurance Company of Hartford was founded shortly thereafter on this same premise.

The Industrial Revolution created industries in which some of the labor performed was hazardous because of the machinery being utilized. Injuries increased and employers turned to insurance companies for protection against workers' lawsuits and the resulting judgments against the employer.

As a result, between 1900 and 1910, the employer's liability laws were adopted by many states, but left something to be desired for the injured employee since the burden of proving employer negligence rested solely with the worker.

The first workers compensation laws were enacted in 1911, providing coverage for job related injury and sickness and relieving the employee from the burden of proving negligence.

In 1915, group disability income took its first bow. It was patterned after the already available group life insurance program. Employers began to offer group disability and, in conjunction with the new Workers' Compensation laws, settled into a fair and reasonable disability income program for employees.

The Social Security Act, passed in 1935 during Franklin Delano Roosevelt's New Deal, put into effect an old age, survivors and disability income (OASDI) plan for most Americans. World War II brought wage controls that caused labor unions and employers to examine employee benefit programs more closely as an important element of an employee's total compensation package. Disability income (at least, short-term disability income) was often included in the labor negotiations performed on behalf of the employees.

Today's individual disability product began to take shape after World War II, but had its roots in the prior history of the disability income insurance plan.

"Own occupation" coverage, a job-specific definition of total disability, came into its own in the 1950's with a gradual enhancement of the language following over the next two decades. This tinkering finally resulted in "lifetime own occupation" protection in the 1970's under which the disability income contract contained only one simple definition of total disability; that an individual be unable to perform the duties of his or her regular occupation.

"Residual disability" coverage was introduced in the early to mid 1970's, generally under more controversial circumstances than one might suspect in view of its widespread availability and importance in disability income contracts today. It was a natural outgrowth of an earlier "partial disability" benefit which paid benefits over a much shorter period of time. (For more on residual disability, and its history, see Chapter 14, Personal Disability Income Policies: What The Contractual Language Really Means.)

The "cost of living rider" concept was first introduced in the early 1970's, but went largely unnoticed. A period of high inflation during which the prime rate went as high as 21 percent in the late 1970's and early 1980's revived this benefit as an alternative to a level benefit claim check.

The "social insurance offset" riders appeared in the latter part of the 1970's as well. These optional benefits offered a solution to programming problems created by the potential availability of Social Security disability benefits, workers compensation and other federal, state and local programs providing disability benefits. (For more on the origins of this rider, see Chapter 5, The Art Of Programming Benefits.)

The industry has come a long way from its ancient Chinese origins in substance and in style, but the basic underlying concept remains the same: insuring against the loss of valuable property, in this case, the income of the breadwinner.

The historical data in this Prologue was taken from several sources including the 3rd edition of the *Life and Health Insurance Handbook* (1973); the Insurance Information Institute's *Sharing the Risk*, 3rd edition, 1989; *The Complete Guide to Health Insurance* (1988); and an article entitled "The Historical Background of Health Insurance" from Monarch Life Insurance Company's *Health Underwriting Manual*.

Part I:
THE SALE AND SERVICE

Part 1 reviews the concept of disability income and follows the sales process from initial identification of qualified prospects through the basic sales presentation, underwriting of the risk, delivery of the policy, and after-sale service and follow-up.

Chapter 1

DISABILITY INCOME: A MARKET IN NEED

Some of the leading consumer publications are telling the working public the story of disability income insurance.

"Even if the odds favor you, if you work you shouldn't risk going without a long-term disability insurance policy to replace lost income."[1]

Money Magazine, June, 1994.

"Unless you can afford to live comfortably without holding down a job — in which case, why are you working? — you need to have some disability insurance. It's as simple as that. You've got to have a backstop to help pay your bills if you get hurt, especially if you're single or if you depend on only one salary."[2]

Smart Money, August, 1993.

"Affordable Insurance That Works When You Can't" (Headline of article from Personal Business column).[3]

Business Week, August 29, 1994.

"Many do not plan for the possibility that they will suffer a debilitating accident or illness during their working years... A young professional with several children, for example, should consider disability insurance a necessity."[4]

Consumer's Research, February, 1993.

With all of this independent publicity, disability income insurance seemingly would be coverage nearly everyone who works and earns an income would own. This is not true. Eighty percent of the work force remains untouched by individual disability income coverage.

Why haven't more consumers demanded this product? Why haven't insurance agents sold more of it? Why haven't insurance companies marketed it more conspicuously? Good questions. If ever there was a market in need, this is it. This chapter will try to provide some answers.

CONSUMERS

We are all consumers. Yet how many times have you thought about disability? Or that a serious illness or sickness might stop your income? We are indestructible, of course, especially when we are young. Nothing can happen. Sickness is something that our grandparents go through. Accidents are news items we read in the paper.

To be fair, none of us are as oriented to disability income insurance as we are to other types of protection. In Florida (as well as other states), one needs automobile insurance to renew his car registration. If one has a mortgage, the bank insists on homeowners coverage. We certainly know about health insurance, especially after the 1993-94 national reform debates in Washington, D.C. Finally, haven't we all been told about the importance of life insurance? Even our parents have talked about that subject.

We hear about life insurance, but not disability insurance. Why? One reason may be that significant advances in medicine have occurred only recently. The big killers — heart disease, hypertension, cancer, diabetes and cardiovascular disease are "controllable" to the point where, instead of death, the victim may face a long term disability.[5] Life insurance purchased to protect against death from any one of these catastrophes provides financial help only if an option called an "accelerated death benefit" is attached to the plan. (This provision calls for an earlier payout of a portion of the policy face amount in the event of certain catastrophic disabilities.) Otherwise, the life insurance face value sits, unattainable, until death.

Articles like those quoted at the outset of this chapter reflect an increasing awareness of disability and the threat it presents. Third party influence was sporadic at best prior to the 1980s. On occasion, a Sylvia Porter column or a letter in "Dear Abby" would discuss the potential for financial disaster caused by a sickness or injury. But it was not until *Consumer Reports* magazine published its "landmark" article in March, 1983 that a relative avalanche of information about this subject started.

The March, 1983 article about disability income was a first for *Consumer Reports* on this subject. Insurance analysts and industry executives were stunned by the amount of erroneous and even misleading information contained in the report. Yet few can argue about its impact on the average consumer who subscribed to the magazine.[6]

For the first time, many people, unaware of disability income's existence, read, "CU [Consumers Union] usually recommends life insurance only for people with dependents, but we encourage the purchase of disability income insurance by almost anyone who earns a fairly good income and who can afford the coverage."

In preparation for this article, Consumers Union contacted a number of disability insurance advocates, myself among them, for assistance. While we applauded and encouraged the effort to increase public awareness of this product and the protection it can provide, we cautioned *against* using a simple rating system (such as Consumers Union uses with comparisons of such items as refrigerators and automobiles) to compare disability products.

The ratings were used and, as expected, many companies responded angrily to the results. It is not easy to compare disability income policies, for there are many factors to consider and not all of these are consistent from company to company.

The backlash resulted in the eventual printing of a follow-up article in July, 1983. In this issue, Consumers Union said, "We have decided that the policy-selection criteria for the ratings in our March report were not adequate" and advised consumers not to use them. These repercussions over-shadowed the real value of the publicity that disability income products received. Here was a leading consumer publication telling us that almost everyone should consider disability coverage.

Other publications followed suit in stressing the importance of disability income. The magazines quoted at the start of this chapter are recent examples of articles that often appear on a monthly basis, extolling the virtues of this type of coverage. Consumers today are, in general, more knowledgeable about the products they buy. Insurance is no exception. Third party support from a magazine like *Money* is outstanding back-up for a story insurance agents tell and a source that many consumers know and trust.

Nonetheless, we have not reached the point where insurance agents merely take orders for disability. It is not a required purchase like automobile or homeowners coverage. It must be sold. In addition, many individuals believe they have disability income protection through work. This is sometimes true, but the extent or quality of coverage often leaves the disabled employee short of the protection he thought he had.

Thus, it is up to the insurance agent to present the need for disability income and to explore the sources of income the consumer will have available during a disability.

INSURANCE AGENTS

People in sales will sell what they have been trained to sell. Since fewer than one percent of the insurance companies train their agents to sell disability income rather than life insurance as a primary product, it makes sense that life insurance has a far greater market penetration.

After being trained first to sell life insurance, most agents never leave that comfort zone. Life insurance selling is about understanding the numbers. How much coverage can be bought and what interest rate can be earned tax deferred are the main considerations for the average consumer. Most individuals know that if they die, they should leave something for their families to maintain their standard of living. Others look to the policy cash value for emergency needs or planned withdrawals for such things as sending a child to college.

Claims for life insurance are usually straightforward. The agent is comfortable with the simplicity of it all including the fact that there are fewer demands for after-sale service. This allows the agent to concentrate on perfecting the life insurance sales presentation.

Disability income insurance seems far more complex by comparison. The numbers are here, too, but payment at the time when the claim is made depends on contractual language. No two disabilities ever seem to take the same course. There are many more "what ifs" associated with disability income than with life insurance. If the agent is selling a product that is easy to explain, why attempt to sell anything that is more difficult to understand with the risk that there may be difficult questions to answer?

This is human nature. Reluctance on the part of companies to train agents in the sale of disability income has kept these products from widespread distribution. Factor in the recent poor experience in the disability industry with companies defecting from the market more and more and you can see why many agents tend to stay away from this product rather than utilizing the excellent third party testimonial from a leading consumer magazine as a lead-in to a sales presentation on this important protection.

Still, agents risk careers by ignoring this type of coverage for their clients. In today's litigious society there already have been lawsuits filed against insurance agents alleging gross negligence for failure to sell a disability income product. Agents sell their clients other forms of insurance, yet when the client becomes disabled, these coverages do not replace his income. In fact, they do not pay anything at all.

Agents, financial planners, and investment advisers have come to realize the importance of disability income as a critical part of the financial planning process (more on this in Chapter 2, Filling A Financial Planning Gap). Today, more industry related educational programs than ever are aimed at disability income training. Managers of insurance agents are encouraging them to learn more about disability income and diversify their portfolio.

Insurance companies, while recognizing the need for the product, balance their emphasis on disability income with the losses this product line has undergone over the last few years.

INSURANCE COMPANIES

Comfortable with the profit margins of their life insurance products prior to the introduction of universal life insurance in the early 1980s, most insurance companies have left the marketing and training of disability income to a few insurers. These companies placed their main emphasis on disability income and have staid the course through the roller-coaster ride of high profits and losses over the past 25 years.

The introduction of universal life and other interest-sensitive life insurance coincided with a period of excess profits for disability income. This success followed a major retrenchment in the 1970s when marketing and contractual excesses had led to significant losses. But the "feel good" 1980s served as a rebirth for the disability income product as insurers concerned about the smaller margins in their new-look life insurance products, went full force into the disability income market.[7]

The 1980s saw the disability income product marketed by many new companies eager to take advantage of the product with the outstanding return on investment. This entry produced more competitive products and more exposure of the product to the insurance agent. The end result was a widespread availability of the product for several years — before the bills came due. Many more consumers were approached as a result, leading to consistent, if not unusually high, increases in premium volume each year.

These new carriers didn't experience the results of the more practiced insurers in the disability income market. Because of poor experience, a major retreat by the vast majority of these companies occurred as they struggled with overall financial solvency and the "beefing up" of their balance sheets for stockholders, policyholders, and regulators. Certainly, this has affected disability income publicity to agents and consumers.[8]

Yet, all of the outstanding reasons to sell this product still exist. The threat of loss of income has been made even more immediate by the loss of jobs due to mergers, buyouts, takeovers and other business financial moves. Reserve requirements for the product are still lower than life insurance, persistency is generally better, and the consumer magazines are willing advocates.

The market, consisting of virtually anyone who earns an income, is still in dire need of this product. Baby boomers, once the "spend now - worry later" generation, have turned over a new leaf. Delayed parenting and work pressures have made them more cognizant of the importance of having income. Many fear a disability and are willing to talk to insurance agents about this type of protection. Future financial commitments — child's education, parent's medical costs, their own retirement — are jeopardized if a disability should occur.

Consumers are ready. Good disability products are still available for sale by insurers riding out the current, stormy disability experience. It remains for the insurance agent to seize the opportunity presented to extend disability income coverage to the nation's workforce.[9]

CHAPTER NOTES

1. "How To Insure Your Paycheck With A Sound Disability Policy", *Money*, June, 1994, p. 33.

2. "Not So Easy Riders", *Smart Money*, August, 1993, p. 139.

3. "Affordable Insurance That Works When You Can't", *Business Week*, August 29, 1994, p. 88.

4. "What To Look For In Disability Insurance", *Consumers' Research*, February, 1993, p. 21.

5. The reference to the increasing morbidity of heart disease, hypertension, cancer, diabetes, etc. comes from several sources including the Life Insurance Marketing and Research Association (LIMRA).

6. "Disability Income Insurance", *Consumer Reports*, March, 1983, p. 122.

7. "Turbulent DI Market Shows New Strength", *Life Association News*, January, 1994, p. 84.

8. The reference to disability insurers' major retreat comes from several sources including the *Wall Street Journal* and the *National Underwriter*.

9. "Picking A Winner", *Best's Review*, September, 1992, p. 75.

Chapter 2

FILLING A FINANCIAL PLANNING GAP

How important is disability income coverage to a wage earner? It should be the cornerstone of any sound financial plan. If it is not, he risks losing everything that he has worked towards in achieving his financial objectives.[1]

It is that important. For example, a savings plan started for a child's college education, contributions to an annuity which will generate sufficient income for retirement and longer life spans, and similar financial plans will never be completed unless the ability to work and earn an income to fund them is protected.

One injury or one sickness that cuts off an individual's income can not only destroy these plans but also the ability to provide the basic necessities for that individual and his family. One never knows when it will happen or how long it will last. All of the life insurance, annuities, savings accounts, and mutual funds are only as good as the contributions that can be made to them.

IS THERE A GAP IN YOUR FINANCIAL PLAN?

This question should not only be asked of a client or prospect by the insurance agent, but the same inquiry should be made about the insurance agent's own plan.

Fewer than one of every five workers has an individual long term disability program. This is a significant number of people who leave their financial futures up to fate.

Many people do not realize they have a problem. Ask people if they have disability income insurance and many will tell you that they are covered at work. Some are, but many are not. At least not adequately. And those who are will have coverage for only as long as they stay in their job at that company. How assured can anyone be of that?

An article appearing in the *Wall Street Journal* stated:

"Even if your group plan seems adequate, it may make sense to look into individual policies anyway. In an environment of mergers and buy-outs, 'executives who change jobs, or get smitten with the entrepreneurial bug' need individual policies."[2]

The federal legislation, COBRA, does not apply to disability income coverage. If one leaves a job, the option to continue eligibility for medical (and, possibly, dental) insurance may be there, depending on the size of the company. Yet there is not an option to continue the group disability income plan. Conversion, yes; usually an overpriced, streamlined plan. Continuation of what one had — no.

The gap is there and it is too large to ignore. Financial planners who do not recommend disability income coverage as an integral part of any financial plan are not doing a thorough job.

The task for the planner-insurance agent is simple: offering the client a way, through a disability income policy, to replace the ability to earn money through gainful employment.

THE BABY BOOMERS FACE THE TWENTY-FIRST CENTURY

The largest segment of the disability income market is made up of the 82 million people born between 1946 and 1965; the traditional baby boomers. The members of this group are between ages 30 and 50 today, the prime ages for considering disability income insurance.[3]

This population segment lived high in the 1980s, often with two-incomes, two homes, two cars and the latest in virtually any fashionable trend. However, the realities of the 1990s have hit home for the boomers. Among today's considerations:

1. *Delayed Parenting.* It was easy to spend when the costs of caring for children were not a concern. But the fear of missing something caused many to rethink their priorities and a number of people observed both a 40th birthday and the birth of a child at the same time. The delight of parenthood has been slightly balanced with the financial task of setting aside money for a future college education (or two).

2. *Aging Parents.* A greater percentage of boomers' parents are still alive, often retired and slowing down due to age and illness. Longer life spans are great, but the last few years may be ones of dependence and high medical costs. While a number of retirees are in better financial shape than their predecessors, many will run out of money before their body quits. Who will be there for them? The probable answer is their children.

3. *Retirement.* Dreams of early retirement have vanished, but there is hope that boomers will have enough money to retire at some point. The per capita savings in this country is at its lowest level ever and with the pressures of daily expenses, future college educations and nursing home costs, retirement savings is low on the list.

From this picture, one can easily see how critical every penny of income has become for this group of middle-aged Americans. One disability could turn an entire household upside down, affecting both immediate and extended family members. A conversation about financial planning, brushed aside five years ago, is more easily pursued today. Boomers remain the best candidates for disability income in view of the overall financial planning necessary to achieve successful college funding, retirement and the possibility of taking care of aging parents.[4]

The boomers aren't the only prospects. Today's college graduates, the generation X'ers, seem to be more financially motivated at an earlier age than the boomers ever were. While they may not yet hold the better paying jobs, they may be more interested in beginning a financial plan now than you'd expect from individuals in their twenties.

A majority of the generation does not hold out much hope for Social Security benefits to be paid at their retirement. The assumption is that they're on their own. As a consequence, this group will begin financial planning sooner than their elders.

OTHER PROTECTION

The life insurance and annuity programs that are being put in place for clients are self-completing plans through protection of the ability to make contributions in the event of disability.

The waiver of premium benefit ensures that the premiums or contributions made to these plans will continue even if the insured is totally disabled and unable to work. Any agent or financial planner should, at least, add this optional benefit to the life insurance or annuity contract sold.

Disability income coverage is meant to provide the basic necessities of living and help maintain the standard of living that existed prior to the disabling illness or injury. But insurance and annuity savings plans should also be protected so that contributions that are funding future plans will continue.

Protecting your clients' current and future earnings begins by recommending disability income as an essential part of their financial plan.

CHAPTER NOTES

1. "Using Disability Insurance To Expand Your Practice", *Stranger's Investment Advisor*, April, 1991, p. 62.

2. "Your Money Matters", *Wall Street Journal*, April, 1990.

3. "Making A Catch in the DI Marketplace", *Best's Review*, November, 1993, p. 69.

4. "The Power of Cohorts", *American Demographics*, December, 1994, p. 22.

■ *Chapter 3*

BREAKING INTO THE DISABILITY INCOME MARKET

"Nothing else in the world, not all the armies, is so powerful as an idea whose time has come."

— Victor Hugo

Understanding that there is a need for disability income is significant progress for those that do not own or have never sold disability income coverage. But if you don't progress beyond this understanding, your clients' financial needs remain exposed to the serious threat posed by an untimely disability.

Witness the story related by *Money* magazine in the April, 1992 issue. A man who owned his own construction business and earned $60,000 annually had an opportunity to review a disability income proposal, but declined. At age 35 and healthy, he didn't seem to have much chance of an extended illness or injury.

But in April of 1990, a heart attack forced him to close up shop. He has recovered but is unable to find work in his field because of his health history. He and his spouse had over $70,000 in various savings vehicles when the disability began. Within two years it was nearly gone.

Money's conclusion? "Don't try to get by without long-term disability insurance."[1]

Closing the sale should have been accomplished by the agent presenting the disability proposal. The business owner didn't take the coverage because he wasn't convinced that disability posed a real threat to him.

Of course not! He was healthy and working! Why should he think about disability and furthermore, be motivated to buy it?

That's the agent's job: to persuade *healthy* people that this protection is critical for them. There's very little one can do after the disability has occurred. The work has to be done before anything happens.

Armed with an understanding of the need, now it's time to learn how to apply this knowledge to the point of sale.

The majority of agents are quite comfortable talking about life insurance with their clients. There are several ways to turn a life insurance close into a disability income sales presentation.

As you read this, remember a key thought: the disability income product provides *income* just as a life policy does. Both offer similar solutions, but to different problems.

There are many reasons why the life insurance agent does not make a disability income sale. Most often, it is because the agent never offers disability income so that the prospect or client has a chance to buy. Among these reasons, and in no particular order are:

1. *Fear of losing life premium dollars.* This is a real concern to the life-oriented agent. A considerable amount of time has likely been spent in the design and preparation of a life insurance plan for which premium has been committed. Now, by bringing up disability income, the agent imagines the client may decide that this is as important as life insurance and say something like, "I'll buy that disability income policy, but I don't want to spend, in total, any more than I was going to pay for the life insurance plan."

2. *Lack of understanding of the disability product.* Certainly there has been turmoil in the disability insurance industry lately leading to significant change. Under a disability income contract, benefit payments hinge on policy wording. If an agent feels that he isn't up to date on the latest changes, there is a reluctance to present the product. There are many situations in which an individual could qualify (or not!) for benefits under the terms of the contract. And if an agent doesn't feel comfortable with the policy language, the product may stay on the agent's shelf. Life insurance is easier: death is undeniably easier to prove at time of claim.

3. *Reluctance to be asked a question and not know the answer.* The "vagueness" of disability income policy language makes this more likely. Prospects and clients can often bring up "what if" claim scenarios for which a concise answer is not possible.

4. *Concern about calculating a rate for the product.* There are many variables in a disability contract that affect the premium and, in turn, complicate the rate calculation process. Several insurers today are "unbundling" their contracts, making many features optional and further complicating proper rate calculation. While software is available, this often doesn't assist an agent at point of sale unless a laptop or portable computer is handy.

5. *Uncertainty about approval for the policy.* The disability income underwriting process is more stringent than for life insurance. There are many medical conditions that can cause a disability but not premature death. Tighter financial underwriting restrictions and thorough searches into an applicant's medical history can cause delays in the approval of the plan that would not ordinarily happen with life insurance.

Let's examine each of these reasons and shift the perspective of the life-oriented agent.

1. *Fear of losing life premium dollars.* A fellow agent admitted to me recently that he'd been wrong when he told me that discussing the disability concept at the conclusion of the life sale would probably reduce the amount of money the client was willing to invest in a life insurance program. This agent had just completed a life and disability sale where he had closed the life plan with a premium commitment of $1,200 a year and then switched to disability using one of my "five easy methods" (more on these to follow in this chapter). After understanding the need for disability income, his client invested $1,925 a year in a disability program to cover 60 percent of his income.

My friend's conclusion was that he never would have been able to convince the client to put $3,125 a year in a life insurance program. If he had not brought up the need for disability income, the sale would have remained at $1,200 a year and the disability risk still exposed. "The additional $1,925 was there," he concluded. "It was the need for disability that uncovered it." You will be surprised at the premium an individual is willing to pay to cover his most valuable asset, his income.

2. *Lack of understanding of the disability product.* Yes, there have been many substantial changes in disability income products today and there will be more to come. But this misses the point. It is not the product that should necessarily be understood, but the concept of why disability income is important. If you cannot work, you do not get paid. If you do not get paid, you and your family may not eat. That is the disability concept. If your clients grasp these basics, they will take measures to protect themselves. The product is quite often secondary.

Many insurance companies are accessing their disability income portfolio from carriers who specialize in this field. These carriers have disability income representatives who can help an agent learn the contract language and even accompany you on the sales presentation.

But don't forget the real reason for the presentation: to explain the *Concept!*

3. *Reluctance to be asked a question and not know the answer.* With repetitive questions, an agent will quickly learn the right answers. Generally, the question that cannot be answered is one that the insurer's claims department cannot answer either. Often, these types of questions can be answered only at the time of claim. Make a presentation! Take a chance! By studying the concept of disability, you will know more than your client. If a question comes up that you cannot answer, admit it. Tell your client that you will call the home office and obtain the answer. People appreciate that; no one has all the answers.

4. *Concern about calculating a rate for the product.* Today, computer generated proposals usually have a page entitled "Alternative Plans." This will list premiums for variations of the main proposal, quoting prices for other elimination and benefit periods and assorted optional benefits. This should address most of the money questions a client will have while trying to stay within his budget.[2]

   Some companies publish "cheat cards" that summarize the pre-calculated premiums for a variety of benefit amounts and parameters.[3] If your company doesn't offer them, compile a card yourself. Calculate the annual premium for $1,000 a month of disability income for 60, 90, and 180 day elimination periods (the length of time before benefits are payable after the start of a claim) and both five year and to-age-65 benefit periods for ages 25, 30, 35, 40, 45, 50, and 55. Do not add the policy fee. If the client wants to know a rate other than what is on the "Alternatives" page, use the pre-calculations. Pick the elimination and benefit period combination and multiply by the number of thousands (for example, 2.5 for $2,500 a month). Then add the policy fee and subtract any non-smoker or volume discount factors. This can be accomplished quickly with a calculator. If the client is 38, interpolate between ages 35 and 40. All of this can be done with relative speed. Practice with the card, carry the "Alternatives" page and learn how to quickly calculate a rate.

5. *The slow underwriting process.* This should be sold as a positive to the prospective insured. If it takes time to receive approval, it must be important protection, or at least not easy to obtain. An agent can help control the amount of underwriting time by completely filling out the application, providing as many details as possible; arranging for the medical examination (if necessary); and following up with the client's physician to obtain medical records (if needed). The more thorough, the faster the process.

Now that we have dealt with the reasons to avoid writing disability income, here are five easy and proven methods for making the switch from life insurance agent to disability income salesperson.

METHOD ONE: WAIVER OF LIVING COSTS

If you are not currently adding *waiver of premium* to your life insurance policies, begin doing so. It protects the client's ability to pay the premium on the policy if disabled and allows completion of the life insurance program.

When delivering a life insurance policy with waiver of premium, your explanation of it should be saved for last. After reviewing the essentials of the life policy itself, discuss the importance of waiver of premium. It is meant to pay for the policy while the insured is totally disabled. During a disability, the dollars will be more difficult to come by and are likely not to be used to pay for the life insurance policy. This provision waives the need to pay for the plan until the insured is recovered from an injury or sickness.

After this explanation, ask, "How would you like to have a waiver of personal living expenses as well? I have a plan that would also waive your mortgage payment, grocery bills, car payments, phone bill, and clothing costs while you are disabled. Would you be interested in that type of protection?"

There. That was simple. You have just made the transition from life insurance selling to disability income selling. Waiver of premium is only the tip of the disability income iceberg. A disability income policy provides income to pay the majority of the insured's personal living expenses. Disability insurance is not far removed from life insurance; disability is, in actuality, a living death.

METHOD TWO: TWO KINDS OF LOST INCOME

After delivery of the life insurance policy, say, "There are really two kinds of lost income, not just one. We've just taken care of the income lost to your family if you die, but what if you don't die? With the advances in medical science today, injuries and sicknesses that killed people yesterday are now totally disabling them. If you die, you are out of the picture, but your family needs to survive on an income the life insurance policy will provide. If you don't die, but instead, become disabled, both you and your family must have an income on which to survive.

"Right now you're only half-insured. Would you be interested in reviewing a plan that will take care of both you and your family if you become disabled?"

The key point to remember here is that if your client does not buy enough life insurance to support the family after death, he will not be around to know it. However, that same client is still a consumer after a disability and will feel the effects personally if the income is not there when it is needed. Arguably, the family income need is greater during a disability. A family of four whose breadwinner dies leaves a family of three; a family of four whose breadwinner is disabled is still a family of four.

METHOD THREE: THE BUSINESS CARD APPROACH

After delivery and review of the life insurance policy, hand your client your business card. Ask him to turn it over and write the names of three people on the back of the card who will help pay his rent, make car payments and pay other bills if he is disabled and unable to work. After waiting an appropriate time, and assuming no response, turn the card over for the client and say, "I can."

Yes, you can help pay the bills with a disability income check from your company.

METHOD FOUR: THE SIX MONTH VACATION

After reviewing the provisions of the life policy, congratulate your insured on the purchase and ask, "When was the last time you took a six month vacation?" The insured will certainly protest that a six month vacation is hardly affordable in today's economic climate. Your response is, "What if you were forced to take six months off? What if a disability occurred without warning, and put you down for six months? Who would pay your bills?

"Let me show you how we can protect you if that catastrophe happens. It's the second part of the income protection program, that we started with your life insurance policy."

METHOD FIVE: THE COCKTAIL PARTY OPENER

If you go to a social gathering and you don't feel like talking to someone, tell them you're in the insurance business. Only kidding! Actually, you are attending functions in the hope of getting to talk to a few people about what you do. Next time, try this:

Invariably, the conversation at any type of function you attend turns to what you do for a living. My response is, "I provide income for disabled business executives." Much of the reaction is in the form of questioning how I could possibly furnish dollars for someone that cannot work. Once questioned, I explain the waiver of personal living expenses concept and — presto! — you're into a disability income sales presentation. It works! Use it![4]

These are five easy methods of breaking the ice, to making the conversion from life salesperson to life insurance *and* disability income specialist. As you can see, it is not a long, involved procedure. You can quickly initiate discussion about disability income and you will be surprised at the reaction. It's not an idea many people are approached on, yet most people are concerned about the bottom line and know that if they cannot work, financial trouble looms.

You are now on your way to the disability sales presentation.

CHAPTER NOTES

1. "Protect Your Wealth Against Risks", *Money*, April, 1992, p.142.

2. The "Alternative Plans" page is a staple of most disability income proposals today. It makes it easier to quote other plan designs if the original one presented is not acceptable.

3. The Principal Financial Group publishes just such a "cheat card" for their agents' convenience.

4. Method number five came directly from teaching the Life Underwriter's Training Council (LUTC) Disability Income course. If you have not taken it, I encourage you to do so.

Chapter 4

THE BASIC SALES PRESENTATION

The basic sales presentation outlined in this chapter can be used for any client, but is a must for the working individual who has no coverage in the event a disability strikes. Since more than 80 percent of the working population does not have individual long term disability coverage, the prospect list for this presentation is substantial. With the new emphasis of the insurance companies on the middle income wage earner ($30,000 - $75,000 annually), concentration on these prospects is highly recommended.

Any basic sales presentation places the emphasis on need, not product. If the prospect understands what is being purchased and why, an agent will close most sales. If an agent spends too much time on the product before the client understands the need, it may take forever to close the sale and begin to put this important coverage in place.[1]

For any sales presentation to be effective, the prospect be must involved. Ask questions frequently and listen carefully to the answers. They usually reveal a lot about the person's state of mind concerning the product concept and buying mood. Be alert for the sign that says, "I need this protection and I'm ready to buy it."

There are four key points that should be presented while trying to elicit agreement from the prospect:

- Your greatest asset is your ability to work and earn an income.

- Disability can and does happen at a time you least expect it.

- Income decreases or stops and expenses increase after disability strikes.

- There are no acceptable alternatives to a disability income policy for protecting your income.

KEY POINT 1: Your greatest asset is your ability to work and earn an income.

Ask the question: "Can you tell me what you think is your greatest asset?" The answer of course is, "My ability to work and earn an income." From my experience, only about ten percent of the people who were asked that question answered income. Most will say it is their home, car, spouse or children before income.

In trying to show the importance of income, I often take out my checkbook and flip through a few pages while telling the prospect that I pay, every month, Barnett Bank for my mortgage, Southern Bell and MCI for the phone, Florida Power & Light for electric, Martin Marietta Credit Union for the car; and I am able to do so for one reason: I am able to put money in the deposit column every month. I know I can count on those bills finding me every month. But can I be sure I will be able to make sufficient deposits to make the bill paying a routine affair? What if I were unable to work? Would I still be paid? If these deposits are not made, how will these bills get paid?

The checkbook brings it closer to home. Many times it will start the prospects talking about all the bills that must be paid every month, and the reaction to the realization that their monthly deposits are quite powerful and impossible to do without, is both interesting and satisfying. Always remember: you have an important story to tell that could change the life of this person. Every time you step up to the sales presentation line, it's the Super Bowl for both you and your prospect. Stay focused and enthusiastic! Give it your best effort every time!

KEY POINT 2: *Disability can and does happen at a time you least expect it.*

Statistics can be tricky to use in a presentation. Too many statistics may confuse the prospect. Conversely, using no statistics may cause the prospect to question the immediacy of the need for this coverage. There is some middle ground, however.

I would recommend one of the following approaches. First, ask the prospect what he thinks are the chances of disability prior to age 65. Then proceed with one of these statistically-based concepts.

1. Compare the chances of disability to death at any given age. The likelihood of being disabled for more than three months is greater than the likelihood of dying in any given year. At age 30, a person is about three and one-half times more likely to suffer long term disability than death; at age 40, the likelihood of disability is approximately three times greater; and at age 50, chances of disability are twice as great. These statistics stress that disability income coverage is probably more important to a family than life insurance during the working years.[2]

2. Point out the types of insurance coverage we do buy to protect certain items. Ask the insured if he has automobile, homeowners or life insurance. We have automobile insurance to protect the car, homeowners insurance to protect the home, and life insurance if we die prematurely. But do we protect the income that pays for all of this insurance, plus the mortgage, the car payment, and the electric bill? According to the U. S. Government, nearly half of all mortgage foreclosures in the country are the result of disability.

3. My favorite statistic appeared in the September, 1988 issue of *Financial Advisor* magazine in an article entitled, "Cast of Thousands". This article reported that the need for disability protection has increased over a period of time. The article says, "The four leading killers of those 45 to 65 years old — hypertension, heart disease, cerebrovascular disease, and diabetes — now are more likely to disable than kill. Between 1960 and 1979, there was a 32 percent decline in the death rate for all four maladies, but a 55 percent increase in chronic long term disability." Prospects can relate to the "big four." The main idea is that while life spans are getting longer, it's due in large part to sustaining a lengthy disability instead of death.[3]

After using one of these three statistical explanations, talk about a disability that actually occurred. It is more convincing if both you and the prospect know the individual, but it is not necessary. The company you represent in the sale of disability income can provide you with actual claims detail and data. Figure 4.1 is an excerpt from a third party piece used by a disability income insurer.[4]

Figure 4.1

Period In Force Months-Days	Occupation	Cause of Disability	Age	Residence	Total Amt. Paid in Premiums	Amount Paid To Date
0 - 26	Mechanic	Brain Hemorrhage	33	IL	$15.55	$900.00
3 - 8	Store Manager	Lower Back Sprain	33	OH	$29.25	$24,000.00
6 - 11	Delivery Driver	Acute Low Back Strain, Contusion	29	VA	$375.57	$14,860.00
1 - 3	Auto Mechanic	Lower Back Strain	41	DC	$28.20	$2,328.33
0 - 12	Salesman	Tear Left Medial Meniscus	45	NH	$6.10	$40,800.00

KEY POINT 3: *Income decreases or stops and expenses increase after disability strikes.*

Those of us who are not independently wealthy work because we must, if only to provide the necessities for ourselves and our families. Without an income, we would lack food, shelter, clothing, and other essentials we need to maintain our standard of living. Most prospects will agree with this.

Draw a small graph to illustrate this key point. On the left side, show the normal relation of income and expenses. Normally, if an individual is healthy and working, his income line is higher than the expense line. (See Figure 4.2.)

Figure 4.2

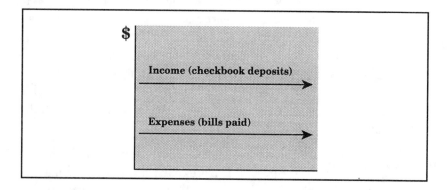

When disability occurs, income stops and the expenses associated with treating disability cause them to increase. The result, after the lines cross, is deficit financing, which only the government is allowed to do. (See Figure 4.3.) Now, the entire picture has changed. What was once taken for granted is now a financial as well as a physical nightmare.

Figure 4.3

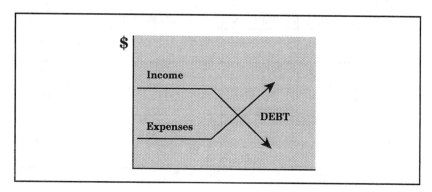

Expenses can increase in ways you might never predict. One individual I know who had a spinal cord injury and was permanently confined to a wheelchair had to have ramps built in his home for wheelchair access, an expense not covered by his medical policy.

KEY POINT 4: *There are no acceptable alternatives to a disability income policy for protecting your income.*

Without the deposits to put in the checkbook, a disabled individual must look elsewhere for a source of income to pay the bills. Review with your prospect the various income alternatives from which to choose.

One alternative is savings. Ask him to think how long his family can live on its savings. If you would like, calculate the number of months by dividing the savings by monthly expenses. The chart in Figure 4.4 can help itemize these expenses.[5]

Figure 4.4

Mortgage	$	_____
Car	$	_____
Food	$	_____
Clothing	$	_____
Utilities	$	_____
Gas	$	_____
Insurance	$	_____
Telephone	$	_____
Emergency Expenses	$	_____

Total these numbers and divide the total into the amount of savings. Usually a 90 day, or longer, disability will eliminate the savings of most people. It takes a long time to build up savings and the recent track record of most Americans indicates that our national savings rate is at an all time low. This cash can be used up very quickly during a disability.

Another possibility is to borrow the money. Ask the prospect this: "If you were a banker making a decision on a loan, would you consider a disabled person a good risk?" Ask if the prospect could borrow money from relatives or friends. How much and for how long?

Liquidation of assets can produce some dollars. Ask if selling the house would be a possibility to raise money. If you agree it is a possibility, add that the prospect and family would now have to find a place to live. It is likely the house would not sell for what it was worth, because of the pressure to accept an early offer.

Finally, point out that the prospect may be eligible for Social Security benefits. The reaction to this possible income source has changed over the years. Many people I have interviewed do not even consider Social Security a remote alternative at the time of claim. A recent survey of generation X'ers found that this young group believes it more likely they will sight a UFO than collect anything from Social Security.[6]

I will never forget watching on television successful heart transplant patient Barney Clark sitting in his hospital bed being visited by then President Ronald Reagan. When asked by the president if there was anything he could do for Mr. Clark, the patient replied that there was: have Social Security approve his claim which had been there for several months without results. Within a few days, Barney Clark had his first check from Social Security.

It is difficult to qualify for Social Security benefits. This will be explored in more depth in Chapter 5, The Art of Programming Benefits. The amount of Social Security disability benefits in 1995, for example, can range up to around $1,400 a month for an individual and more than $2,100 a month for a family. These amounts depend upon income, age and how long contributions have been made to the Social Security system. In most cases, Social Security will not do as a sole source of income.[7]

Now ask the prospect if any of these alternatives is a perfect solution. The majority of people agree that every one of the choices offered leaves something to be desired.

Up until now, disability income insurance has never been mentioned. Simply by exploring the concept of the need for income during disability, you have set the product up as the most ideal solution. And it is! Disability income insurance is a way for the insured to put a small amount of money aside today to provide a substantial source of income if disability strikes. Yes, it is another bill to pay today, but it can make a big difference in the future. Contrast the situations of the two people in Figure 4.5.

Figure 4.5

PERSON #1		
Today's Monthly Earnings:	$3,000.00	
Earnings if Disabled:	-0-	
PERSON #2		
Today's Monthly Earnings:	$2,800.00	
Earnings if Disabled:	2,200.00	tax-free

Is there a choice? Sure, one can gamble on being disabled or not being disabled. But a single person is his sole source of income and a married person often has a family dependent on his paycheck.

Disability income makes sense as the best answer as to where, in the event of disability, the money will come from to put in the checkbook each month so that the bills can be paid.

Your next step is to find out how much disability income the prospect needs, when benefits begin, and how long the income is needed.

CHAPTER NOTES

1. The basics of the sales presentation here have been used long before I was born and are part of the training regimens of the disability income-oriented companies like Paul Revere and UNUM. I have added my own ideas over the years.

2. Statistics are from 1985 Society of Actuaries CIDA Table, an update of the 1964 Commissioner's Disability Table.

3. "A Cast of Thousands, Part One", *Financial Advisor*, September, 1988.

4. This claims data is extracted from various disability insurers' published information on their claims results.

5. "Do You Have Enough", *Smart Money*, August, 1993, p. 141.

6. The reference to generation X'ers came from a Luntz Research survey of 1,000 U.S. residents commissioned by Merrill Lynch and discussing financial attitudes.

7. *1995 Guide to Social Security*, William M. Mercer, Inc., Louisville, Kentucky.

■ *Chapter 5*

THE ART OF PROGRAMMING BENEFITS

There are no set programs for disability income. There is no one answer for everyone's disability financial planning. If there were, an agent could sell one plan to everyone with the same benefit amount, elimination period and benefit period.

The essential purpose of disability income is to provide money during a disability that is equivalent to a substantial percentage (50 to 70 percent) of gross earnings. It is never intended to replace the full earnings amount, but to furnish enough income to enable the disabled insured (and his family) to maintain a reasonable standard of living during recovery until the insured returns to work when higher income can be realized.

The elimination period, the length of time before benefits start, will be selected by the insured based on his individual ability to survive for a specific period of time after disability commences. Every client's financial situation will be different, and there are a variety of choices from which to select the most appropriate elimination period. Of course, the shorter elimination periods (30 and 60 days) no longer enjoy a widespread availability, and the cost of these time frames has become prohibitive. This recent trend will have some effect on the choice of elimination period, too.

Benefit periods are a matter of individual preference as well, although most people prefer the longest period they can qualify for, up to lifetime, if available. Company trends show a movement away from offering lifetime coverage, tendering a lengthy, but finite period (such as to age 65 or 70) in its place for consideration. Selection of benefit periods even shorter, such as five years, may also be a matter of affordability.

While the choices have narrowed, there are at least several options to choose from when selecting elimination period and benefit period. Monthly benefit amount, the other key variable in designing a disability insurance plan for a potential insured, is based on a variety of factors. This is where the concept of programming becomes important.

KEY PLAN DESIGN VARIABLES

The objective in designing an individual plan tailored to meet the precise needs of the client is for the agent to construct a program in concert with the prospect. The more specific input the agent receives from the client, the greater the likelihood of the client's understanding why the policy is being purchased. For an agent, the ideal situation is to use the client's numbers; it will be easier for the client to recall later where these figures originated.

The three main variables to consider when programming a client's disability income plan are: elimination period, benefit period, and monthly income.

Elimination Period

The length of time before benefits begin is the starting point of the programming process. Factors such as accounts receivable, savings and sick leave will give the prospect an idea of how many days of disability and reduced earnings can be tolerated before insurance company funds will be necessary. The longer the individual can wait, the lower the price that is paid for the policy. Lowering the cost of the plan by extending the elimination period has become more important in recent years due to the substantial rate increases for both the 30 and 60 day choices. Once the number of days the insured can self-insure is identified, try and keep the elimination period extensions to no more than 30 days, if possible.

While companies offer elimination periods down to 30 days (there may be a few companies that offer 14 days), along with selections at 60, 90, 180, 270, 365, and 730 days, the most utilized choice is the 90 day elimination period. For one, this is the place where insurance companies have become very competitive in rating. Second, the high costs of elimination periods of less than 90 days have made them unattractive to the average consumer. It's not always the best choice. If the financial analysis of a client's cash flow situation reveals a shortage following 30 days of disability, waiting until 90 days (120, actually, since benefits are paid in arrears) may be the longest stretch for the disabled person and their family. If the disability appears to be lasting the full term of the elimination period and the likelihood of receiving benefits virtually assured, many creditors will be willing to let the payments slide for a couple of months. It's not an ideal situation, but the reality of the market is that consumers will have to take care of short-term liabilities, while a disability policy will help them if they need it — long term.

Benefit Period

The benefit period option in the disability program defines how long benefits can be paid. Common benefit periods offered for sale are: one year, two years, five years, and to-age-65. Less frequently seen now is the lifetime benefit period which, when combined with a noncancelable feature and a liberal definition of total disability, can mean exceptionally high claims losses for insurers. The substitute-apparent may be a new *to-age-70* benefit period — slightly longer than to-age-65, but at least a finite period of time. Very short benefit periods such as six months may also be found within a disability insurer's portfolio.

Most individuals want to elect the longest benefit period available to them. The agent should always quote the maximum choice available and be ready with additional quotes on shorter benefit periods if price is a problem. Remember, almost all disabilities are resolved within 365 days of an injury or illness, so there is some flexibility and safety in lowering this variable based on price. The shorter the benefit period, the lower the cost of the plan.

Monthly Income

Identifying the monthly income need for an individual is the easiest part of working with this variable. Identifying the key expense areas and totalling up the costs needed to cover these if no other income is available is the simple part of the process.

If there are other income sources that will provide dollars at time of disability, these should be noted. Items like other private insurance coverage, Social Security benefits, workers compensation payments, state cash sickness benefits and employer-provided group insurance or salary continuation that offer income for some period of time should be quantified and written down. These amounts will reduce the benefit that is available for purchase. There's no need to duplicate coverage and spend money that isn't necessary. A dual income family may be able to count on the healthy spouse's income during a disability, so this should also be considered.

These other income sources may or may not give the insured enough to live on during a disability. If not, the coverage being proposed can make up the difference between the current income sources and the percentage of gross income that can be insured under a company's monthly income guidelines (known as issue and participation limits).

A SHORT HISTORY OF PROGRAMMING

Modern day issue limits, i.e., the amount of benefit the insured can qualify for based on gross earnings, evolved through a series of changes, enhancements, and additions over the years. To understand how these current numbers were established, a look back into programming history is appropriate.

As you read this, remember that while companies differ slightly in amounts offered at distinct income levels, the process used to arrive at these numbers is very similar.

The basic policy monthly benefit is the cornerstone of any disability income policy. These are the dollars received to help pay bills during disability. Added to what could be received from Social Security, this total amount represents a significantly high percentage of the individual's earnings.

Social Security benefits were first available in January of 1937. In 1994, Social Security provided retirement, survivor, and disability and health benefits to 43 million people each month in the form of Social Security and Medicare payments.

In the early stages of developing guidelines upon which to base the amount of benefits a company would issue in relation to earnings, one could not ignore Social Security disability benefits. Thus, the early issue limit tables were calculated based on a percentage of gross earnings (50 to 60 percent) less the potential Social Security disability benefit.[1] For example, if an individual earned $60,000 ($5,000 a month) and one assumed an average Social Security benefit of $750 per month, the issue limit would be $2,250 a month ($5,000 x .60 = $3,000 less $750 = $2,250). Limits were calculated at other income levels using a similar formula.

What these limits do not account for is:

(a) the likelihood of actually collecting (or being denied) Social Security benefits based on the definition of disability under the Social Security Act, and

(b) when these benefits are actually received.

Supplemental First Year Coverage

The companies dealt with problem (b) first. By definition, there is a five month waiting period for Social Security disability benefits. An application for benefits may be filed before the end of this five month period and evidence provided that the definition of disability is met. A decision will not be made until the waiting period of five months has passed and, in many cases, judgments are not rendered for an average of six or seven months after that time, due primarily to the disability claim backlog that the Social Security Administration is trying to whittle down — so far, unsuccessfully.

Once approved, benefits are retroactive to the sixth month of disability. During this interim period (from the end of the waiting period until a decision is made), however, creditors wait for payments that cannot be made until the benefit check is sent.

The basic limit approach unintentionally left many people short of their financial goals during a disability due to the slowness of the Social Security system. These issue limits belied the notion that a disability policy would replace a substantial enough portion of earnings to help the insured maintain a reasonable standard of living during a recovery period. Without the Social Security disability payment, the insured was well short of the income necessary.

This led to the creation of supplemental first year coverage under which the issue limit table was expanded to produce a higher first year benefit payable. This additional first year benefit usually was paid for either one full year or, in most cases, the balance of the first year of disability after the elimination period. This means that if a 90 day elimination period was elected, the length of time the additional first year benefit was paid was nine months.

In the example above, the basic limit available to an insured making $60,000 a year was $2,250 a month. Under the new issue limit approach, the new eligible limit would be $3,000 ($2,250 + $750 supplemental benefit based on average Social Security payment) in the first year of disability, reducing to $2,250 thereafter for the balance of the benefit period.

The Social Security Offset Rider

The assumption now after this latest approach is that Social Security benefits will commence after 365 days of disability. This is the point where a company's monthly income benefit reverts back to the basic limit regardless of what actually happens. But what if the insured is *denied* Social Security benefits because of an inability to qualify under the Social Security definition? Denial left a void beyond the first year that needed to be addressed. This is the problem mentioned above at (a): the failure of the limit to take into account the likelihood of collecting Social Security disability benefits under the Social Security definition.

Under Social Security, disability is defined as the inability to engage in any substantial gainful activity by reason of any medically determinable physical or mental impairment which can be expected to result in death or which has lasted or can be expected to last for a continuous period of not less than 12 months.[2] A person must not only be unable to do his previous work or work commensurate with the previous work in amount of earnings and utilization of capacities, but also be unable, considering age, education, and work experience, to engage in any other kind of substantial work which exists in the national economy. It is immaterial whether such work exists in the immediate area or whether a specific job vacancy exists, or whether the worker would be hired if he applied for work.

As you will see in later chapters, the definition of disability under a private insurance policy is much more liberal than the one written for potential Social Security recipients.

At last check, Social Security was initially denying more than two-thirds of the applications for these benefits and, after the lengthy appeals process, approving only enough to drop the overall denial rate to about 50 percent.

This problem was addressed in the mid-1970s by the creation of the third piece in the programming puzzle: the Social Security offset rider. This rider went into effect, for most companies, when the supplemental first year benefit period ceased. The amount of the benefit was commensurate with the additional first year coverage and was payable in full if no benefits were received under Social Security for disability. The insurance company even offered to help file the Social Security claim for the insured as a service and a way to ensure that the claimant did follow through on claim application and was not simply relying on this rider.

With the addition of these two coverages, the issue limit table for $60,000 reads $3,000 a month, consisting of:

Basic Benefit $2,250
First Year Additional 750
Social Security offset rider 750

A more complete description of the various Social Security riders that are available on the market today is given in Chapter 15, Personalizing The Disability Plan With Optional Benefits.

These are the reasons for the appearance of most issue limit tables published by each company and used by the agent to determine the amount of coverage that can be written for a specific client. Many tables use at least two and sometimes three pieces (as the example above), that collectively determine the total amount of protection the client needs to survive until a return to work is possible.

OTHER INCOME SOURCES

Programming is not limited to the amount of Social Security benefit for which the insured is eligible. Often, the Social Security offset rider functions as a Social Insurance Offset rider and includes other potential income sources such as workers compensation, occupational disease, and other federal and state programs. Let's examine the more common forms of other coverage which will affect the amount of benefit that can be issued on a given individual.

Social Security Benefits

The actual benefit calculation process is a complex one under the Social Security rules. The "Primary Insurance Amount" for the disabled insured is equal to the retirement benefit at normal retirement age (presently at ages from 65 to 67 based on the year of birth). However, adjustments are made to this Primary Insurance Amount based on other sources of income, the date of disability and the Consumer Price Index, among others factors.

For ease of advising the approximate Social Security disability income monthly benefit of an individual with a typical earnings history, the benefit consulting firm of William M. Mercer, Inc. publishes a handy reference chart that is easy to use and reasonably accurate based only on a few variables.[3] The information in that chart is adapted in Figure 5.1.

Figure 5.1

	Monthly Benefit at Disability							
	EARNINGS AT PRESENT							
	$20,000		$30,000		$44,000		$61,200+	
Age in 1995	Insured	MFB*	Insured	MFB	Insured	MFB	Insured	MFB
65	$739	$1108	$985	$1477	$1123	$1684	$1199	$1798
64	744	1116	992	1488	1135	1702	1217	1825
63	760	1140	1015	1522	1167	1750	1256	1884
62	747	1120	997	1495	1151	1726	1244	1866
61	748	1122	998	1497	1156	1734	1255	1882
55	729	1106	974	1478	1149	1743	1280	1942
50	709	1089	948	1456	1128	1733	1283	1974
45	714	1097	955	1467	1136	1745	1318	2027
40	710	1095	951	1467	1127	1739	1319	2035
35	672	1060	901	1422	1064	1679	1249	1971
30	676	1066	907	1430	1068	1684	1255	1979

* Maximum Family Benefit is the total amount of benefits that all members of one family may receive based on the earnings record of the insured.

Some companies arrange their issue limit table to coordinate exactly with the actual potential Social Security disability benefit, but most simply use an average for ease of explanation. Whatever the display, there is no denying that the presence of Social Security benefits controls the issue limit guidelines.

Workers Compensation

Workers compensation laws are designed to provide benefits for an occupational disability and relieve employers of liability from negligence. There are six basic objectives of these laws,[4] as outlined in the U.S. Chamber of Commerce publication, *1995 Analysis of Workers Compensation Laws*. These objectives are:

- to provide sure, prompt and reasonable income and medical benefits to work-accident victims, or income benefits to their dependents, regardless of fault;

- to provide a single remedy and reduce court delays, costs, and workloads arising out of personal injury litigation;

- to relieve public and private charities of financial drains incident to uncompensated industrial accidents;

- to eliminate payment of fees to lawyers and witnesses as well as time-consuming trials and appeals;

- to encourage maximum employer interest in safety and rehabilitation through an appropriate experience-rating mechanism; and finally

- to promote frank study of causes of accidents (rather than concealment of fault), thus reducing preventable accidents and human suffering.

These noble pursuits resulted in the enactment of workers compensation laws in each of the 50 states, the District of Columbia, and the territories of American Samoa, Guam, Puerto Rico, and the U.S. Virgin Islands.

The amount of benefits payable under these laws has risen dramatically in recent years and is a cause for programming concern at the income levels of $25,000 - $30,000 and below.

Some companies establish a minimum income level of $20,000 to $25,000 or even higher to be eligible for any type of disability income coverage. This eliminated the concern about the amount of money received under workers compensation. But most companies handle this outside income source by including workers compensation benefits in their Social Security offset riders, as explained above.

Figure 5.2 depicts the maximum weekly benefit payable by law in each state (and the District of Columbia) and the equivalent monthly benefit that this figure represents.

Figure 5.2

State	% of Wages	Maximum Weekly Payment	Equivalent Monthly Benefit
Alabama	66 2/3	$427.00	$1850.00
Alaska	80*	700.00	3033.00
Arizona	66 2/3	328.00	1421.00
Arkansas	66 2/3	270.00	1170.00
California	66 2/3	406.00	1759.00
Colorado	66 2/3	443.00	1920.00
Connecticut	75**	660.00	2860.00
Delaware	66 2/3	346.00	1499.00
D.C.	66 2/3	702.00	3042.00
Florida	66 2/3	444.00	1924.00
Georgia	66 2/3	275.00	1191.00
Hawaii	66 2/3	481.00	2084.00
Idaho	67	361.00	1564.00
Illinois	66 2/3	735.00	3185.00
Indiana	66 2/3	428.00	1855.00
Iowa	80*	817.00	3540.00
Kansas	66 2/3	319.00	1382.00
Kentucky	66 2/3	416.00	1803.00
Louisiana	66 2/3	319.00	1382.00
Maine	80*	441.00	1911.00
Maryland	66 2/3	510.00	2210.00
Massachusetts	60	586.00	2539.00
Michigan	80*	499.00	2162.00
Minnesota	66 2/3	516.00	2236.00
Mississippi	66 2/3	253.00	1096.00
Missouri	66 2/3	476.00	2063.00
Montana	66 2/3	362.00	1568.00
Nebraska	66 2/3	350.00	1517.00
Nevada	66 2/3	432.00	1872.00
New Hampshire	66 2/3	714.00	3094.00
New Jersey	70	469.00	2032.00
New Mexico	66 2/3	343.00	1486.00
New York	66 2/3	400.00	1733.00
North Carolina	66 2/3	478.00	2071.00
North Dakota	66 2/3	366.00	1586.00
Ohio	66 2/3-72	493.00	2136.00
Oklahoma	90	368.00	1594.00
Oregon	66 2/3	489.00	2119.00
Pennsylvania	66 2/3	509.00	2205.00
Rhode Island	75*	474.00	2054.00
South Carolina	66 2/3	422.00	1829.00
South Dakota	66 2/3	388.00	1681.00
Texas	70	464.00	2010.00
Utah	66 2/3	417.00	1807.00
Vermont	66 2/3	648.00	2808.00
Virginia	66 2/3	466.00	2019.00
Washington	60-75	531.00	2301.00
West Virginia	70	423.00	1833.00
Wisconsin	66 2/3	479.00	2076.00
Wyoming	66 2/3	421.00	1824.00

*   of spendable earnings
** of after-tax income

As you can see from the amount of benefits in most states, an injury on the job prompting payments under workers compensation laws will substantially replace an individual's lost income up to the $25,000 to $30,000 income range, depending on the state. It is important for the agent to recognize this when discussing any offsets for workers compensation that might be made in a given disability policy or rider.

State Cash Sickness Benefits

Another variable which may affect programming at lower income levels is the availability of a state disability benefit provided by five states: California, Hawaii, New Jersey, New York, and Rhode Island.

This branch of the social insurance system provides cash payments during short-term periods of sickness or illness due either to injury or disease, and not by employment conditions.

The purpose of these benefits is to provide temporary replacement of lost earnings because of a worker's "off the job" disability. The elimination period for those benefits is one week and benefits are usually payable for up to 26 weeks. California is an exception. Here, benefits may commence upon actual hospitalization and continue for up to 39 weeks.

Other Available Federal, State, or Local Programs

There are literally dozens of government-sponsored programs that an individual may potentially qualify for when disability strikes. The occupation of the individual will signal whether the agent must probe more to ascertain what other coverage the client may be eligible to receive. In some cases, the prospect may not even know about these benefits. Generally, any person that works for a government (federal, state, or local) entity, probably has some type of coverage that may be found by reviewing the retirement plan booklet given to the employee at his place of employment. The underwriter at the home office who will be reviewing this case will need to review this booklet to determine what coverage, if any, can be offered, to the client.

Other Disability Income Coverage

If the individual owns other types of disability coverage issued by another carrier, or through a group plan, or has association-sponsored benefits, the benefit amounts under any and all of these contracts must be counted in determining the amount of new disability coverage that can be offered based on the current earnings level of the client.

A PROGRAMMING EXAMPLE

Having reviewed the various sources of income that could be available to an individual at time of disability, the agent can program the benefits and identify the gap, if any, between coverage owned and income needed at time of claim. The following example illustrates the process.

Oprah, age 45, earns $60,000 a year and has a husband and two children. The agent lists the necessary monthly living expenses, as follows:

- Housing (includes mortgage, taxes and insurance) .... $ 800.00
- Utilities (oil, gas, electric, water) 150.00
- Food 800.00
- Clothing... 200.00
- Transportation (car payments, insurance) 500.00
- Medical 100.00
- Education 150.00
- Entertainment and Miscellaneous 300.00

Total Living Expenses needed at time of disability $3,000.00

Other Sources of Income

Salary Continuation: 60% of income ($3,000/mo.) for 60 days

Insurance: Individual D.I. policy: $1,000/month with a 60 day elimination period and a *to age 65* benefit period.

Social Security Benefits: (children are both still in high school)
— Primary Insurance Amount: $1301
— Maximum Family Benefit: $2000

With this information, you can illustrate Oprah's financial situation after disability utilizing a chart, as in Figure 5.3.

Figure 5.3

Disability Income Distribution
Expenses that must be covered

$3,000 _____

$2,000   Gap between needs and current coverage

$1,000 _____

covered by current disability income policy
$1,000/mo., 60 day elimination period, *to age 65* benefit period.

-0- _____

  0   30   60   1   2   5   Age 65
     Days   Years

As you can see, there is a gap of $2,000 a month after 60 days that must be met for Oprah to maintain the standard of living that she and her family have enjoyed until now. Since her husband is a self-employed writer whose income is sporadic and cannot be counted on during Oprah's disability, her income is the critical factor in keeping their standard of living.

If Social Security does pay, the family could receive between $1,300 and $2,000 a month to help make up the gap. Counting on Social Security, however, is not a practical solution. In addition, the children are almost out of school, thus reducing Oprah's Social Security benefit to the primary insurance amount. When programming, if Social Security is going to be used at all, the primary insurance amount should be the figure counted in determining issue limits. If the maximum family benefit is payable, this will give the insured and family some extra money for emergencies, but will not cause the client to be overinsured.

Therefore, a proposal of $700 base and $1,300 to be offset with Social Security payments would solve the gap left by loss of income. As discussed above, the $1,300 portion of the coverage can be written one of two ways, depending on the insurance company. The entire $1,300 can be written in an offset rider starting the same day as base coverage (60 days). Or the $1,300 can be split between a first year amount and an offset rider following this benefit, as shown in Figure 5.4.

Figure 5.4

Disability Income Distribution

Expenses that must be covered

$3,000

$2,000/mo. **new** coverage written as either

$2,000 $700/month base, 60 day elimination period, *to age 65* benefit period

+

$1,300/month Social Security offset rider

or

$700/month base, 60 day elimination period, *to age 65* benefit period

+

$1,300/month supplement, 60 day elimination period, 10 months coverage and $1,300/month Social Security rider

$1,000

Covered by current disability income policy

$1,000/mo., 60 day elimination period, *to age 65* benefit period

0	30	60		1	2	5		Age 65
	Days				Years			

With the introduction, by many insurers, of universal life insurance policies the demands on a more sophisticated computer technology to handle the flexibility inherent in such plans increased rapidly. These new data processing systems have also assisted disability insurers in programming around existing coverage more closely. The following example illustrates this improved ability.

Mr. Gump has a disability income need of $4,000 beginning after 90 days and extending to age 65. He currently owns a short-term disability income policy which would pay him $2,000 after 180 days for two years. Illustrated in Figure 5.5 is the *gap* in Mr. Gump's disability income program.

Figure 5.5

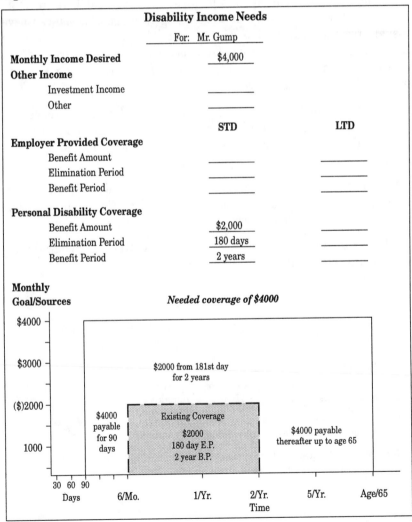

As you can see, Mr. Gump has three specific gaps:

1) From the 91st to 180th day, there is a $4,000 need.

2) From the 181st day for the next two years, there is a $2,000 gap.

3) From that point forward to age 65, the gap is again $4,000.

With the new flexibility from several disability insurers, Mr. Gump can probably buy a policy that fills in these gaps exactly — all within the same policy. Thus, his disability plan would begin on the 91st day at $4,000/month. On the 181st day, it would drop to only $2,000. Then after two years at that level, the policy would once again increase to $4,000/month.

Companies cannot always match the gaps perfectly, and there are limits to the number of increases and decreases in coverage that you can have (usually two changes are allowed in one policy). But the technology that has handled the new complexity of today's insurance policies can be used in a positive manner to handle even the most difficult programming around existing disability income coverage.[5]

The importance of programming is only secondary to the concept of disability income. If the client understands both the need for the coverage and how the benefit numbers were derived, this policy will be sold and the client will keep it and regularly pay premiums.

There is no magic. The dollars needed at time of disability depend on the client's own specific financial circumstances. The agent has to work with the numbers at hand to properly design the appropriate program.

Understanding the programming process makes this design much easier to calculate and explain.

CHAPTER NOTES

1. *1995 Guide to Social Security and Medicare*, published by William M. Mercer, Inc, Louisville, Kentucky, p. 2

2. The disability definition and denial rates are provided by the Social Security Administration.

3. Figure 5.1 is adapted from a chart on page 22 of the *1995 Guide to Social Security and Medicare*, published by William M. Mercer, Inc., Louisville, Kentucky.

4. Workers compensation law objectives and numbers for Figure 5.2 are from the *1995 Analysis of Workers Compensation Laws*, published by the U.S.Chamber of Commerce, Washington, D.C.

5. The charts used to illustrate the programming examples are from material published by Royal Maccabees and the Principal Financial Group.

■ *Chapter 6*

CLOSING THE DISABILITY INCOME SALE

The stage has been set. The need has been clearly defined. You and your prospect have determined the monthly benefit and elimination period. Lifetime protection (if available), or to age 65, or the longest benefit period available for this risk has also been determined.

Now, he or she buys, right?

Well ...

... not exactly. While you have unveiled a gap in your prospect's financial planning and quickly proposed a solution to the problem, spending money to buy more insurance may be as appealing as a root canal.

Disability income coverage, especially noncancelable plans where the insurance company cannot change the premium under any circumstances until age 65, is not cheap. As you will read in Chapter 13, Comparing Personal Disability Income Policies, you *do* get what you pay for with disability coverage. A quality product is not inexpensive.

While premium is not the only hurdle to closing the sale, it is the dominant one. The movement by insurers away from noncancelable coverage and more towards needs-based, lower-cost products may make closing somewhat easier with more affordable premiums. In any event, be prepared for price questions by illustrating what the real value of the product is to the prospective client.[1]

If you have already sold a life product to this individual (and perhaps you have just delivered it), compare the disability income plan and premium to it.

One company's target annual premium for a $100,000 universal life standard non-smoker policy with waiver of premium is $866.00. That same company's annual premium for a $3,000/month, 30 day, to age 65 noncancelable disability income plan is $1,239.66.

On the surface, this does not look very saleable:

$866.00 for $100,000

$1,239.66 for $3,000/month.

Change the monthly benefit to total potential monthly benefit and you will turn around the cost questions. At age 35, the benefit payment potential of a disability income plan with a to-age-65 benefit period is 30 years. At $3,000 per month, the benefit payout potential expressed in dollars is $1,080,000 if the individual were to become totally disabled in the first year ($3,000 x 12 months x 30 years).

Your new comparison is:

$866.00 for $100,000

$1,239.66 for $1,080,000.

Now, the universal life seems like the less attractive deal.

Although it is true that the disability benefit will decrease since in the next year the benefit period potential will reduce to 29 years and $1,044,000, think of it as a decreasing term benefit. How long before the benefit potential is down to $100,000? Quite a few years!

Remember: always express disability benefits in total potential dollar value, not only in terms of monthly benefit.

There will be many occasions where the prospect truly has difficulty in buying the complete program needed as proposed, because of affordability. When you realize this, ask first if he believes in the need for this coverage. Most will answer positively. If he does not, you should review the need for the coverage again.

If he does believe in the plan, ask how much could be set aside each month for the disability income program. Once you know the dollar amount, you can calculate some alternate proposals.

Rates for disability income are based on several variables. Age and occupation, are two factors not alterable. Monthly benefit, elimination period, and benefit period are adjustable. The order of adjustment is: benefit period, monthly benefit and, lastly, elimination period. When making these adjustments, be sure the prospect understands exactly what you are doing and the logic behind the new proposed coverage.

Despite what you may hear, the elimination period is the very *last* part of the program to be adjusted. Because of the poor claims experience of the 30 day elimination period, this alternative has been either eliminated as an offering by insurers or the rates raised so high that it is unaffordable. Sixty day elimination period plans are also experiencing the same process, leaving 90 days as the first reasonable elimination period variable. Increasing the elimination period from 90 to 180 days will lower the total premium. The difference in premium is not dramatic enough to offset the loss of *three* months of benefits.[2] In the example given above, the prospect would save $150 annually by increasing the elimination period to 180 days ($1089.27 vs. $1239.66). $150 savings and $9,000 in benefits lost in just one claim. The premium savings over the 30 year lifetime of the policy would only be *half* of the benefits lost ($150 x 30 years = $4,500). Do not alter the elimination period except as a last resort.

While it is important to quote the maximum benefit period for which the prospect is eligible, this is the first premium savings possibility. Most disabilities are over in the first 12 months and nearly all in the first 24 months. Generally, the savings from reducing the benefit period from lifetime to age 65 is 25 to 30 percent; from age 65 to five years, 30 to 60 percent, from five years to two years, 10 to 20 percent, and from two years to one year, 15 to 20 percent. (These averages will vary from company to company.)[3]

As you can see, there are significant savings when changing the benefit period from age 65 to five years. Five year (and even two year) benefit periods are reasonable alternatives if the proposed long term coverage is out of the prospect's budget range.

If the savings, after reducing the benefit period, is not enough the monthly benefit can be reduced further. While not the optimum solution, this choice is usually more acceptable than raising the elimination period to 180 days.

The monthly benefit amount you have established is the maximum the prospect can purchase based on his income. Review the monthly necessities chart where you noted the dollar amount of the critical bills that must be paid. Discuss each one and establish a priority list for payment. Determine the least amount of monthly income that the prospect and his family can live on following a disability. Then determine the cost in $100 increments between the "lowest level" and the maximum amount that could be purchased and see where these premium levels fit in the prospect's budget. Between the benefit period reduction and the election of a lower monthly benefit amount, the plan should be affordable.

One other premium saving alternative can be found in the premium variations a company may offer.

Many carriers offer a "step-rate" program for their better-rated occupation classes at the younger ages. A low, initial premium is offered to these risks for a specified period. (five years, to age 35 and to age 40 are examples of the lengths of time for which the low premium is applicable.) The premium then increases to a second, set level (guaranteed at time of issue in a noncancelable contract) that remains the same until age 65.

The longer a policy is kept, the insured eventually will pay more than if the level premium was elected in the first place. However, this premium variation allows initial premium savings and defers higher costs towards later years when affordability may not be as great a problem. The opportunity to convert to a level premium at an earlier time is also available if the insured can afford a higher premium earlier than the scheduled increase.

Some companies offer a rate schedule to purchase disability that looks very much like term life insurance. Under this method of payment, the rates increase slightly *each* year with higher increases coming at the older ages. The premiums are guaranteed for noncancelable policies and allow the insured to save as much as 40 percent on the purchase of disability coverage. The insured can then keep the program as proposed (without changing the variables - monthly benefit, benefit period, and elimination period) and still stay within budget by adopting this premium payment concept. Conversions to a level premium are also offered under this funding arrangement. Unfortunately, recent claims experience has been poor and has nudged this premium schedule towards extinction.[4]

Many prospects will agree with your plan recommendations but will want to wait before making a final decision. Not only is there a risk that a disability may occur before the program is put into effect, but it usually costs money to wait.

To delay is natural. Most healthy people cannot see themselves becoming disabled. Convincing people in the age range 25 to 45 that disability is a real threat during their working years is not easy unless they already know someone who is disabled. Even then, it is hard to persuade them that it could actually happen to them. Therefore, a more direct demonstration of the cost of delay is sometimes appropriate in closing the sale.

At age 30, a $2,000/month, 90 day, to-age-65 policy can be purchased from one company for $685.44 annually. If the insured keeps the policy to age 65 the total premium outlay is $23,990.40. Instead of buying the plan today, suppose the prospect decides to wait until age 50 when the threat of disability seems greater. While we know the ratebook premiums are going to change in 20 years, the least this individual can expect to pay, at age 50, and at today's rates is $1,580.22 annually. If this plan is kept until age 65, the total dollar amount spent is $23,703.30 in 15 years, virtually the same as the 35 years of premiums for the plan bought at age 30.[5]

So what has the prospect lost? Waiting 20 years has not changed the total premium outlay if the policy is held until age 65. The individual has lost *20 years* of protection for the *same* dollar amount. Furthermore, at age 50, the plan can be purchased only if the individual has remained healthy.

If the individual had bought the policy at age 30 and suffered a long term disability at age 40, $6,854.40 would have been spent in premiums for a benefit potential of $600,000 ($2,000 x 12 x 25 years) and a net return of $593,145.60. If the prospect had waited, the benefit available would have been zero. It saves nothing to wait and only increases the exposure for the healthy individual to a risk that, from the family's viewpoint, he cannot afford to take.

Another method of closing used is the "medical close." This is used in life insurance, but has a dramatic effect with disability insurance. Disability coverage is, after all, health insurance, and a number of medical questions must be answered by the prospect before the company agrees that this is a good risk and issues a policy.

When finishing the discussion of the need for coverage and the plan details for that prospect, take out an application and say, "Let's see if we can get you qualified for this program." While the majority of all policies are issued standard, extensive review of an applicant's history is necessary for a company properly to assess its liability. Premium rates are fixed based on the majority of policyholders being in reasonably good health. This keeps the costs down for the average insured.

If the prospect knows that this coverage is difficult to obtain, it may be the motivation to purchase the plan now. Our health is fragile; you have only to read the newspaper every day to appreciate that. Stressing this at the right time during the sales presentation can close the case for you and put into motion the wheels that will eventually turn out a policy for the insured to help replace vital income when disability strikes.

You will not close every sale. Even Pete Sampras loses a few tennis matches. If the prospect absolutely refuses to solve the financial problem disability represents, you should then complete a form with the individual's help called *Financial Funding Alternatives In the Event of Disability*. This document, a sales piece originally published by John Hancock Life Insurance Company, is an excellent tool that is both a financial reference tool for the agent and client and a final attempt to close the sale by revealing how precious few dollars will actually be available at time of claim.

The form has three sections to it. The first covers the basics of the individual's current savings and investments programs. (See Figure 6.1.)

Figure 6.1

Client's Name _____   Date of Birth _____

What types of savings or investment plans do you currently own?

_____   _____

_____   _____

_____   _____

_____   _____

Of these, do any have fulfillment provisions in the event of a total disability?

_____   _____

_____   _____

The second lists assets and liabilities (some of which may already be done if you've sold life insurance to this client). (See Figure 6.2.)

Figure 6.2

ASSETS:		LIABILITIES:	
Savings	_____	Mortgages	_____
Checking	_____	Bank Loans	_____
C.D.	_____	Other Loans	_____
C.V. Life Insurance	_____	Charge Accounts	_____
Residence	_____	Loans On Life Ins.	_____
Real Estate	_____	Property Taxes	_____
Mutual Funds	_____	Leases	_____
Annuities	_____	Income Taxes (not withheld)	_____
Stocks/Bonds	_____		
IRA/Keogh	_____	Other Debts	_____
Business	_____		
Personal Effects	_____		
Other Assets	_____	**NET WORTH**	_____

The last section asks the tough questions. (See Figure 6.3.)

Figure 6.3

How much are you currently contributing to your savings and investment programs on a regular basis? _____

How do you feel about managing your investments in the event of a total disability?

If you were to manage your own investments, how important would it be to provide a hedge against inflation now and in the event of a disability?

In your opinion, what would be a fair return on invested money over a long period of time?

What percentage of your invested assets would you wish to deplete in the case of a disability?

In the event of a disability, how would you rank these financial priorities:

$/Mo.

_____	_____	Savings and investment for education
_____	_____	Savings and investment for retirement
_____	_____	Income tax reduction or deferral
_____	_____	Estate creation or family security in the event of your death
_____	_____	Overhead expenses of your business
_____	_____	Overhead expenses of your household

What percentage of your assets would you like to maintain as liquid assets in the event of your disability? _____ %

Approximate Tax Bracket _____ %

Gross Income Previous Year _____ %

Net Income Previous Year _____ %

Do you see a substantial increase in income over the next —

Five years? _____ %

Ten years? _____ %

Twenty years? _____ %

The answers to these questions may show the individual that the savings and investment programs in place are not sufficient to meet the dollar needs of a long term disability. Moreover, it is not an easy item to budget. No one knows when disability will occur. It could be the next day, week, month, or 10 years from now. Or not at all. One can never be sure that enough money will be on hand to pay expenses unless sufficient funds are already in place. Since that is rarely the case, this form can focus on the specific deficiencies that will become obvious when a disability happens. It will increase your sales closing ratio.

One other form has become important in the today's litigious society. If after completion of the *Financial Funding Alternatives in the Event of Disability* form, the prospect still does not wish to complete the program today, have the individual sign a waiver form. (For a sample form, see Figure 6.4.)

Figure 6.4

I, _____ , acknowledge that _____ (hereinafter, "the agent") has alerted me to the potential loss of income in the event of physical disability. The agent has urged me to purchase a disability policy in order to insure myself against potential loss as a result of physical disability.

Regardless of the above, I choose not to apply for a plan of disability income protection at this time. Therefore, I release my agent from any liability in the event that I do become disabled from a sickness or an accident.

I do not expect the agent to contact me in the future regarding the purchase of a disability income policy. I agree to contact the agent and/or another insurance professional if I decide to consider the purchase of disability income coverage in the future.

_____   _____
(Date)   (Client)

There have been too many cases where an agent has been sued by a disabled client for not offering or selling disability income coverage. Do not make this mistake! Have the prospect sign the waiver form and keep it in your files along with the *Financial Funding Alternatives in the Event of Disability* form.

If you have closed the sale, congratulations! It is time to complete the application and follow it through the underwriting process, a procedure that should be adhered to closely and carefully to ensure prompt return of the application in the form of a policy to be delivered to the insured.

CHAPTER NOTES

1. "Paul Revere Unveils NonCan DI Targeted At New Markets", *National Underwriter Life & Health / Financial Services Edition*, January 2, 1995, p. 23.

2. "Dilemmas for Agents in DI Market", *Insurance Sales*, January, 1993, p. 42.

3. The rate calculation percentages are based on an average of five different DI carriers and their prices as of January, 1995.

4. The "term DI" program, called Annual Renewable Disability Income was tried unsuccessfully by several disability insurance carriers.

5. Rates are from products sold by the Principal Financial Group as of December, 1994.

Chapter 7

FIELD UNDERWRITING

The objective of the sales presentation is to obtain an application for disability coverage and, if possible, a deposit to bind the coverage. After the agent presents the disability income policy as the solution to protecting one's income, the next thing to do is to see if the client can qualify for coverage.

An application magically appears from your briefcase and the questions relating to medical history should then be asked. This begins the application process in a simple, straightforward manner.

Two important concepts should be noted:

1. Disability income coverage is not easy to obtain if occupational and income stability are not present. The agent is not kidding when he says, "Let's see if you qualify for this coverage." It may sound like a gimmick, but insurance companies do not issue this coverage indiscriminately. Today, more than ever, disability underwriting is extremely difficult. (The medical and financial underwriting processes are discussed more fully in the next two chapters.)

2. The agent, by asking the medical questions, has begun the critical practice of field underwriting. In taking the application, the agent can almost always affect the speed at which this form makes the transition from inquiry to policy.

In a perfect world, the agent would ask all of the questions in a slow and deliberate manner; the prospect would answer accurately and in great detail; the agent, in turn, would write *all* of the information down on the application form.

Realistically, all three of these actions happen in concert only some of the time. Human nature takes a hand quite often. Agents are salespeople and, as such, are not generally "detail" people. They are unintentionally selective about what appears on the application because it is easier to write three words instead of ten and still feel that the gist of the information is there. The home office underwriter spends a significant amount of extra time trying to discover the other seven words that more clearly define the risk involved for the insurance company. This search adds extra days and even weeks to the issue time; a delay that frustrates agent and potential insured alike.

It is also human nature for the prospect to edit the data given to the agent. Not many people are free with details of either their medical past or their financial present. Thus, important information necessary for an accurate underwriting decision does not appear on the application because the agent never had the opportunity to write it down.

But how would the home office underwriter ever know, you ask? This will be discussed in more detail in the next two chapters, but there are independent information sources that the underwriter relies on either to substantiate data included or to alert him that there is more information about the prospect that has yet to come to light. The journey to identify the missing pieces causes the delays in the underwriting process.

Hence, Underwriting Rule Number One: The better the *field* underwriting, the faster a policy will be sent for delivery to the insured. The goal of this chapter is to make the agent an improved field underwriter and for the prospect to realize the importance of complete answers.[1]

THE MEDICAL QUESTIONS

While the medical questions are never located in the front of the application, we will start with this section since it is where many agents begin. When using the medical close, the answers can dictate whether the rest of the application should even be completed.

Depending on the age of the prospect and the amount of coverage being applied for, a medical exam may be necessary to qualify for the coverage. While the exam covers the same ground (and more) that the application medical questions do, completion of these is still important for two reasons:

1. It gives the home office underwriter a chance to begin reviewing medical data and start the evaluation process even before receiving the results of the exam. Today, most disability insurers require the medical portion of the application to be completed even if there is an exam needed.

2. It gives the agent an idea about the medical history of the client and better alerts him to the likelihood of a standard issue (coverage issued as applied for) or a substandard issue (modification by the company of the coverage applied for). Preparing the insured for a substandard issue *at the time application is made* is important to the future success of the agent in placing this case.

Medical question formats may vary, but they all ask about the same general subjects. Figure 7.1 is an example of the medical questions (often called Part 2 of the application) that usually appear on an application.

Figure 7.1

	YES	NO	IMPORTANT!
To the best of your knowledge and belief has any person proposed to be insured:			Give complete details, dates and results of treatment, name of doctor or hospital and complete address (attach additional sheet if necessary). Specify to whom history applies and reference by number.
19. Within the past ten years had diagnosis or treatment of:	☐	☐	
(a) The lungs or respiratory system including hayfever or other allergies, asthma, bronchitis, tuberculosis or emphysema?	☐	☐	
(b) The heart or circulatory system including high blood pressure, heart attack, heart murmur, or chest pain, irregular heartbeat or varicose veins or phlebitis?	☐	☐	
(c) The digestive system including ulcer, gastritis, intestinal disorders, colitis, gall bladder, hemorrhoids, hernia or disorder of the pancreas, liver or spleen?	☐	☐	
(d) The nervous system, including epilepsy, convulsions, seizures, headaches, paralysis, mental disorders, nervousness or psychiatric treatment?	☐	☐	
(e) The genito-urinary system including any kidney disorder, kidney stones, cystitis, prostate trouble, or bladder infections?	☐	☐	
(f) Diabetes or sugar in the urine, thyroid, goiter, breast or other glandular disorder?	☐	☐	
(g) The muscular or skeletal system including arthritis, gout, rheumatism, any back or spine disorders or treatment of muscular disorders or joint disorder, rupture or syphillis?	☐	☐	
(h) Cancer, tumor, cyst, or growth of any kind?	☐	☐	
(i) Eyes or ears including impaired sight or hearing?	☐	☐	
(j) Any disorder of the generative organs, including irregular menstruation or pregnancy complications?.	☐	☐	
(k) AIDs (Acquired Immune Deficiency Syndrome) or ARC (AIDS Related Complex)**.	☐	☐	
20. Is any Proposed Insured now pregnant?	☐	☐	
21. Ever had surgery (including cesarean section) or has surgery ever been recommended?	☐	☐	
22. Had an EKG, EEG, chest x-ray, or blood study of any kind in the past five years? If yes, give name of physician completing test and results.	☐	☐	
23. Currently taking medication or receiving medical treatment of any type?	☐	☐	
24. Ever been treated for alcoholism or drug addiction or ever a member of Alcoholics Anonymous or used narcotic drugs or similar agents other than as prescribed by a physician?	☐	☐	
25. Had any other illness, injury, medical treatment, or consulted with any physician during the past five years not reported above?	☐	☐	
26. Have any physical or mental defect other than shown above?			** AIDS Related Complex (ARC) is a condition with signs and symptoms which may include generalized lymphadenopathy (swollen lymph nodes), loss of appetite, weight loss, fever, night sweats, diarrhea, malaise, lethargy and tiredness, oral thrush, skin rashes, unexplained infections, dementia, depression or other psychoneurotic disorders with no known cause.
27. Gained or lost weight in the past year? If yes, ... Name_____ Lbs. Gained_____ Lbs. Lost_____ Cause_____	☐	☐	
28. Name and address of family doctor of insured adults.	☐	☐	
29. Name and address of children's doctor, if insured.	☐	☐	

Depth of answers is important. The actual symptoms or condition, date first treated, duration, and names *and* addresses of physician(s) seen for same must be on the application.

There are many more medical conditions that cause a disability than there are medical conditions that result in death. Therefore, disability income underwriting evaluates many more illnesses or injuries than life insurance underwriting. Those agents familiar only with life underwriting must be especially sensitive to noting details they are unaccustomed to taking in the field underwriting process for life insurance.

For example, a knee injury and operation would not warrant a significant amount of detail on a life insurance application, but these details are important for disability income underwriting. Depending on the severity of the trauma, the recency of the operation and the type of occupation (is the knee used a lot?), this information must be evaluated to formally underwrite the application.

As the agent becomes more experienced with how the home office evaluates a risk, he can prepare the client after reviewing medical history. For example, a prospect who replies to an inquiry about any back or spine disorder by saying, "I've had back trouble off and on for the last three years," should know that the probability is strong that the disability policy will be issued *with* an exclusion of any coverage for the back. The agent should speak generally in saying, "I'm not sure what our underwriting department will do, but back trouble is a source of concern to the company and they may not offer coverage for your back on this policy. But it will cover *all* of the other unexpected health problems you may incur over your working career."

It will be easier to place the policy at delivery time if the applicant is initially prepared during the taking of the application.

Remember, the more details you provide the underwriter now, the less likely a search (causing delay) for the information will need to be done and the faster you will have a policy to place.

Most application forms today require the applicant's signature on a notice and consent form to do blood testing. The test is primarily done to check for the presence of human immunodeficiency virus (HIV) antibodies. It may not be done routinely. In most states, the policy application has to be over a certain amount, such as $2,000/month in benefits. In a few states, notably California and Florida, the consent form usually requires a signature. The agent should check with the specific insurance company for whom they are writing the disability income coverage to determine its requirement. Figure 7.2 shows a sample of this type of form.

Figure 7.2

NOTICE AND CONSENT FOR BLOOD TESTING WHICH MAY INCLUDE AIDS VIRUS (ANTIBODY) TESTING

To evaluate your insurability, the insurer named above (the insurer) has requested that you provide a sample of your blood for testing and analysis to determine the presence of human immunodeficiency virus (HIV) antibodies. By signing and dating this form you agree that this test may be done and that underwriting decisions will be based on the test result. A series of tests will be performed by a certified laboratory through a medically accepted procedure.

Pre-Testing Considerations
Many public health organizations have recommended that before taking an AIDS-related blood test, a person seek counseling to become informed concerning the implications of such a test. You may wish to consider counseling, at your expense, prior to being tested.

Meaning of Positive Test Result
The test is not a test for AIDS. It is a test for the HIV virus, the causative agent for AIDS, and shows whether you have been exposed to the virus. A positive test result does not mean that you have AIDS but that you are at significantly increased risk of developing problems with your immune system. The test for HIV antibodies is very sensitive. Errors are rare but they do occur. Your private physician, a public health clinic, or an AIDS information organization in your city might provide you with further information on the medical implications of a positive test.

Positive HIV antibody test results will adversely affect your application for insurance.

Confidentiality of Test Results
All test results are required to be treated confidentially. They will be reported by the laboratory to the insurer. The test results may be disclosed as required by law or may be disclosed to employees of the insurer who have the responsibility to make underwriting decisions on behalf of the insurer or to outside legal counsel who needs such information to effectively represent the insurer in regard to your application. The results may be disclosed to a reinsurer, if the reinsurer is involved in the underwriting process. The test may be released to an insurance medical information exchange under procedures that are designed to assure confidentiality, including the use of general codes that also cover results for other diseases or conditions not related to AIDS, or for the preparation of statistical reports that do not disclose the identity of any particular person.

Notification of Test Result
A positive test result will be disclosed to a physician you designate. If you do not designate a physician, a positive test result will be disclosed to the Florida Department of Health and Rehabilitation. Because a trained person should deliver that information so that you can understand clearly what the test result means, please list your private physician so that the Insurer can have him or her tell you the test result and explain its meaning.

Name of physician for reporting a positive test result: _____

Address: _____

Consent
I have read and I understand this Notice and Consent for AIDS-Related Blood Testing. I voluntarily consent to the withdrawal of blood from me, the testing of that blood, and the disclosure of the test results as described above.

There is also a form inside the blood profile kit which must be read and signed. If you choose not to sign below on this form or the form in the kit, we will be unable to process your request for coverage. If you wish for us to continue processing, sign below.

I understand that I have the right to request and receive a copy of this authorization. A photocopy of this form will be as valid as the original.

_____

Signature of Proposed Insured or Parent/Guardian

_____

Date Signed

GENERAL INFORMATION

After completing the medical questions, return to the first part of the application to obtain the basic information about your client. Name, date of birth, gender, address, Social Security number are all part of these questions. They are easy to ask and the prospect almost always has a quick answer. An example of this part of an application is shown in Figure 7.3.

Figure 7.3

1. PROPOSED INSURED(s) NAME: Title Last First	Middle Initial	Relationship to Primary Insured	Birthdate Mo. Day Yr.	Ht. Ft. In.	Wt. Lbs.	Age	Sex	Birthplace State or Country
a.		Primary Insured						
b.		Spouse						
c.								
d								
e.								
f.								

2. ADDRESSES: Send correspondence to: ❑ Residence ❑ Business
Length of Residence at Current Address_____

	Number Street	City	State	Zip Code

Residence_____

Phone # ( )

e. Soc. Se. No. ☐☐☐ - ☐☐ - ☐☐☐☐

Business _____

Phone # ( )

OWNER: ❑ Primary Insured ❑ Other _____

Phone # ( )_____ **The Owner must sign this application on the next page where indicated.**

Accuracy is of obvious importance here as this is the source of the company's permanent record of the insured. Future billing notices will be sent to the address shown. Age is a key variable in the calculation of the cost of the coverage.

EMPLOYMENT INFORMATION

Occupation classification is another component of the rate calculation process. The more stable the occupation, the lower the premium charged for the coverage. For many companies, the more secure the occupation, the more liberal the definition of disability in the policy.

The more complete the description of the duties of the client (see Figure 7.4), the easier it is for the home office underwriter to classify the occupation. A title such as Vice President, Acme, Inc. is not very useful. However, described as the national sales director for a tire manufacturer, the job is more clearly defined. Acme, Inc. could be a munitions factory, and the client's duties could require the planting of explosives which would definitely alter the rating of the policy if it could be issued at all. Yet both people are Vice Presidents. Both work for Acme, Inc. But there is a world of difference in job risk. Be specific!

Figure 7.4

Occupation &
Duties in Full: _____

Name & Address	b. Length of Service: _____
of Employer	c. Are you actively at work? ❑ Yes ❑ No

(a) Type of business ❑ Sole Proprietor ❑ Partnership ❑ Corporation ❑ S Corporation
(b) Number of employees Full-time _____ Part-time _____ Contracted _____
(a) Is your business or office at your residence? ❑ Yes ❑ No (b) Percent of time working there ____ %
Distance between business and residence _____ feet or miles (circle one)
Other occupations in the last 5 years and duration worked in each _____
_____

Describe any part-time jobs _____

INCOME INFORMATION

Financial data is not always easy to obtain from a prospect. As a society, we are conditioned not to divulge our earnings to many people. Despite agent assurances, we are convinced that everyone, including the Internal Revenue Service, will be privy to this information.

But, in addition to net worth and unearned income, income dictates the amount of monthly benefit the prospect can buy. A more detailed discussion of financial underwriting will be found in Chapter 9, Financial Underwriting. There are standard income questions on the application (see Figure 7.5). This will probably not be all that is required. Today, most disability insurers also require further documentation: tax forms and schedules. Pages 1 and 2 of the 1040 form must be submitted to substantiate income. Businesses will also need to submit Schedule C, Schedule E (F for farmers) if filed, 1120 or 1120S for corporations and perhaps even W-2 forms. Agents should check with their specific disability income company for their actual requirements.[2]

Some insurers ease the "pain" of submitting tax forms with the application by extending a discount off the policy premium for doing so.

Figure 7.5 illustrates a sample income question on an application form.

Figure 7.5

---

a. What were your earnings from your occupation or profession last year? (Gross income less business expenses) $ _____

b. What was "other income" last year from dividends, interest, rents, royalties, estates and trusts, etc.? (Circle items) $ _____

c. In answer to 21b, how much was income from the business in which you are an officer or partner?
   $ _____

d. What was contributed to IRA, HR10, qualified pension or profit sharing plan? Is this included in 21a?
   ☐ Yes ☐ No $ _____

The income that can be insured is gross earned income *after* business expenses and *before* taxes. Unearned income is income that is likely to continue whether the insured is disabled or not. A large net worth usually indicates the lack of need for long term coverage depending upon the nature of these assets and how quickly they can be converted to cash for assistance at time of disability.

OTHER KEY QUESTIONS

There are general questions (see Figure 7.6) that do not fit into any one category, but they are important. The answers give the underwriter an idea of activities that could affect the chances of a disability. A CPA who spends three weeks a year making deep scuba dives in the Bahamas represents a greater disability risk than the CPA who spends vacations sitting on the beach in the Hamptons.

Figure 7.6

	Yes	No
17. Have you, or do you plan to engage in ultra light flying, scuba or sky diving, car or other type of racing?	☐	☐
18. Do you plan to fly or have you within the last five years flown as a pilot, student pilot or crew member?	☐	☐
19. Do you plan to live or travel outside of the U.S.?	☐	☐
20. Have you ever had life or disability insurance rated, ridered, modified or declined?	☐	☐
21. Driver's license number_____ . In the last 3 years have you been charged with or had 2 or more motor vehicle moving violations or accidents, suspension or revocation of your license, driving while intoxicated?	☐	☐
22. Have you in the last five years been arrested for other than traffic violations?	☐	☐
23. Within the last 5 years have you been treated or counseled or joined an organization for alcohol or drug use or used amphetamines, barbiturates, sedatives, LSD, marijuana, cocaine, heroin, or morphine?	☐	☐
"Yes answers to 17 and 18 require Sports and/or Aviation Statement respectively. Explain or give reasons if "Yes" for questions 19-23.		

OTHER COVERAGE IN FORCE

Since there is a limit on the amount of coverage a company will insure for disability income protection, based on the insured's income, it is necessary to check to be sure that *all* disability coverage owned by the insured stays below this limit (see Figure 7.7).

Figure 7.7

Accident and sickness insurance in force? ☐ Yes ☐ No   Types 1. Individual DI   2. Group   3. State Disability
4. Individual Overhead Expense   5. Individual Buy-Out   6. Association

Insurance Carrier	Type of Coverage	Amount Per Month	Elimination Period	Benefit Period
_____	_____	_____	_____	_____
_____	_____	_____	_____	_____
_____	_____	_____	_____	_____

(a) Will policy applied for replace or change any other accident and sickness insurance? ☐ Yes ☐ No
If "yes," complete item 15(b) (submit state replacement forms if required, and give details) _____

An insured with more benefits available from disability income coverage than earned income is financially better off if he is disabled. These questions try to ensure that this does not happen.

Field underwriting revolves around completion of the application. The more details you provide the home office underwriter, the more easily and quickly an issue decision can be reached.

Field underwriting does not end with the application. Assisting in obtaining medical records of the insured if they are needed can be handled by a phone call to the insurance claims and records person in the doctor's office. Briefing the client on the possibility of being contacted by a third party (an inspection service representative by phone or in person or a home office person by phone to verify some of the questions on the application) can adequately prepare your client. Avoid surprises!!

Assisting the home office underwriter in compiling the information required for a decision strengthens the relationship between the agent and the home office and assures the client of receiving a product accurately based on his personal and business situation.

CHAPTER NOTES

1. The application forms illustrated in this chapter are samples from the Principal Financial Group, Royal Maccabees Life Insurance Company and American Pioneer Life Insurance Company.

2. The income tax schedules required are essentially the same from company to company. While there may be some minor variation, disability insurers today want proof in the form of Internal Revenue Service forms to substantiate income.

Chapter 8

HOME OFFICE UNDERWRITING

The agent has done the job expected. An application has been completed and forwarded to the home office. Now comes the most misunderstood process that occurs in the insuring of an individual for disability income: underwriting.

Contrary to popular thought, the home office underwriter generally does everything within his power to issue a policy. The majority of disability income applications sent to the home office are issued, many of them on a standard basis. Most underwriters understand that premium income to the insurance company is paid only if the contract they approve is placed.

They also have an obligation to the company for which they work. The law of large numbers governs. Some cases issued are going to become claims. Many will not. The underwriter must ensure that the company is protected from the poorer risk (a certain claim) by screening during the underwriting process. A recent history of deteriorating claims experience has forced the underwriter to be even more careful than ever in reviewing and approving an application.

This is not a simple task. Underwriting, I was once told, is an art. The underwriter develops a sense for the case he can take a chance on and the one he cannot. Above all, an underwriter must be creative. A decision must be made that both protects the company and gives the agent an equitable policy to place. With more stringent underwriting guidelines today, the underwriter's ability to satisfy the company, agent and potential insured is somewhat impaired. Cases of a certain nature with a specific history must be declined. Others have to be modified. Still, most are issued as applied for even given the latest underwriting constraints.

This chapter takes a closer look at this issue process.

THE INITIAL SCREENING

When an underwriter first reviews an application, some quick notes are made to refer to later as the case develops. Age, gender, height and weight, income, occupation, and eligibility for the plan applied for are the first facts noted on a review of the application forms submitted by the agent.

The application is the key to how quickly the underwriting process will flow. Complete, accurate answers assist the underwriter in deciding whether or not to approve or investigate further. If further investigation is warranted, the more details furnished on the application, the more likely that the underwriter will go to the right source for additional details.

Two forms usually compose the initial underwriting process: the application and the medical examination report (including the HIV testing form). In cases where a medical examination is not required (where the benefit level applied for is low), the application asks sufficient medical questions to serve this purpose. The report of the medical examination provides further information in the narrative medical history and reports on build, pulse, blood pressure, and the heart. In addition, a urinalysis and (now) a blood profile often accompany the medical exam form.

A word about blood profiles. This requirement came into existence as a result of the increasing presence in our society of Acquired Immune Deficiency Syndrome (AIDS). During the incubation period of the AIDS epidemic in this country, many applications were underwritten and approved, creating a large block of business that was issued prior to the blood profile becoming a part of the underwriting process. This created a large exposure to potential AIDS claims for which the issuer of noncancelable policies has no protection. With a few company exceptions, the AIDS claims actually incurred have been less than originally forecast. It remains, however, a medical condition which must be recognized and underwritten; thus the use of the blood profile.

This blood profile requirement has been producing valuable results for underwriters since one can test blood for more than just the presence of HIV antibodies. Now, the underwriter receives a report detailing more medical knowledge of the proposed insured than the result of the AIDS test. Levels of cholesterol, triglycerides, liver enzymes and glucose, among others, can indicate higher risk factors than any narrative history could ever tell. The blood profile, originally a protection for companies against future AIDS claims, has also given the underwriter a substantial amount of new information upon which to make an underwriting decision.

ADDITIONAL DATA REQUIRED

After a review of the application and initial medical data, many underwriting decisions are made. These decisions often result in the approval of the coverage as applied for. However, the underwriter may not have enough information upon which to make a proper decision. There are additional tools for underwriting which can provide enough data for a decision.[1]

- *Attending Physician Statement (APS).* If the underwriter wants more information about a medical condition, a doctor's office, clinic or hospital can frequently provide more details regarding symptoms, prognosis, medications, and duration. An APS request is sent directly to the address of the institution or office of the attending physician. The company pays a fee for this information. Many physicians, clinics, and hospitals bill the company for the fee; however, some require payment in advance. If you, as the agent, are aware of the medical personnel in your area who do charge before releasing any information, let the home office know. It saves time during the underwriting process.

- *Inspection Report (IR).* This report typically verifies answers to questions on the application but also provides information about the insured's habits, moral reputation, business background and motor vehicle record. A third-party organization can be hired to contact the insured. More often today, designated home office personnel perform this task as a *Personal History Interview (PHI)*. When writing the application, it is helpful to prepare the proposed insured for this contact. In the case of the PHI, the best time to call the applicant will be listed somewhere on the application for completion.

- *Supplemental Health Statement.* A quick way to obtain more details about a medical condition, other than through an APS, is to contact the applicant directly for more details concerning the condition. The more information provided in the application, the less likely the need for this additional requirement, but if necessary a request for a supplemental health statement will be sent to the applicant for completion and return.

- *Questionnaires.* Several questionnaires are available to the underwriter to elicit more information about a specified subject or condition. These forms are specifically focused on the relevant subject: aviation, hazardous sports participation, chest pain, blood pressure, alcohol and drug usage, and diabetes are the more common of these fact-finding sheets.

- *Other Lab Tests.* If necessary, an additional lab test may be requested to complete the underwriting file. Chest x-rays and electrocardiograms are the most common of this kind of test. If a urinalysis has been furnished with the exam form and proves abnormal, additional specimens will be requested to pinpoint whether a problem exists, the test results were incorrect, or there was a minor problem that has corrected itself. The presence of sugar in the urine can compel the underwriter to order a *Glucose Tolerance Test* to further determine if this is a problem which may affect issuance of the policy.

All of this data will help the underwriter make the most appropriate and fair underwriting decision. This information is not ordered purposely to delay a case. In many cases, it costs a significant amount of money to obtain these facts. Once they have been compiled, the overall view of the risk narrows down the range within which an underwriting decision is to be made.

TYPES OF UNDERWRITING DECISIONS

1. *Standard.* A majority of cases reviewed are issued as applied for. This is the decision every underwriter wants to make. It is not always possible, but even in disability underwriting many cases leave the company on a standard underwriting basis.

2. *Exclusion Rider.* It is sometimes necessary to use an exclusion rider, under which no coverage is provided for a certain condition. Back riders, for example, are very common, primarily because of the unpredictability and the likelihood of a recurrence associated with this ailment. Except for the exclusion rider, all other coverage is standard. Most exclusion riders attempt to be specific about the condition being eliminated from coverage.

3. *Rating.* Some conditions do not lend themselves to an exclusion rider, such as excessive hypertension or diabetes. In these instances, where coverage can be issued, an extra premium is added to cover the higher risk of disability associated with these conditions. This does *not* exclude coverage: disability due to the condition(s) for which the rating is assessed will be covered. The extra premium is meant to help meet the expected claims costs of the higher risk.

4. *Benefit Modifications.* There are times when the variety of risk factors present make it necessary for the underwriter to adjust the parameters of the policy applied for in order to make an offer of coverage. Decreasing the benefit period (for example, from to-age-65 to five years) or increasing the elimination period (from 60 to 90 days, for example) enables coverage to be offered rather than declined or issued at an excessively high extra premium or with multiple exclusion riders. In

addition, a limit on the monthly benefit amount may also be necessary to lower the overall dollar risk.

5. *Limited Condition Rider.* This is a form of exclusion rider that provides some type of coverage for a specific condition without altering the other benefits applied for. The underwriter may be able to extend coverage to a condition on a limited basis rather than completely exclude it because the risk factor is lower, although still present on some basis. For example, let's say an individual applies for a 60 day elimination period and a to-age-65 benefit period and has a peptic ulcer that flares up every so often. A limited condition rider can be placed on the peptic ulcer providing coverage from the 91st day. All other conditions are covered from the 61st day and even the peptic ulcer is covered to age 65 following its special 90 day wait. In this situation, the underwriting concern was with the 60 day elimination period rather than the to-age-65 benefit period. A limited condition rider accomplishes the underwriting purpose without having to place a full exclusion. This is a method designed to help the agent place substandard cases and is very effective. This creativity in the underwriting process accomplishes the task of protecting the company, but gives the agent a fighting chance at placing a policy that offers reasonable protection for a known medical condition.

All of these various decisions are made daily by the underwriter and make up the medical underwriting portion of the issue process.[2]

Before closing the medical underwriting portion of this chapter, two additional comments concerning trial applications and field underwriting guides are necessary.

TRIAL APPLICATIONS

The trial application is an informal inquiry from the applicant to the company regarding the possible issue of disability income coverage. If the insured has extensive medical history that suggests a policy is likely *not* to be issued other than on a highly modified basis, rather than be put through the procedures of a medical exam, the individual completes the medical portion of the application, furnishes medical records or authorizes their release to the company and asks for an offer of coverage.

The underwriter reviews the information and either makes no offer as the risk is too high to take or advises the limits within which coverage can be issued, usually subject to the fully completed application and current medical examination.

No money to bind coverage is collected in this situation. The individual is seeking an offer with the trial application. If the offer is acceptable, the normal application-taking process can then be followed.

FIELD UNDERWRITING GUIDE

To assist agents in the question and answer process surrounding the proposed insured's medical information, companies often publish a guide to medical underwriting which provides a synopsis of requirements and possible underwriting decisions associated with a specific medical condition.

This type of information can be very useful to the agent (and applicant) in previewing the type of coverage (based on the underwriting decision) that may be forthcoming. Discussing this at the time application is made can help to set up the agent's return visit to place a case that is not going to be issued as applied for.

The guide generally describes the condition, medical requirements, and underwriting process on an abbreviated basis. Obviously, *all* factors affecting insurability will have an impact on the final underwriting result, but this guide is helpful as an educational tool.

Figure 8.1 is an example of the type of entries found in this guide.[3]

OTHER UNDERWRITING FACTORS

While medical underwriting is an important part of the overall underwriting process, there are other significant areas that affect a decision on a case. Financial underwriting will be discussed in detail in Chapter 9, but occupation and job duties, prior insurance history, other coverage in force, and avocations are also considerations for the underwriter.

Occupation

The insured's job and surrounding duties is one of the critical factors in disability income rating. The less hazardous and more stable the occupation, generally the better the risk.

In addition, the better the occupation class, the more liberal the definition of disability under the contract. (Various definitions of total disability are described in Chapter 13, Comparing Personal Disability Income Policies and Chapter 14, Personal Disability Income Policies: What The Contractual Language Really Means.) This places some extra responsibility squarely on the underwriter's shoulders in determining occupation class.

Figure 8.1

SAMPLE FIELD UNDERWRITING GUIDE

Condition	Medical Requirements	Underwriting Process
ANEMIA. Blood disorder.	APS with details of cause of the condition and a complete report of all blood tests.	1. Blood Loss Anemia- Usually standard if blood count has returned to normal.
		2. Secondary Anemia- Usually standard if successfully treated with iron and blood count has returned to normal.
		3. Aplastic Anemia-Decline
		4. Pernicious Anemia-After one year, blood tests normal, rate 50%. After two years, 25%; three years - standard.
		5. Sickle Cell Anemia- Decline.
		6. Thalassemia Major: Decline.
		7. Thalassemia Minor: If blood count is normal- standard. If below normal, rating of 20-50% depending on level.
		8. Hemolytic Anemia. Without splenectomy, decline. After successful operation, standard after 12 months.
ANGINA. Mild ischemia of short duration due to narrowing of the coronary arteries as a result of arterio-sclerosis.	APS with details of incidence, frequency and prognosis.	Usually decline.
ANXIETY REACTION. A condition of unreasonable fear and apprehension.	APS Psychiatric Question- naire or analysis.	1. If condition is currently present, app. should be postponed.
		2. Others: Depends on recency of symptoms. If less than 5 years ago, probable decline. If more than 5 years ago, decision based on specifics of the condition.
APPENDICITIS. Inflamation of the appendix.	Part II completion only.	1. If operated on, standard after three months.
		2. Not operated, standard with 90 day EP.

Most companies publish an occupation listing (by no means complete) which lists the more common occupations and assigns them a rating class. Occupations are usually rated in similar fashion from company to company, but the type of rating assigned can be confusing. Some companies call their best occupation class Class One. Others call it 4A; still others 5A; others list their best class as Preferred, or P.

Whatever the nomenclature, the best occupation class consists of the professional risk who has invested a considerable amount of time in education, is in a stable job situation not subject to seasonal or economic swings, is a high income earner in a position where personal services are the key to success. Occupations in this category include most physicians, attorneys, CPAs, pharmacists, engineers, psychiatrists, osteopaths, architects, optometrists, and high income corporate executives. By coincidence, actuaries, who normally rate the policies, are also in this category. This group is dwindling as poor claims experience has taken risks like dentists, surgeons, and podiatrists out of this higher level.

The second classification, eligible for coverage that may be as liberal (or with slight modifications to disability definitions), but at a higher premium rate, lists occupations that are upper to middle income type positions. Included here are positions where the individual's personal services are not necessarily as critical to the overall success of the business, where the duties are still not hazardous, where risk exposure is slightly higher, and claims experience slightly worse. Some of the members of this group were formerly in the top classification (anesthesiologists, emergency room physicians) but have been dropped a notch due to unfavorable claims experience. Other occupations here are middle income corporate executives, psychologists, nurse anesthetists, physician's assistants, higher earning experienced insurance agents, small animal veterinarians and some stockbrokers.

A third classification with a higher premium and less liberal contractual language than the second class covers other white collar occupations, some gray collar jobs and those in the management end of manual labor-oriented work. These risks present a higher risk for the insurance company than the previous two classifications. These types of jobs include real estate salespeople, manufacturer's representatives, personnel recruiters, some opticians, dentists, paralegals, librarians, registered nurses, teachers, copywriters and commercial artists.

The fourth occupational grouping consists primarily of other gray collar jobs and some blue collar professions that have higher premiums still and more limited benefits. These risks might qualify for the to-age-65 benefit period, but may be limited to only a five year benefit period. There is usually a cap on the amount of coverage that these risks can purchase. Specific occupations in this class are members of the clergy, photographers, clerical workers, switchboard operators, chiropractors, building inspectors, dental hygienists, hotel managers, lithographers, medical lab technicians, packing plant foremen and silversmiths.

The final listing is for the most hazardous jobs which only a few companies will actually write. Benefit periods are often restricted to two years, or at most five years. Some companies will write these risks only if a "Return of Premium" rider is added. This rider requires a substantial extra premium, which will be returned to the insured at a later date only to the extent that premium paid exceeds claims paid. These occupations include chefs, service station managers, shoe repairers, welders, waitresses, piano tuners, painters, plumbers, stock clerks, and carpenters.

The underwriter looks at duties performed when classifying these risks, *not* the job title carried. Thus, a Vice President of Acme, Inc. may be a high income corporate sales executive or the person who assembles the explosives that Wily Coyote never seems to plant correctly. Both risks would be classified quite differently even though both individuals are Vice Presidents of Acme, Inc.

When completing the application, the more specific an agent can be about job duties, the easier it is for the home office underwriter to assess occupation class and avoid delays in trying to clarify the correct occupational classification.

Business Owner Classification

Just as it's difficult to distinguish between the Vice Presidents of Acme, Inc. without more detail, classifying a business owner for rating purposes requires more than a description of job duties. For example, the owner of a plumbing business may seem easy to classify. In a company underwriting guide under "plumber" it usually is the lowest classification level which pays high premium rates for somewhat limited benefits. But is it really easy?

What if there were two plumbers who each owned his own business? One is a sole proprietor, works alone, does all the estimating of jobs when not actually performing the usual plumbing duties and has an office manager who handles the essential paperwork. The other has a larger business with three plumbers working for him. This business owner spends the bulk of his time estimating new jobs and inspecting past and current ones. He dons the plumber's uniform only on the rare occasion that one of the plumber employees is out and a job needs to be finished. He earns about $75,000 per year and has been in business for 12 years. The sole proprietor who does it all, earns $30,000 and is a four year veteran of the plumbing industry.

Should each be classified the same way?

One could easily make an argument for a higher classification for the owner/boss who contracts jobs that employees perform. This person is a long-time business owner, a high earner and performing less hazardous work since he rarely spends any time performing the duties of a plumber.

To address this business owner classification inequity, companies have developed a business owner classification grid. This approach utilizes several variables concerning a business owner rather than only the type of business. These key qualifiers are:

- age
- income
- years in current business
- number of full-time employees

These standards give a better picture of the type of business owner the underwriter is attempting to classify. Experience, earnings and size of business will assist in placing the more successful business owner into a higher level of occupational classification than would otherwise happen based solely on occupation and job duties.

Typically, points are assigned to these various factors and a final point total is used to assess classification. Illustrated below is a sample grid.[4]

AGE:			INCOME:		
	Below 25	1		Below $25,000	1
	25-34	2		$25,001-35,000	2
	35-44	3		$35,001-50,000	3
	45+	4		$50,001-65,000	4
				$65,001-80,000	5
				$80,001 +	6

YEARS IN CURRENT BUSINESS (OR SIMILAR OCC.):		
	Less than 3 years:	1
	3-6 years	2
	6-10 years	3
	10 years +	4

NUMBER OF FULL-TIME EMPLOYEES:		
	Less than 10	1
	10-24	2
	25-49	3
	50-74	4
	75-99	5
	100 +	6

Point Totals:

6-10:	elevate one classification
11-16:	elevate two classifications
17+:	elevate three classifications

This is merely a sample grid and each company will have its own set of administrative rules for classification purposes. For example, a plumber (our example) may only be elevated as high as two additional classifications even if the person's point total was 17 or higher. Be sure to read the guidelines carefully. There is usually a limit to the amount of physical labor that can be performed to make the business owner eligible for an upgrade. Usually there is a minimum ownership percentage, such as 25 percent, required to be eligible.

Whatever the specific rules, the agent should recognize that business owners merit different considerations when it comes to occupational classification. That being the case, the agent should know what variables are important and seek this information out at time of application making the job of classifying easier for both agent and underwriter.

Prior Insurance History

The disability application always asks whether the applicant has ever had prior insurance coverage declined or modified in some way. Here, the underwriter looks to see if the applicant has had difficulty in obtaining insurance in the past.

Prior problems do not always mean bad news, though. An exclusion for a peptic ulcer on a prior disability income application issued seven years earlier may not be necessary on the current application if no problems have existed since then and the proposed insured no longer needs medication for the condition. The agent might even recommend, in this case, contacting the insurer to see if the exclusion can now be removed.

Accuracy in information is important here. The more specific the agent and proposed insured can be about the individual's insurance past, the less likelihood any delay will occur.

Other Coverage In Force

Disability income is the only insurance I have sold where a client has told me, "I wish I could buy more." Disability income has a finite limit illustrated in the tables that companies publish showing the amount of monthly benefit that can be purchased based on specific earnings levels.

The limits to what the insured can purchase are meant to maintain a "corridor" between the amount of money the insured will receive if disabled and the income that would have been earned if the insured had remained healthy and working.

This corridor is intended to provide an incentive for the insured to return to work since he would be financially better off by doing so.

For this reason, a complete disclosure of other coverage in force is important. All the sources of income available to the insured at time of disability are added together for determination of what the company can issue in benefits. There is no point in holding out with this information. The underwriter can access a data bank which has a listing of prior insurance coverage applied for by the proposed insured. (See Chapter 5, The Art of Programming Benefits and Chapter 9, Financial Underwriting, for further discussion of this subject.)

Avocations

One other detail the underwriter notes is the presence of any unusual hobbies the insured may undertake on a regular basis. These can range from the extreme (auto car racing with Paul Newman or parachuting into professional football stadiums on Sunday afternoons) to the daredevil (hang gliding, scaling Mount Everest) to the more common vacation pursuits (scuba diving).

Since these extracurricular activities present a greater risk of disability, the type of avocation, frequency of participation and policy elimination period (length of time before benefits commence after disability) all are factors in issuing coverage.

Frequently, a full exclusion of the activity is placed on the policy. In other cases, an extra premium may suffice. Normally, the avocation does not mean an outright decline, and coverage will still be available for the medical problems, outside of these activities, that the policy was intended to cover.

CONCLUSION

The disability income underwriter reviews a substantial amount of data about a given individual and from this information, identifies the risk the insured presents to the company. In many cases that risk is minimal and coverage is issued as applied for. Certain conditions or problems may cause modification of benefits or the inability to issue any coverage because the risk is too great to assume.

There is one additional piece to the underwriting puzzle: financial underwriting, covered in Chapter 9.

CHAPTER NOTES

1. "Bank of Insurers: New Ailments", *New York Times*, November 28, 1994, p. D1.

2. Medical underwriting sources included Monarch Life's *Health Underwriting Manual* and Paul Revere's *Health Underwriting Manual*.

3. The field underwriting guide is not from any specific insurer's books, but a sample utilizing several carriers' guidelines.

4. The Business Owner Classification Grid illustrated is of my own making. However, many disability insurance carriers take a similar approach in attempting to label a business owner with an occupational classification.

■ *Chapter 9*

FINANCIAL UNDERWRITING

The financial underwriting of a disability income policy is a critical and often complicated process that must be done in the course of approving the case for issue. As has been true with the entire disability income industry, financial underwriting has undergone some dramatic changes over the past three or four years.

Much of what the underwriter reviews in the course of financial underwriting has already been explained during the programming portion of the sales interview (see Chapter 5, The Art of Programming Benefits).

The purpose of the disability policy is to provide a source of dollars so that the insured can maintain a reasonable standard of living during a disability. The purpose is not to replace the entire amount of income lost during the injury or illness. This *gap* between policy benefit amount and actual earnings lost is meant to provide an incentive to return to work and the full-time earnings level achieved prior to disability.

It is the job of the financial underwriter to be sure that this *gap* is maintained. The underwriter's job was complicated somewhat throughout the 1980's as insurers increased substantially the amount of monthly benefit that could be written on a given insured.

When I began my insurance career back in 1975, the highest amount of personal monthly benefit a company would issue was $3,500/month. Less than a decade later, companies were issuing $35,000/month disability income policies. Studies have now shown that these increased income replacement ratios increased the rate of claims for insurers. According to disability studies performed by the Society of Actuaries, a one percent increase in replacement ratios leads to a similar increase in the rate of claims. You will need a calculator to determine the increase in claims when you move issue limits from $3,500/month to $35,000!

Increased claims incidence has led to a reexamination by companies of the financial underwriting process and an overall tightening in not only the amounts that are being issued but in substantiating the accuracy of these amounts as reported on the application.[1]

EARNED INCOME

Financial underwriting starts with an individual's earnings. Earned income consists of salary or draw, commissions, fees, bonuses or other forms of remuneration for services performed in the insured's occupation.

The benefit amount that may be purchased is based on the gross earned income before taxes. Where an individual is either self-employed or in a partnership or S corporation, business expenses are subtracted from the gross earnings figure to determine benefit eligibility.

Generally, the rate of income for the past calendar year is used to determine an individual's current income level. However, the current year's income is considered in conjunction with the past two to three years of income results to establish the *average* income over a period of time. This is especially important in the case of widely fluctuating yearly income figures.

Earned income must often be substantiated by tax forms today. Some companies require tax forms for all disability income business written while others only review tax forms if the amount applied for exceeds a certain level ($2,000/month for example).[2] In some states, notably California and Florida, tax forms are usually a requirement no matter what the monthly benefit amount.

The tax forms usually required are:

*Sole Proprietor: 1040, pages 1 and 2
Schedule C
Schedule F (if client is a farmer)
Schedule E (if filed with the return)

*Partnership: 1040, pages 1 and 2
Schedule E

***Limited Liability
Company:** 1040, pages 1 and 2
Schedule E
W-2 form if spouse employed outside the home

*S-corporation 1040, pages 1 and 2
Schedule E
1120S
W-2 form if spouse employed outside the home

*C-corporation 1040, pages 1 and 2
Schedule E
1120C
W-2 form if spouse employed outside the home

There is usually a minimum income that the applicant must earn to be considered at all for disability insurance. That level will vary from company to company but is often in the $13-18,000 range.

Some companies ask for either the tax forms or a signed copy of IRS Form 4506 which authorizes the IRS to send a copy of the filed tax return directly to the underwriter.

Once the earned income level has been established, the agent will consult a company-produced table of earned incomes and the corresponding maximum benefit levels the insured may purchase. At the lower income levels, the replacement ratio of benefits to earnings (gross less business expenses) can be as high as 70-75 percent. As the income level increases, this ratio declines to 25-30 percent for the upper incomes ($40-50,000/month in earnings). This ensures that the *gap* between earnings while healthy and earnings while disabled continues to exist. It also limits the liability of the company for any one insured risk.

In Chapter 5, The Art of Programming Benefits, we discussed the necessity for recognizing the possibility of Social Security disability benefits as a source of potential income at time of disability. At lower income levels, the Social Security benefit amount could be sufficient to replace a large portion of income if the insured can qualify under the stringent disability definition.

In recognition of this, many companies require the insured to elect both basic coverage and a Social Security offset rider which provides an additional monthly amount that will be reduced if Social Security actually does pay a benefit to the insured. (For a more complete explanation of how this rider works, see Chapter 15, Personalizing The Disability Plan With Optional Benefits.)

The amount of the Social Security offset rider benefit is expressed at all income levels, even though it has somewhat less impact at the upper income levels. Use of the Social Security offset rider is required at lower income levels. However, all applicants can choose to utilize this benefit amount or to take the entire amount available (basic plus Social Security rider) as basic coverage without any amounts offset if the insured receives Social Security benefits.

The typical table used by insurers to identify the amount of coverage that can be written varies among the income levels. However, the variance is not usually significant. An example of a portion of a *personal earned income* table is shown in Figure 9.1.[3]

Figure 9.1

Annual Earned Income	*Personal Earned Income Benefits*				
	Basic	+	Social Security Rider	=	Total Amount
$15,000	$ 200	+	$ 700	=	$ 900
21,000	500	+	800	=	1,300
27,000	800	+	900	=	1,700
36,000	1,300	+	900	=	2,200
45,000	1,700	+	1,025	=	2,725
60,000	2,300	+	1,150	=	3,450
84,000	3,025	+	1,375	=	4,400
102,000	3,600	+	1,400	=	5,000
120,000	3,950	+	1,400	=	5,350

The issue limits in Figure 9.1 continue on for most companies now up to a maximum personal earned income issue limit of $15-20,000/month. That's a drop from the example of $35,000/month cited earlier in this chapter. Some companies were writing much higher benefit amounts, but this has tempered now in the face of increasing claims costs and the correlation between higher issue limits and higher claims.[4]

Personal earned income issue tables like the one above are developed for cases where the individual is buying coverage and paying the premium with *after-tax dollars*. As such, the benefits when received are *not* taxable to the claimant.

There are many instances, though, when an individual is not paying for coverage with *after-tax dollars*. If a corporation buys disability income coverage on an individual and deducts the premium from the company's income tax as a business expense (perfectly legal), benefits, when and if received, are taxable.

As another example, suppose an individual was participating in a Section 125 Cafeteria plan and paying for disability income coverage with *pre-tax dollars*. This, too, would result in taxation of the disability benefits when and if received. (For more discussion of Section 125 plans, see Chapter 27, Section 125 — The Cafeteria Plan Market.)

A taxation rule of thumb for disability benefits is that if the premium for the policy is paid on a tax-favored basis (deduction, pre-tax), the benefits will be taxed at time of receipt. If the premium is paid for with *after-tax dollars*, benefits will be paid income-tax free.

Because of the taxability of benefits in certain situations, insurers publish a second table (see Figure 9.2) to illustrate the different, higher level of benefits that the applicant can buy. The benefit amounts are higher to offset, as much as possible, the resulting taxability of the benefits.

Using the same income levels as illustrated in Figure 9.1, note the difference in benefit level from the *personal earned income* table to the *employer-paid* table, as shown in Figure 9.2.[5]

Figure 9.2

Annual Earned Income	Personal Limits	Employer-Paid Limits
$ 15,000	$ 900	$ 900
21,000	1,300	1,400
27,000	1,700	1,850
36,000	2,200	2,500
45,000	2,725	3,125
60,000	3,450	4,125
84,000	4,400	5,350
102,000	5,000	6,150
120,000	5,350	6,650

What the insurer is trying to accomplish here is to give the insured approximately the same benefit as would have been available under the personal earned income table. The higher amount in the employer-paid table, less taxes, will be relatively close to the personal earned income limit. The employer-paid table simply recognizes the presence of taxable disability benefits.[6]

A third table has been recently introduced to enable individual disability income coverage to be written. In addition to group long term disability more employers today are providing some form of salary continuation coverage. In some cases, this takes the form of buying group LTD coverage for the entire firm.

When an employee is disabled, the group benefits are almost always taxable to the employee in addition to being integrated with Social Security, Workers' Compensation and other forms of social insurance. Rather than simply subtracting the group LTD amount from what the applicant could qualify for under either the personal earned income or employer-paid table, a separate group limits table is used which recognizes that the actual LTD benefit will be reduced at claim time. The result is a higher benefit level.

Companies publish the table with both personal earned income and employer paid benefit levels pre-established. Some vary based on the percentage of income insured by the group LTD plan (60, 66-2/3 , 70 for example). Others require a slight calculation before determining the benefit amount.

Whatever the method, this separate table is intended to issue a higher benefit because of the taxability and integration of the group LTD benefit. The entire amount is written as *basic* coverage as the need for a Social Security offset rider is eliminated due to the group LTD integration already considered.

OTHER FACTORS AFFECTING EARNED INCOME AND BENEFIT LIMITS

There are a number of other variables the financial underwriter must evaluate in the financial underwriting process. Other disability coverage owned by the insured limits the amount that can be issued. Unearned income and net worth are the two major factors that may affect the selection of benefit based on adjusted gross earned income as shown in the previous tables.

Other Coverage

You know that companies use a separate table to calculate the amount of benefit that can be issued when the applicant has a group LTD policy in force. Individual coverage owned by the applicant must also be considered in determining the benefit amount that can be approved.

This is of even greater importance now as companies carefully monitor the insured's total coverage in force to be sure the amount does not exceed a company's maximum issue and participation limit. Private individual coverage owned by the insured will directly reduce benefits available. For example, if the insured earns $84,000 per year and could qualify for benefits of $4,400/month, but already owns $2,500/month policy, only $1,900/month can now be written ($4,400 - $2,500) in addition to the coverage already owned.

If the prior policy was replaced in full, then the entire $4,400/month could be written. In view of several portfolio rate increases, the disappearance of shorter elimination periods and some liberal definitions of total disability, replacement will most likely *not* be warranted.

It is important to ask about prior coverage the applicant holds since it directly affects the amount of benefit that can be written. Information of this nature is available to the financial underwriter through a database that most insurers have access to which contains information on past insurance buying activity of the insured.

Government Benefits

Employees in a federal, state or local government capacity are often eligible for some form of disability benefits through a special retirement plan. The amount, eligibility date and duration of benefits vary from plan to plan but will be a factor in financial underwriting. The agent should always try to obtain a copy of the actual benefit plan and forward it to the financial underwriter for review.

Many companies simply choose not to write any coverage on government employees. Those that do limit the occupation classes that can qualify (usually the top two or three classes only), the maximum benefit amount, the elimination and benefit periods that can be written, and the issue age. Those that write federal employees assume a certain level of other coverage in determining benefit amounts. In the case of state, county or city employees, the amount of other coverage determined depends on the specifications outlined in the employee's actual benefit booklet. (Hence, the importance of securing this document).

What is often overlooked is that the definition of total disability in these programs is very restrictive and it is not easy to qualify for benefits. Personal disability coverage offers more liberal coverage approaches and should, if possible, always be the primary source of disability benefits for an individual. Rather than judge in advance that sufficient benefits will be available at time of disability, it is easier to place an offset rider with the policy that will reduce benefits at time of claim *if* (and this a big if) the other coverage does pay. Attaching the rider can discount the cost for the basic coverage by five to ten percent since there is a possibility of reduced benefits payable at claim time.

Suggested language for such a rider is shown in Figure 9.3.

Figure 9.3

OCCUPATIONAL DISABILITY BENEFITS

Due to the nature of your occupation, you are eligible for disability income benefits through your employer. We can only provide you insurance coverage if you agree to the terms of this amendment.

Benefit Co-ordination and Calculation

At the time your disability starts, we will calculate the policy monthly benefit payable to you based on the lesser of (a) and (b) where:

(a) is 60 percent of your gross monthly salary (72% if purchased by your employer or paid under a Section 125 salary reduction arrangement) *less* any disability benefits you receive from your employer as a result of your disability; and

(b) is the policy monthly benefit shown on the policy schedule page.

This rider would eliminate the need to determine how much the coverage under the retirement plan will be, especially since this amount will undoubtedly change between the time of policy issue and time of claim. The company could also assist the insured in applying the government benefits since any amount paid will reduce the amount that the company will pay under the policy.

Workers Compensation

Eligibility for workers compensation is confined to on-the-job injuries or illness and is a concern only at the lower income levels where receipt of benefits could replace a substantial portion of income. Many companies' Social Security offset riders also offset workers compensation benefits in order to successfully coordinate the total amount received by the claimant.

UNEARNED INCOME AND NET WORTH

When the insured is applying for coverage, questions concerning the individual's unearned income and net worth are asked — for a reason. In the past, companies utilized a confidential financial statement to be completed by individuals applying for benefit amounts of $3,000 and higher. Today, much of this information has been transferred to the application form plus applicants must often send in their tax forms.

Unearned Income

This is income that the insured will receive whether disabled or not. Net rental income, stock dividends, bond interest and a monthly trust fund are all examples of income unaffected by the insured's ability to work and earn an income.

In determining unearned income, add these sources up, but be sure the figure is net of any expenses or offsets. For example, rental income will be offset by the expenses of maintaining the property, and these expenses should be deducted accordingly from income before determining the final figure.

Unearned income's affect on issue limits is dependent on the financial underwriting rules of the company. Two separate methods for determining issue limits based on unearned income are illustrated below.

(1) Unearned income: Earned income limits will be reduced by the amount of any unearned income in excess of 20 percent of the client's earned income.

> Example: Hillary has $84,000 in earnings and $30,000 of unearned income in stock futures annually. The usual amount issued if no unearned income existed would be $4,400. Disregard 20 percent ($84,000 x 20%) or $16,800. Subtract $16,800 from $30,000 which equals $13,200. Convert to monthly numbers ($13,200 divided by 12) which equals $1,100. Subtract $1,100 from $4,400. The result, $3,300 is what can be issued.

(2)

For earned incomes of:	Reduce monthly benefit by 4% of unearned income in excess of:
up to $100,000	$10,000
$100,001 to $200,000	10% of earned income
$200,000 and above	$20,000

> Using the same example above, Hillary would fit into the up to $100,000 income category. She has $20,000 of unearned income over the $10,000 limit. Four percent of $20,000 is $800 which would be subtracted directly from the $4,400 to arrive at a $3,600 issue limit.[7]

Net Worth

Individuals with a very high net worth are not usually good candidates for long term disability coverage because of the large amount of assets available. Critical to the financial underwriter's determination is the make-up of this net worth and the resulting liquidity. A large percentage of net worth tied up in a business, for example, will be heavily discounted by the underwriter simply because the business value will deteriorate rapidly during the extended disability of its principal.

Generally, a three to four million net worth requires little or nothing in the way of additional financial underwriting. Over four million of net worth will create some adjustments in either or both the monthly benefit amount or the maximum benefit period, figuring that net worth can be liquidated over a period of time to provide sufficient income. If the net worth is made up of highly liquid assets, it may not be possible to write any coverage on the individual. Net worth in excess of six to seven million dollars often disqualifies an applicant for any personal disability income coverage.

OTHER CONSIDERATIONS

Pension Contributions

If an individual is contributing to a pension or profit sharing plan, all or a portion of that contribution may be added to an individual's earned income in determining the monthly benefit amount that can be issued. For example, someone earning $100,000 who contributes $20,000 to a pension or profit sharing plan over and above these earnings will look in the earnings tables under $120,000 of annual income (rather than just $100,000) to ascertain the monthly benefit level available.[8]

Some companies are even separately insuring the pension contribution, enabling the contribution to still be made even during an extended disability. Since many individuals depend on their pension benefit during retirement, this can be an attractive benefit.

Fringe Benefits

Fringe benefits are those extras that the individual may receive in lieu of cash. Or a company may provide fringe benefits by paying certain of the employee's expenses in addition to regular compensation. The use of a car or payment of a mortgage may be lost during a disability, creating more of an economic hardship than loss of stated earned income. For this reason, financial underwriters analyze the tax returns of individuals like S corporation owners to calculate a total compensation amount upon which an issue limit can be based. Most CPAs are trying to help the business owner keep income as low as possible, thus close scrutiny of the tax return can identify certain fringe benefits which can be added to salary in arriving at an income figure.

The world of financial underwriting has changed. Some underwriting departments today have hired an accountant or a tax specialist to decipher the inner workings of the various tax forms an individual may have to file. This financial data is vital to making a determination of the monthly benefit available.

Once the financial information has been compiled, the underwriter either agrees with the monthly benefit amount applied for or makes appropriate adjustments. The policy is then issued and sent to the agent to place with the potential insured.

CHAPTER NOTES

1. "Restoring Individual DI", *Best's Review*, November, 1992, p. 53.

2. While disability insurance companies are all asking for the same general forms, these specific guidelines are those of the Principal Financial Group.

3. Figure 9.1 is from the issue limit tables of the Principal Financial Group.

4. "Agents Bemoan Disability Changes", *National Underwriter Life & Health / Financial Services*, February 20, 1995, p. 7.

5. Figure 9.2 is from the issue limit tables of the Principal Financial Group.

6. "Managing Disability to the Client's Benefit", *Best's Review*, November, 1993, p. 73.

7. Unearned income calculations are from the Principal Financial Group and CNA.

8. Both Paul Revere and UNUM have offered coverages which insure an individual's specific pension contribution.

Chapter 10

PLACING THE POLICY

Good news! The policy has been issued and it is time to contact your client, deliver the contract and formally make the insured a policyholder. You now have something tangible you can show as evidence of the important coverage just purchased.

It is not always easy to place the policy, however. As a result of the underwriting process it may have taken some time to issue the contract and the agent may be faced with having to re-sell the concept of disability and risk. The policy may have been issued on a modified basis and an explanation of this will be necessary in placing the case. "Buyer's remorse" may also have to be addressed as the client now wonders if it really is worth spending $150.00 each month on this disability program.

While everyone has his own style of policy delivery, there are some general methods that can assist at this important time, helping to seal the relationship between agent and client and set the stage for future sessions together.

POLICY ISSUED AS APPLIED FOR

When a policy has been issued on a standard basis, the agent can concentrate on stressing the key points of the contract and lay the groundwork for the next policy update.

If there has been a long delay in the underwriting of the case for whatever reason, or if the client has had second thoughts about why this coverage is necessary, begin the delivery process by reviewing the *need* for this plan. Talk about the gap in the individual's financial plan that will continue to exist and threaten the completion of other dreams if this program is not put in force. Point out what happens after disability strikes, when expenses increase and income stops. Review again, if necessary, the income sources that are available to the insured if disability happens and the usual paycheck stops coming.

Once the need has been re-emphasized and understood, focus on the specific items you have to deliver:

(1) the policy

(2) policy card

(3) outline of coverage (if required)

(4) claim form

(5) buyer's guide (if required)

The Policy

Delivering a disability policy can be a long and unsatisfactory process if the agent spends too much time on contractual language that may be confusing. There are many terms and definitions in the contract. Most insurance agents, even those with many years of experience, will not understand, at first reading, all of these provisions. It is unrealistic to believe that the average insured, with no prior exposure to the product, can absorb every word of the policy.

Instead, concentrate first on the policy schedule page. This is the *declarations* page of the insurance contract and specifies the individual components of importance in the policy. Moreover, it is a page that your clients can easily absorb *first* before you begin treating them to the review of specific policy definitions.

The key to helping someone understand the policy easily is to turn the various disability definitions or provisions into actual dollars. Using the policy schedule page as a reference, run down the items listed and try to attach a monetary value to each one.

For example, the policy schedule page will indicate the monthly benefit, the policy elimination period and the benefit period. Let's say those numbers are $2,000/month benefit, 90 day elimination period and a to-age-65 benefit period. The person's age or date of birth should also be listed on the schedule page. If the person is 40 years old, the total policy benefit is potentially worth $600,000 (2,000 x 12 x 25 years). Write that down and note it will decrease by $24,000 each year.

Next, look at the space indicating "total disability coverage". Write down "$600,000 to start" next to it. Then note the space indicating "residual disability coverage." Write down "percent of $600,000 to start" based on income loss. Next, look at the waiver of premium. Assuming it's a 90 day retroactive benefit, as most are, write down an amount equal to the monthly premium amount multiplied by three since this is the amount that the insured will directly save. Since waiver of premium continues for the length of disability, you could also indicate that the monthly premium savings is an ongoing benefit for the remainder of the claim.

Continue this procedure down the length of the page, putting dollar benefits next to rehabilitation provision, presumptive total disability, cost of living rider and so forth. The more you break down the *language* of the policy into *dollars*, the more likely the insured will understand what really has been purchased. The client didn't buy words. He bought the promise of future dollars if needed and this exercise underscores this point.

Now, you can proceed to the rest of the policy, covering:

- the renewability provision, usually listed on the face of the policy

- the pre-existing condition provision on the face of the policy

- definition of total disability

- definition of residual disability

- presumptive (or loss of use) disability

- waiver of premium

- exclusions

- filing a claim (time frames)

- any endorsement(s) to the policy

Take a high-lighter pen and mark these provisions for future reference. You might even want to write in the dollar amounts again where appropriate. Pause after a short explanation of each to gauge the level of comprehension of the insured. Eight provisions and the schedule page plus an endorsement are not overwhelming and will probably stay in the client's mind longer than a complete policy review.

If pressed for time, always review the policy schedule page and the definition(s) of disability. Make another appointment, if possible, to complete your policy review. The agent is the best judge of the client and how much or little to present, but one should always work toward the listed goals.

The Policy Card

Most companies include at least two (and often more) policy cards which list the basic policy information regarding monthly benefit, elimination period, benefit period, premiums and optional benefits with the insured's name, address, policy date and agent also shown. The agent should keep one for reference and the client should have one at the front of the policy, either stapled to it or enclosed in the front of the policy jacket. The agent should also clip his business card to the policy card.

Outline of Coverage

Some states require the company to furnish a special outline of policy benefits with a reminder to "read your policy carefully" on the front of the form. The reasoning behind this is that the insured may be more likely to read a short two or three page form than an entire policy. This form includes some specifically required provisions nearly all of which are in the required policy provision/schedule review list. The agent may choose to use this form rather than high-lighting the policy.

Claim Form

Usually a claim form has been enclosed with the policy for the insured's convenience. The agent should show this form to the client while briefly explaining that the front page of the form is for the insured to complete when the claim is made and on the reverse side is the physician's responsibility to verify the disability. Since the handling of any claim is important to the agent, a business card should be stapled to the claim form together with the note, "Call me and I will help you complete this form." This ensures that the agent will have some control over getting the claim processed as quickly as possible.

Buyer's Guide

Some states also require the delivery of a printed buyer's guide. The contents are in language prepared by the insurance industry's regulatory arm, the National Association of Insurance Commissioners, as revised, in some cases, by the state in which the insured resides. This guide contains general information about a disability income policy and the important things to look for as a consumer. This should be given to the client with the recommendation that he read it.

SETTING UP THE NEXT REVIEW

After reviewing these items with the client, the agent should conclude by making arrangements for the next review.

If the Guarantee of Insurability benefit is attached to the policy (this optional rider is explained in Chapter 15, Personalizing the Disability Plan with Optional Benefits) or if the policy has an Automatic Increase Benefit (see Chapter 14, Personal Disability Income Policies: What The Contractual Language Really Means, for an explanation of this policy benefit), it is easy to set up your next sales call to review the policy benefits for an update.

These provisions make it easy to increase coverage as income increases and thus maintain the correct benefit level. It is critical for the agent to keep up with the insured's needs. Moreover, consistent contact with the client helps keep other agents from coming in and replacing your business. Many agents make the one sale and run. This is a mistake with disability income since this is a policy the insured will keep. Updating the product just gives the insured further reason to continue paying the premiums for this valuable plan.

If the Guarantee of Insurability or Automatic Increase Benefit is not part of the insured's program, ask when the insured next expects to receive a salary increase. Make an appointment now for the week after this raise to review the current benefit level as measured against the new earnings. If the insured is self-employed, make an appointment after the next tax forms are filed to see if an increase in earnings justifies increasing the policy monthly benefit.

PREMIUM MODES

If the insured has not yet paid for the policy, a choice will be made regarding what frequency of premium payment will be best. In general, there are four choices:

(1) *Annual.* This is usually the best method financially because no extra charges are assessed for billing and sometimes a discount is offered for paying 12 months in advance. Not all insureds can afford to pay the entire annual premium at once, but if affordable, it should almost always be done.

(2) *Semi-Annual.* With only two billings per year there is usually a slight extra charge for handling an extra bill, so the insured, while paying more than the annual mode, has divided the large annual bill up into two more palatable parts. While not the most popular mode, some insureds like having to see a bill only twice a year and in more manageable payment increments than annual.

(3) *Quarterly.* Many companies have eliminated this mode or added such a high extra surcharge for handling that even if available, it is rarely elected. The high surcharge is the result of poor persistency. Policies with quarterly billing arrangements just *lapse* that more often. There are four chances each year to question the value of the bill when it comes due and the agent isn't always around to remind the insured of the policy's value. The insured is better off with a monthly bank draft mode.

(4) *Monthly Bank Draft*. This may be the most popular method since the insured does not have to write a check. Instead, with the insured's consent, the company contacts the insured's bank, and the bank automatically deducts the policy premium on a specific date each month. In some cases, there is no extra charge to do this as the insurance company tries to encourage this method of payment because of excellent persistency. Some insureds do not want to have automatic drafting of their account in the event that sufficient money to pay the premium is not there. It is not always easy to change banks, either. Next to annual payment, though, this is the most popular premium payment method.

CHANGE IN THE INSURED'S HISTORY

If changes have occurred in the insured's medical, occupational or financial history since the application was taken, the agent needs to make note of these changes and contact the home office underwriting department. The policy was issued on the basis of answers given in the application and any change could affect the underwriting decision. This notification should be done when no premium has been collected with the original application.

If premium has been collected for either the premium mode desired or enough of a deposit to bind the coverage, then new history, medical or otherwise, may not affect the underwriting decision provided the application and any medical examination required predate the new history. It is, nevertheless, important to contact the underwriting department or the company to ensure that all is still acceptable as done.

PLACING THE SUBSTANDARD CASE

The policy that has been modified on some basis and is issued other than as applied for needs extra time at policy delivery to explain the differences from the policy originally applied for. This is when an agent who was aware that a substandard situation might exist when the applicant's answers were initially recorded, should be rewarded for properly preparing the client for the substandard issue (see Chapter 8, Home Office Underwriting). There are various ways benefits may have been changed in order to issue the policy as an acceptable risk:

- Addition of an exclusion rider

- Addition of an extra premium

- A change of benefit period or elimination period

- A change of monthly benefit amount

- Removal of an optional benefit

- A change in occupational classification

- A different policy form altogether

Exclusion Rider

This type of rider excludes coverage for a medical condition in whole or in part. For example, an exclusion rider might provide "No coverage for any disease or disorder of the lungs." Or the rider may be a limited one providing some coverage. For example, the preceding exclusion could read, "No coverage for any disease or disorder of the lungs for the first 90 days of disability," or "No coverage for any disease or disorder of the lungs for more than 24 months."

The agent must explain that while this condition is not covered (in whole or in part), the client is aware of the medical condition and (usually) taking care of it through some form of treatment. More importantly, there are thousands of other illnesses or accidents that could happen for which the insured is covered. Does it make sense not to take a policy because only one condition is not covered, thereby losing coverage on all other conditions?

Extra Premium

In some instances, the underwriter can approve the policy for issue with an extra charge for the risk without having to exclude it. The agent should place emphasis on this complete coverage approach, even though the risk was higher. Handling it as an extra premium means only that there will be a higher charge per premium payment and any and all conditions will be covered in accordance with the policy specifications.

Changes in Elimination and Benefit Period

This is often done in conjunction with an extra premium, but can be done also to avoid placing the additional charge for the extra risk. Again, the emphasis should be that all injuries or sicknesses will be covered within the new time frame(s). If it avoids an extra premium, stress this point. The insured may have the option of taking an extra premium or exclusion rider (or both) if he does not wish to have the elimination and benefit periods altered. It's important to know that substandard decisions can be a little flexible in how the coverage is actually modified.

Change in the Monthly Benefit

This change is usually made if the benefit applied for is too high in relation to actual earned income. It is rarely done because of medical history, but the monthly benefit could be reduced for this reason too. The agent should explain the relationship between income and benefit and how much the company is willing to write based on the income level determined through the financial underwriting process.

Changes in Occupation Class

It is possible to classify an insured incorrectly in an occupation especially if the occupation is not listed in a company's occupational listing guide. Any change made is usually to a higher risk classification at a higher premium which may also change the contractual definition of disability to a more restrictive wording. This can make it very difficult to place the policy since the responsibility rests squarely on the agent's shoulders. The client does not select the occupational class for rating purposes. It is important to check in advance about an occupation that the agent is unclear about or that is a borderline risk that could easily be a higher premium class than the one quoted. If the agent is unsure, he should always use the higher classification for quoting purposes and request that the client be upgraded to a better classification if appropriate. It is easier to come back with lower premiums and, perhaps, better coverage than the reverse.

Different Policy Form Altogether

As mentioned above, improper occupational classifications could alter the policy form the insured is eligible to buy. The policy form could also be changed by the underwriter to limit the risk exposure. If the original policy applied for has, for example, both total and residual disability (explanations of these benefits are in Chapter 14, Personal Income Disabilities: What The Contractual Language Really Means) and the underwriter wishes to remove the residual coverage due to the applicant's health history, a different policy form will be issued that contains only total disability coverage. Or it may simply be a way of raising the rate and restricting the definitions of disability just by issuing a different policy form. Either way, the new policy and its benefits must be explained in full.

In all of these situations, the agent should be prepared to give an explanation that makes sense. The substandard issue may take the agent by surprise if the underwriting decision is based on information not originally disclosed by the prospect.

Work through the explanations with the insured. The substandard risk already has a problem and should understand the need for disability insurance even more than a healthy individual.

■ *Chapter 11*

SERVICE AFTER THE SALE

Disability income insurance is, technically, health insurance, but the service work, when compared to major medical-type coverages, is minimal. Like all service work, though, the agent who provides the extra support keeps the confidence of the insured and continues to earn renewal commissions for the effort.

Renewal commissions for the agent are much higher for a disability income policy than for a life insurance contract. The incentive to perform in the few areas of after-sale service connected with the policy is higher and agents who work successfully in the disability income market take full advantage of it.

The major categories of service work are:

- guarantee of insurability or automatic benefit increase updates

- claims

- product enhancements

- miscellaneous policy changes (address, beneficiary)

GUARANTEE OF INSURABILITY UPDATES

This is the easiest service work leading to an additional sale that exists in the insurance business. The entire concept behind disability income protection is the replacement of a certain percentage of earned income during an extended injury or sickness. As income increases, so does the need to increase the monthly benefit level under the policy to maintain the same replacement percentage of income. Adding a Guarantee of Insurability Rider to the policy is meant to ease the process of keeping up with increases. This rider permits increases to basic coverage on specified future dates (sometimes annually, or every two years) with a minimum of paperwork.[1]

Most agents plan annual reviews with their clients. This rider guides you in setting a date, often one to two months prior to the policy anniversary date. The agent can review the insured's current financial situation

---

measuring this against the issue limit tables the company publishes. If there is a sufficient increase in income, the insured can exercise the guarantee of insurability option and elect additional coverage.

A short-form application is generally used and asks *no* medical questions. Financial evidence is important here and the questions on this form are confined to this area of information. The agent assists the insured in completion of the form and sends it to the home office underwriting department.

First-year commissions are available on the increased benefit amount and, since the policy stays in force, renewal commissions continue to be earned on the original program. This is policy service work that is both easy and rewarding.

The underwriting department reviews the financial data and, if the application is approved, either sends out an additional policy in the amount of the increase or, more likely, amends the original policy schedule page to reflect the increased amount and the new total monthly benefit under the policy.

A complete description of the Guarantee of Insurability benefit option can be found in Chapter 15, Personalizing the Disability Plan with Optional Benefits.

AUTOMATIC BENEFIT INCREASE UPDATES

A number of policies today have a feature built-in which, in actuality, is a simplified version of both the guarantee of insurability and cost of living riders.

This feature, generally known as an Automatic Benefit Increase, resembles the Guarantee of Insurability Benefit in that it increases the monthly benefit automatically during the early policy years. In addition, this provision resembles the Cost of Living rider in that the increases are measured more in terms of Consumer Price Index increases (five to ten percent) than the more substantial amounts associated with the Guarantee of Insurability Benefit.

The purpose of the benefit is to keep the monthly benefit in step with inflation. In this instance, virtually no paperwork is involved unless the insured does not want the increase and the resulting higher premium that accompanies it. (In some contracts, the increase is not an option but will occur automatically with notification of benefit change and new premium sent to the policyholder.)

Regardless of the mechanics, it is another opportune time to make a service call and all agents should take advantage of it. Contacting the insured to review this feature and increase may uncover a greater benefit level increase need or other needs not previously addressed. If the agent who wrote the initial policy does not make the call, someone else may and a change in agents could occur.

CLAIMS

One of the satisfactions of the disability income business is the ability to deliver a claim check to the individual who purchased the policy. A life insurance claim check is given to the insured's beneficiary; the disability check goes right to the agent's client.

When you sell a disability plan, or any insurance product, you are selling dollars to be delivered at a future unspecified date, having only a policy as tangible evidence of the promised dollars. At claim time, these dollars become a reality and can mean the difference between recovery or ruin.

It is more than another reason to contact your client. A claimant on disability has suffered physically, emotionally and financially. The agent is one of the most important people in the disabled insured's life at this time.

When the agent is first contacted or becomes aware of the claim, the first thing to do is to call the insured or a family member to see what assistance can be rendered. A call to the home office with notification of the claim is appropriate and, if the agent does not have a claim form, he should obtain copies from the claim department.

The claim form is usually a one page piece printed on front and back with information to be provided by the insured on one side and details to be given by his physician on the other. Fill out as much of the insured's information as possible when meeting with him. Then track down the physician and help to speed up the completion process on the rest of the form.

After mailing in the claim form, give the home office claims examiner a few days to review it, to order any appropriate reports relevant to the claim, and to make a decision. Stay in touch with the insured and family to keep them informed of claim progress.

When the check is finally sent, be sure it is mailed to you for delivery. It is fine to wear the white hat when you can and there is no better chance to do this than at the time of a claim. Delivery of claim checks not only brightens the lives of your client and his family, but often leads to referrals now that the client sees how this policy really works.

There was a television show in the 60's called "Branded." At the beginning of each show, the star, Chuck Connors, was seen having his stripes ripped off the shoulders of his uniform. (He did not deserve it and he spends the rest of the series trying to prove it, but that is beside the point.) In my opinion, any agent who is not involved in delivering at least the first claim check should undergo the same procedure Chuck faced at the beginning of each show, and then be drummed out of the insurance service.

A recent claims case I followed involved an insured who broke some bones in his back at a job site some 90 miles away from his home (and from his agent's place of residence). The agent drove out to see him in the hospital, ran around picking up medical information, helped to have the claim form completed, walked it through the claim department and even requested an advance payment of two months' benefits because of the potential long duration of the claim and the insured's financial status.

The claimant received the claim check from the agent with the extra benefits payable in advance. He made a remarkable physical recovery and was back to work much sooner than anticipated. I later found out that the agent had to persuade the client to pay the premium for the policy only a month before the accident when the insured felt that the coverage was not necessary. This agent has a client for life.

Another way in which the agent may be involved at the time of a claim is by gathering the financial information needed to evaluate a claimant who is partially or residually disabled and receiving benefits based upon earnings loss. The agent may work closely with the insured's accountant to ensure that the home office claim department receives this data on a timely basis.

Claims work can be the most important and rewarding service work of an agent's service career. Do not miss the opportunity to make good on the promises made to the insured at time of application and policy delivery.

PRODUCT ENHANCEMENTS

Disability products have undergone many changes over the past 20 years, most of them positive in nature for the insured. Quite often, changes to the contract are made by policy endorsement, a form that indicates what provisions are affected and substitutes the new policy language that will thereafter be used.

These endorsements should be delivered personally by the agent whenever possible. Take the time to explain the changes, positive or negative. Maximize the impact of liberalizations to the contract and minimize the difficulties that may be associated with changes that adversely affect the contract. Be sure the client understands what the endorsement is trying to accomplish and that he should keep it with the policy. It is also another opportunity to see a client with whom you may not have had recent contact.

Product changes are not always handled by endorsement. In the late '70s, when the Cost of Living Rider was being mass produced for sale, an agent I know contacted every existing client who owned a disability policy to see whether they were interested in adding this new rider to their coverage. Nearly three-fourths responded positively. The agent utilized a simplified form in connection with a 90-day introductory offer to existing clients to add the new option without evidence of insurability. His great service work produced a significant amount of extra commissions without much paperwork.

You should always contact the insured about a product enhancement to avoid having another agent point out the benefit and raise questions about your credibility. Give the client the chance to turn the benefit down. It is surprising what the client will buy when asked.

MISCELLANEOUS POLICY CHANGES

Basic service work that an agent can assist with involves such mundane areas as address changes, name changes, and beneficiary changes.

Name and address changes are cosmetic in nature but an address can cause a missed premium if the notice of payment does not reach the insured. When made aware of these changes, the agent should obtain a policy change form from the home office policyowner service department and have it completed and signed by the insured.

Beneficiary changes are of obvious importance in a life insurance policy, but disability policies, too, can have benefits paid to someone else. A policy provision called a "Transition Benefit" (described in more detail in Chapter 14, Personal Disability Policies: What the Contractual Language Really Means) continues the monthly disability benefit to the insured's beneficiary for a short period if the insured dies while disabled and receiving benefits.

There may also be a premium refund due upon death of the insured for any unearned premium (premium paid in advance but at a point beyond the insured's ability to utilize the policy). This premium credit would have to be paid to a designated beneficiary.

Beneficiary changes can also be handled with a policy change form unless there is a specific beneficiary change form the company requires.

Policyholder service work is both necessary and satisfying in the disability income business. There is not much to do, but the few tasks required are all important and should be personally handled.

CHAPTER NOTES

1. Most disability articles promote the Guarantee of Insurability Rider, among them: "Pre-Disability Income Planning", by Richard E. Cicchatti, published in the April, 1990 edition of *Life Insurance Selling*; "Not So Easy Riders", published in the August, 1993 issue of *Smart Money*; and "Disability Income for Professionals", published in the National Association of Health Underwriters 1991 *Disability Income Sales Reference Manual*.

■ *Chapter 12*

DISABILITY INCOME CLAIMS EVALUATION

The claim check is the payoff in the insurance business. The intangible turns tangible; it is the delivery of dollars sold but not *seen* at time of application. For disability insurance agents, it is a chance to deliver a check to the actual client, the man or woman who needed to be persuaded to purchase the coverage. In life insurance, you cannot deliver that claim check to your client.

Claims can be both a blessing and a curse for all concerned. The disability claim is not always easy to evaluate. Even the same injury may affect two people differently. A broken arm may not disable an attorney but could keep a carpenter out of work for some time.

Timing is critical here, as well. The claims examiner knows the importance of verifying disability but must balance that against the length of time the insured has been without income but with bills to pay.

What about the pre-existing condition? Information not disclosed on the application that surfaces at claim time and has a material effect on paying benefits could jeopardize more than this one agent-policyholder relationship. What if the insured belongs to the agent's largest employer group where more than 40 policyholders paying a substantial premium every month are waiting to see how the first claim is handled? In this situation, the claims examiner can be right *and* wrong; if the claim is denied, the other policyholders may cancel the coverage. Should the claims examiner consider this?

What about the effects of being HIV positive? The actual diagnosis is not necessarily followed by an immediate period of *physical* disability. It may be several years between diagnosis and limitation of ability to perform duties in one's own occupation. Yet if you are a health care professional, your ability to practice is subsequently curtailed even though you are able to work. The result is an economic loss without a simultaneous, corresponding physical problem. How should the claims examiner handle this?

There has been a phenomenal growth in disabilities of a mental and nervous nature. These are extraordinarily delicate claims, difficult to measure and monitor as to effective recovery. How do claims examiners work with these disability scenarios?

The issue amounts during the 1980's and early 1990's were amazingly high: $20,000/month, $30,000/month, $40,000/month and higher! At what point does a claims examiner attempt to negotiate with an insured to try to reduce the company's claims exposure in a manner both accepted and welcomed by the claimant?

This chapter will outline the claims process and the many facets of it that the claims examiner must consider. This is, arguably, the most sensitive area with any insurance company. Yet, how well the claims examiner performs can affect an insured's lifestyle and an agent's livelihood in addition to insurer profitability. If you have thought of the claims examiner's job as an easy one, read on.

MECHANICS OF A CLAIM

Assume a disability policyowner for ABC Company is seriously injured in an automobile accident. The agent for the insured learns of the accident and calls on his client in the hospital to be of assistance in filing a claim.

What can the agent do to assist in the claims evaluation process? A claim form must be completed first. Usually, the company form will be two-sided; the front is for information about the insured to be signed by the insured; the back calls for information by the attending physician verifying disability and inability to work.

The agent can assist in the completion of the form and mail it to the home office claims department. What the agent should *not* do is try to determine the amount of the benefit or whether the insured qualifies. Let the claims examiner do that.

The claim form triggers the evaluation process. The form can be filed even if the insured or the agent does not believe that the claim will last beyond the elimination period. Do not worry about it. Send the form in and start the evaluation. The disability could go on longer than anticipated and this way the preliminary work is finished.

Your company may allow you to file your claim on-line via a computer network or fax the initial data to get a file set up. The faster and easier the process, the better. Some insurers may then appoint a *case manager* for that claim whose responsibility will be to coordinate all facets of the claim including exploring the option of some form of rehabilitation. This will be your (and the claimant's) contact from this point on.

In addition to the claim form, the claims examiner may order medical records about the insured. Often this is a routine procedure. In the first two years of the policy (before the incontestable provision expires), these records often verify that the current medical condition causing a disability is not a pre-existing condition which was not disclosed on the application. An automobile accident is more straightforward, since a pre-existing condition would generally not be a consideration.

The medical records may reveal information that, although not germane to the current claims evaluation, may have altered the initial underwriting decision had this data been available at the time the application was approved. In this case, depending on the extent of the medical history, the original file may be sent back to an underwriter for a *new* evaluation and a different decision may result. The claim will still be handled in most circumstances, but the future of the policy may hinge on the new underwriting decision.

The length of time it takes to accumulate this information will vary depending, in large part, upon the cooperation of the medical office furnishing the records of the claimant. This can be the most frustrating part of the process for both the insured and the examiner. If the claim form has been filed late (after the time when benefits are due), the insured is not pleased with a further delay because income has stopped and creditors may be nervous. The examiner has no control over when the claim is filed, yet he starts at a disadvantage because the pressure is on to make a decision quickly.

Disability benefits are paid in arrears. If a policy has an elimination period of 90 days (no benefits payable in the first 90 days), benefits are not going to be paid until the 121st day. On the 121st day, if disability is verified for the first 120 days, a check is sent to the insured for one month of benefits covering disability days 91-120. Many feel that benefits should be paid in advance, yet without evidence that the disability will last that long, the examiner has no choice. In this example, if payment for one month of benefits was sent on the 91st day and the insured recovered on the 105th day, the chances of recovering the extra two weeks advanced is very small. Policies are priced for expected claims, not for the ones that should not be paid.

Once the initial evaluation has been made, an updated claim form should be sent in each month to verify the ongoing nature of the disability. Benefits are usually paid once a month. A case manager monitoring the claim may be able to generate a claim check with little or no paperwork based on this "hands-on" approach to working with the claimant and the care givers. If the disability is lasting longer than the examiner believes is normal, the company has the right to an independent examination of the insured to confirm the continued inability to work.

PRE-EXISTING CONDITIONS

What is a pre-existing condition? Generally, it is a condition that first made itself known to the insured prior to the date of application. If it was not disclosed to the agent when the application was completed, the company can generally deny a claim based on whether it affects how the application would have been issued or the claim paid. After two years, the claim can be denied only if the company can prove that the insured intended to defraud it. This is nearly impossible to prove and thus reduces the company's line of defense against improper claims based on the pre-existing condition.

For example, an applicant for disability insurance answers a question relating to a back injury "no", and the policy is subsequently issued on a standard basis. Later, a claim is filed based on a back injury. The claims examiner orders medical records and discovers that the insured had been to a doctor several times *prior* to the date of application. If the claim has been filed within two years from the issue date, the claims examiner will likely deny the claim, rescind the policy and refund the client whatever premium had been paid. If the claim is filed *more* than two years past the issue date, the insurer must prove fraudulent intent. Since the insured had seen a doctor several times for back problems, the likelihood of these visits slipping his mind is small and thus the insurer may be successful in his case. If the claimant had only seen a doctor one time for a back injury, this could have easily been forgotten making fraud more difficult to prove. A one-time visit may not have much affect on the claim, either, so the claim may be handled and the coverage not rescinded.

Denial of a claim puts a significant amount of pressure on the agent. The agent sold a promise to the client that the disability coverage would be there to provide income during an eligible disability. A claim denial, however justified, can end a client-agent relationship and perhaps jeopardize other business for the agent.

But some claims must be denied, otherwise a company would include a checkbook with each policy so that the insured could write the claim check whenever he chose. Policies are not priced to pay for pre-existing conditions. This is why application completion *in full* is critical to the underwriting and claims process.

TYPES OF DISABILITY TO CONSIDER

Total Disability

A policy may have one or two definitions of total disability and these must be considered in the total disability evaluation process.

The "own occupation" definition of total disability means that the insured must be unable to perform the major duties of his regular occupation. (See Chapter 14, Personal Disability Income Policies: What the Contractual Language Really Means, for complete discussion of total disability definitions.) For the claims examiner, this means evaluating the disability in one dimension only: can the insured perform the job being done at time of claim?

This is important. Coverage is provided if the insured cannot work in his occupation, but it may not be the same occupation he held at the time the policy was issued. For example, consider a CPA who took out a policy and, after a few years, quit this profession to become a painter but continued to pay premiums and then filed a claim. The claims examiner would be evaluating the claim based on the insured's ability to perform duties as a painter, not as a CPA. The examiner must know what the current job is and what duties are performed. These are listed and then evaluated against the medical condition and doctor's statement to evaluate the disability.[1]

For example, a surgeon may list the following duties:

- Surgery
- Pre-Op
- Post-Op
- Pre-authorization check
- Patient evaluation
- X-ray/records evaluation
- Report completion

If the surgeon has a heart attack and is unable to work completely, the evaluation process is relatively simple. If his heart attack is not the result of pre-existing conditions, the claim is likely to be paid. If this same surgeon broke his arm instead, the evaluation process is more difficult. Now the examiner must decide what duties the surgeon can perform. Certainly, half the duties listed above could be done, but the duty that delivers most of the income to the insured, surgery, is the essential one that cannot be performed. If he is unable to perform surgery, many of the other duties become irrelevant even if the insured could perform them. Surgery is the one that drives the rest of them and generates the income. Yet, if the definition of disability reads, "must be unable to perform the duties of regular occupation," is the client disabled or not? Perhaps technically not, but rare is the claims examiner who would deny this claim.

If the definition reads "must be unable to perform the duties of regular occupation, and is unable to engage in any other occupation for which suited by education, training, or experience," does the answer change? Could the surgeon with the broken arm do something different in the medical field? Probably. If the arm is expected to heal properly so that the surgeon could perform surgery again, do you deny the claim in the interim period because other duties in a related field could be performed? Probably not. What if the end result is that the arm heals but leaves the insured with residual damage that prevents him from performing surgery again? Now, do you enforce the definition of disability to the fullest?

So you think claims evaluation is easy?

Residual Disability

The popularity of this benefit provision in recent years together with a renewed emphasis on the part of insurers to sell policies whose major component is a *loss of income* provision makes this an important feature to understand in the overall claims process.

A policy that pays a benefit for residual disability pays a portion of the total disability benefit based on earnings loss. In order to determine loss of earnings, prior earnings must be established. An examiner may request prior tax forms to be sure of proper income determination. Some companies will allow the insured to use consecutive months, or to go back *five years*, prior to date of disability to establish the *pre-disability earnings* which would be most advantageous for the insured.

Next, current earnings must be obtained. This can also be difficult to obtain but deposit slips, accountant statements, and check stubs can all be used to determine current earnings and pre-disability earnings. This would allow the claims examiner to then determine the actual current loss of income percentage to be used in calculating the claim benefit. Figure 12.1 illustrates an example of residual disability benefit calculation.

Figure 12.1

Pre-disability Earnings	Current Earnings	Income Loss	x	Total Disab. Benefit	=	Residual Disab. Benefit
$5,000/mo.	$2,000	60%	x	$3,000	=	$1,800

The examiner must review current earnings each month along with the claim form which continues to verify disability. There may be an exception to the latter requirement if the company definition requires income loss only and not continuing reduction of time and/or duties as well, to be eligible for disability benefit payments.

For a full review of residual disability, see Chapter 14, Personal Disability Income Policies: What The Contractual Language Really Means.

REHABILITATION

While insurance companies have made the same kind of re-engineering decisions as other industries in the last few years by streamlining and injecting new technology, a key area has actually seen staff increases: claims departments. The extra personnel have been employed for one primary purpose: to try and reduce the overall financial burden of a claim to the company while leaving the claimant in the same or better position than he was prior to disability.

This work has come mainly in the form of rehabilitation efforts and it has significantly changed the claims process for many insurers. Nurses and Certified Rehabilitation Counselors are now major players in the claims process.

Successful rehabilitation is predicated on a number of factors. First, it must be in the best physical and financial interest of the insured. Second, it must be in the long-term best financial interest of the insurer. Third, it may necessitate cooperation from an employer since this person(s) must also agree with the arrangements about to be made. Fourth, the claimant's supervising physician must also sign off on the rehabilitation attempt. Yet if all of these parties agree, the claim could take a completely different turn than even the policy language would indicate.

The driving force behind rehabilitation is to move a claimant from total disability to residual disability and, hopefully, to full recovery. The key to understanding how this works is that *the insured will always collect more in disability benefits by collecting residual benefits plus current earnings than he will by collecting the total disability payment only.*

Look back at Figure 12.1. If the insured was totally disabled, the benefit collected would be $3,000. But the insured returns to work, he is earning $2,000 plus collecting residual benefits of $1,800 for a total of $3,800. This is $800 *more* a month for the claimant, but $1,200 *less* for the insurance carrier. It's a win-win situation.

If you understand this principle, you can see why both sides would be motivated to promote rehabilitation. Naturally, the insured must want to return to work even in a reduced capacity. Moreover, there must be the physical ability to do so as agreed upon by both claimant and physician. It may also require that the employer make some accommodation in terms of workspace, job motivation and duties. Under the *Americans With Disabilities Act*, employers with 15 or more employees must make reasonable accommodations to bring a disabled employee back to work.[2]

The individual non-cancelable policy has often been purchased by people that work alone or with less than 15 employees in a group. Here, claims

---

examiners and rehabilitation case managers can be very creative in returning an applicant to work. For example, let's say a private practice attorney becomes disabled as a result of substance abuse. On claim in a drug rehabilitation program for over a year, he now decides, after kicking his habit successfully, to start a clinic to counsel others with similar problems. The future of his law practice is in doubt because of his past problems and he feels that the stress of the practice contributed to his chemical dependency problems.

His pre-disability earnings level was $150,000 annually or $12,500/month. His total disability monthly benefit is $7,500/month. His benefits are payable to age 65 and he was 42 when the disability began. The total potential payout (assuming a 90 day elimination period) is $2,070,000(!) if he is never able to return to the practice of law. If he agrees to go on residual disability and have his current income as head of a drug counseling service counted in the calculation, this would obviously cut into that two million dollar claim. In addition, the insurer may agree to pay some of the attorney's start-up costs for the drug rehabilitation counseling service. (For actual examples of this kind of claims handling, see the explanation about rehabilitation provisions in Chapter 14, Personal Disability Income Policies: What The Contractual Language Really Means.)

So you still think disability claims evaluation is easy?

HIV POSITIVE AND CLAIMS EVALUATION

The definition of total disability refers to the "inability to perform duties of an occupation." This implies the physical capacity to carry out the normal task of one's work.

The advent of AIDS has contributed to a re-evaluation of the definition of total disability for certain individuals for whom the diagnosis of being HIV positive would mean an inability to practice. This inability wouldn't necessarily be a physical loss. Most HIV-positive individuals can still work and perform their job initially. But the possibility of contagion in certain professions virtually ends the person's career.

The primary occupations affected are those in the medical profession. Doctors, dentists, osteopaths, chiropractors, nurses and similar health care workers will not be able to ply their trade simply due to the potential risk of infecting another in the course of their work.

The normal definition of total disability doesn't cover this possibility. However, most claims examiners are looking at the *economic* impact of the diagnosis rather than the lack of early physical limitations. A dentist who can't practice dentistry will be hard pressed to immediately attain a similar level of economic success in another field. A registered nurse may find new work, but isn't likely to match the level of income.

Rather than use the total disability definition alone, many carriers are applying the residual disability benefit clause to begin claim payments earlier than would normally be the case. There is an obvious economic loss. What remains is how far the insurer wants to take its obligation despite the contract language.

A number of states are requiring that new disability income policies, filed for approval to be sold, incorporate some HIV language into the definition of total disability on behalf of health professionals.[3] This new language would declare an individual in a health care field to be totally disabled upon diagnosis of HIV without regard to the physical ability to perform work.

MENTAL AND NERVOUS DISORDERS

Mental and nervous disorders did not register on the top ten list of disability claims fifteen years ago. Today, it is often the first or second leading dollar outlay for disability insurers. What happened?

Most individual disability contracts contain no exclusion for mental or nervous disorders, including substance abuse. (This is changing, however. See Chapter 14, Personal Disability Income Policies: What The Contractual Language Really Means.) Therefore, any claim for this type of condition has to be considered. These are not medical problems that can be excluded from coverage, so it is highly unlikely policies would be issued with an exclusion rider for a mental or nervous disorder.

Society has changed dramatically in the last three decades. Divorce rates, second and third marriages, step-children, single parent families all have added to a higher stress level. The result has been a major increase in hospitalizations and treatments for this type of illness.

With more than 25 percent of all hospital days in the country accounted for by mental disorders, it is no surprise that some of this should spill over into the disability income claims area. In addition, hospital stays for this type of illness tend to be significantly longer than hospital stays for any other single reason. Longer stays mean longer recovery periods and the probability that an elimination period could be satisfied and a claim paid.

These are difficult claims to handle. Not only is this a sensitive area, but many in the psychiatric and psychological fields disagree on standards of diagnosis and typical lengths of disability for any given condition.[4] Treatment will vary, often dependent on external factors such as environment along with the usual physical make-up of the claimant.[5] And while underwriters are trying to carefully look for past mental and nervous disorders during the application process, these claims are still hitting disability insurers hard.

The agent should understand that evaluation of this type of claim is time consuming. Further, there will not be any significant pattern from one claim to the next since each case is markedly different from the last even when the diagnosis is the same. Any assistance the agent can give in securing medical reports is helpful, but these are delicate claims to administer and best left to the experts in the claims unit.

THE SPECIAL CONSIDERATIONS

Consider a claim in a firm where 41 of the company's 150 employees are insured for disability and the agent has earned (and could continue to earn) a substantial income from the commissions paid on all of these premiums. The agent is also about to interview several other employees whose decision on buying the coverage may hinge on how the first disability claim is handled.

The examiner reviews the papers. He notes that the claimant started having symptoms indicating a lung disorder two months before the application was signed. A doctor was consulted and x-rays were taken. The results were inconclusive but further testing was to be done upon recurrence. The application was signed and none of this information was written in the medical questions section.

One month after the policy was put in force, symptoms recur and an x-ray now reveals a growth on the lung. A biopsy is scheduled and performed; the growth is malignant and chemotherapy is scheduled. The insured will miss work for a time; perhaps the condition will improve, perhaps not.

In the claims examiner's mind, the symptoms existed before the policy date and were not disclosed on the application calling clearly for a denial of the claim. But the agent calls and advises him that the whole company is watching this claim. The annual premium paid by policyowners here is currently about $50,000 and additional insureds could double this amount. Does the examiner decide to pay a month or two in benefits to help the agent save the rest of the case?

It is a tough call. The decision will rest on the total claim dollars expected, the quality of the agent, the amount of premium involved, and the seriousness of the persistency problem if the claim is not paid.

Some companies will decide to pay; others will not. Disability claims are anything but clear-cut, as we have seen.

OTHER FACTORS

The claims examiner must also be aware of economic and social trends that may cause an increase in the number of claims filed and paid. In times of severe economic downturn, a disability claim check may be easier to collect than a paycheck.

One might expect more problems of this type from seasonal occupations or lower income workers, but these circumstances have spread to most of the occupation classes written by disability insurers, including professionals. Claims from physicians are up significantly and one must seriously question whether the deterioration in experience for this occupation is due to poor health or other factors such as the advent of managed care with its decreasing emphasis on large numbers of specialists. Charles E. Soule, President of the Paul Revere Life Insurance Company, points out "demographic projections indicate that there will be an overabundance of professionals in both (physician and attorney) groups as society moves toward the end of the century, and the business should question whether or not this will impact the favorable work ethic the insurance industry has experienced in these markets."[6] Apparently, it already has.

What happens here? A claim is submitted that may or may not be valid. The duration of the claim is stretched since the *motivation* to return to work is questionable. The claims examiner must be aware of all of these factors in making a decision to pay policy benefits.

From the agent's standpoint, it is important to recognize that the first motivation of the claims examiner is to pay the claim accurately and as quickly as possible. There is no incentive to deny a claim which is likely to have negative ramifications for all concerned.[7]

The majority of claims are paid. For the agent, the opportunity to personally deliver the claim check should be taken. This is a service call you should enjoy making. The policy is performing as you said it would; this money is being used to pay for necessities that might not be possible without these dollars.

Many claimants are more than willing to provide *new* prospects for the agent to call on once they have seen the value of the disability policy. Take advantage of it! Indeed, agents who have been in the business a long time may have already made a list of the claim checks they have delivered for use in future sales interviews.

If you do not have such a list, most companies can furnish one which illustrates the policy value better than most visuals can. A sample list appears in Figure 12.2:

Figure 12.2

Period In Force Months-Days		Occupation	Cause of Disability	Age	Residence	Total Amt. Paid in Premiums	Amount Paid To Date
0	26	Mechanic	Brain Hemorrhage	33	IL	$15.55	$900.00
3	8	Store Manager	Lower Back Sprain	33	OH	$29.25	$24,000.00
6	11	Delivery Driver	Acute Low Back Strain, Contusion	29	VA	$375.57	$14,860.00
1	3	Auto Mechanic	Lower Back Strain	41	DC	$28.20	$ 2,328.33
0	12	Salesman	Tear Left Medial Meniscus	45	NH	$6.10	$40,800.00
1	17	Meat Cutter	Torn Knee Cartilage	52	RI	$23.63	$30,125.00
6	21	Safety Engineer	Herniated Disc	36	NC	$220.40	$42,400.00
4	7	Maintenance	Low Back Sprain	41	MA	$181.26	$10,800.00
8	10	Contractor	Cancer - Lip	55	TX	$453.18	$1,260.00
11	2	Upholsterer	Degenerative Disc Disease	53	WA	$221.10	$35,400.00
10	2	Brick-Layer	Herniated Disc	48	WA	$304.00	$51,600.00
11	13	Supervisor	Ruptured Disc	46	AR	$201.83	$33,450.00
11	18	Lobstering	Radiculitis of Lumbar Spine	53	FL	$575.00	$64,500.00
11	0	Private Aide	Dislocated Toe	25	MI	$440.55	$1,740.00

CHAPTER NOTES

1. "Time To Redefine Your DI Line, Part 2", Macmillan Co., New York.

2. MDBO "Disability Post ADA", *Best's Review*, November, 1992, p. 46.

3. Florida is one of the states requiring that the HIV positive language be included in contract language defining total disability.

4. *Handbook of Psychiatric Rehabilitation*, 1992, Macmillan Co., New York.

5. "Treatment of Depression and the Functional Capacity to Work", *General Psychiatry*, October, 1992, p. 761.

6. "Disability Income — Now and in the Year 2000", *Journal of the American Society of CLU and ChFC*, January, 1989.

7. "Consider Rating DI with Motivational Classes", *National Underwriter, Life & Health / Financial Services Edition*, February 20, 1995, p. 16.

PART II:
THE PRODUCT

Part 2 reviews common disability products sold today: personal, business overhead expense, disability buy-sell, and key person disability. It focuses on the contractual language of provisions in disability income contracts and explains optional benefits that are available to meet individual needs. Finally, it explores future trends.

■ *Chapter 13*

COMPARING PERSONAL DISABILITY INCOME POLICIES

WHY CONTRACT LANGUAGE IS IMPORTANT

The disability income contract an agent sells will not be put to a test of its true value until claim time. Unfortunately, if the policy is of little or no merit, it will probably be too late to do anything about it.

The agent, therefore, must be prepared in advance to know what policy provisions are important for a specific client. If the agent is already affiliated with a company that markets a disability policy, obviously, it is critical for the agent to know that company's policy well. It is equally vital, though, for the agent to acquire the knowledge necessary to evaluate the disability income products of other companies.

Today, more than ever, it is important to offer this service. Often, there will be several different types of products available for sale, each with its own strengths and objectives. The ability to match the right product to the client is the key to successful disability income selling. It increases the probability that the policy will do the proper job at claim time.

Each individual works in an occupation and earns an income in a specific way. Disability policy definitions vary as to the type of occupation and income protection provided. Understanding how this contractual language works helps to identify which occupations are more closely aligned with certain definitions. Understanding how benefits are paid as compared to how an individual is compensated can assure the proper match of a disability income program to a client.

It is a great service to be able to review a prospect's current disability income portfolio to ascertain its strength and completeness and its fit into the person's financial situation. Understanding contracts allows the agent to provide just this type of service.

This service will be of greater significant for the agent working in the professional market. Prospects in this market probably already own some form of disability coverage. Many may own the maximum amount of coverage available under today's reduced issue and participation limits. The review and recommendations made in the professional market will rely heavily on an agent's knowledge of the contractual language and market. A review of the existing coverage is part of any discussion with these prospects.

PRODUCT CHANGES

The individual disability income market is well known in the industry for its marked up and down swings as to experience and profits. In the mid 1970's, a serious product retrenchment occurred among several leading carriers, leading to a significant difference in the type of products available for sale.

This made it important to thoroughly analyze product provisions and price. One couldn't rely strictly on one or the other in a comparison; both assumed equal importance. In the early 1980's, product liberalizations were made in a frenzied pace as companies recognized significant profit gains. This led to policy endorsements which enhanced existing contract language. It remained even more important to outline both policy provisions and the premium charged in performing a policy analysis.

By the late 1980's, companies had improved their product language about as much as possible. Moreover, a number of companies had dropped out of the disability income market, leaving it to carriers with more experience. Since there were only three or four companies with the ability to assume this responsibility, product similarity became the norm. At this point, selling disability income policies was almost strictly a matter of premium comparison since there was little difference in the contractual language.

No more. Once again, there has emerged a diversity of products that again emphasizes the importance of comparing both policy provisions and premium. It will always be important to review in-force disability coverage as the agent determines how much additional coverage can be written. Due to current rate increases and a revision in contract language, it is unlikely that existing coverage will be replaced. However, identifying benefit amounts and coverage parameters such as elimination period and benefit period in addition to specific policy definitions will be critical in the overall analysis of an individual's financial goals.

The changes occurring today in the industry will not be easy to absorb, especially for the agent inexperienced in the disability income market. But these changes should be learned. Disability income coverage is an essential part of the overall financial plan for individuals and families. To ignore it because of its potential complexity is to do a disservice to one's clients. The homework done in preparation for a disability income review will make the comparison and analysis easier. The more reviews one does, the more comfortable one becomes with the entire process. Believe me, your clients will appreciate it.

ANALYZING THE PERSONAL DISABILITY INCOME CONTRACT

Much of the disability insurance industry's new emphasis today is on prospects who have not been offered affordable coverage in the past. In this situation it is unlikely that there will be any existing coverage to review. If so, a straight needs sales presentation (see Chapter 4, The Basic Sales Presentation) can be made. Concentration on product language will be in the form of identifying the type of product that best fits the person's occupation and compensation picture.

Looking at contractual policy provisions is needed in a review of an existing policy and in a situation where an agent is competing against another contract and a review of both programs is appropriate. Before discussing specific policy provisions, what they mean, how they developed and how they work at time of claim, let's review the evaluation process and set the stage for further contractual language.

Rule 1: Disability income policy analysis, as previously mentioned, should never consist of only a comparison of contract language. You must compare both provisions and premium cost to be fair and accurate in your assessment. A product today containing several more product features or more liberal language is virtually certain to carry a much higher price tag. If the policy is outstanding, but the prospect cannot afford it, the agent has accomplished nothing.

Rule 2: Conversely, you cannot shop price only. An agent can do this in looking for term life insurance coverage for a client, but with disability income insurance you get what you pay for. The lower the premium, the fewer the benefits. There are step-rated policies that allow purchase of a top-rated policy at a lower initial rate, which increases later and overall will eventually cost more than a level premium. Most of the time, however, lower price means less coverage. This may not mean that lower cost, lesser benefits isn't an option for the client. Some people may not need the more liberal definitions, so why pay for them? But compare both price and provisions!

Rule 3: Avoid using occupational classification designations as a basis of comparison. Most companies use a different scale in identifying the occupation being offered coverage. With the recent downgrading by many companies of physician occupations, there is likely to be an even wider variance in occupational classification nomenclature. Whether an individual is a Class 1 or Class 3A is immaterial. What matters most is what the individual can purchase in terms of benefits and definitions and how much it costs. The occupational classification will identify those more important pieces of the disability puzzle and should be used only to accomplish this.

Rule 4: In preparing a benefit-premium comparison, be sure to review *all* of the main policy features and specifically reproduce the substance of the policy provisions. "Yes" and "No" listings next to a specific feature under a company's heading are misleading and often inaccurate. Also, state insurance departments frown on this practice, especially if used to replace a policy. Policy replacement is *always* on the minds of insurance department officials as they look out for the best interests of the consumer. Don't take any chances! Do the proper comparison and spell out the definitions being compared.

Rule 5: Always look for policy endorsements that accompanied or followed placement of the original policy. A common mistake in policy comparisons is to overlook an enhanced policy provision. The client may receive the policy change and file it with or near the original contract or not file it at all. Do not always assume that the policy provisions shown are "gospel," especially if the definition seems particularly out of date. It will be more difficult to tell these days as the market has undergone both enhancement and cutback. The date of the policy may provide a clue as to whether an endorsement was attached since this was a common practice in the mid to late 1980's. Remember that a noncancelable or guaranteed renewable policy can only have the definitions *improved* after issue, up to age 65. Companies cannot restrict the language further once the policy is in force. (See Chapter 14, Personal Disability Income Policies: What The Contractual Language Really Means.) At any rate, look for the extra piece of paper that may represent an improvement in policy language after issue.

These rules are worth repeating:

1. Always compare both policy provisions and premium.

2. Do not shop price only.

3. Do not use occupational classification designations as a basis for comparison.

4. Write out the substance of each policy provision in the comparison.

5. Watch out for any and all endorsements to the original contract.

If you follow these guidelines, you have an excellent chance of assembling a fair, accurate and reasonable policy comparison that will help you understand the actual differences between the two or more contracts being compared.

PREMIUM CALCULATION

Before doing the benefit analysis, calculate the companies' premiums. Be sure that it is an equal comparison with the monthly benefit, elimination period, benefit period, optional benefits being the same. If there is a significant premium difference there may be a contractual variance and you should be prepared to identify it. If you are comparing a policy that is three or four years old to a current contract, the higher premium under the current contract may be attributable to a bevy of rate increases made to new business over that time period.

There may not be an ability to match either elimination period or benefit period. Older policies may have 30 day elimination periods which are hard to find today. The newer policies will likely cut back on the offering of a lifetime benefit period. Earlier policies containing this option may not have a comparable companion in today's policies. In this case, use the longest benefit period available in your calculation. It may be a to-age-65 or to-age-70 benefit period that will be the new longest standard available today.

Comparison for replacement purposes will be reduced significantly as a result of the recent cutbacks. There is no reason for an individual to give up a noncancelable policy, or a 30 day elimination period or a lifetime benefit period. Writing future coverage in addition to the in-force program is, of course, highly recommended.

A SAMPLE COMPARISON

The comparison form that I use when comparing professional contracts is reproduced in Figure 13.1. This analysis covers the major policy provisions offered to the professional risk today.

When completing this analysis, be sure to define each policy feature in accurate, easy to understand language. Most states require policies to be written in a simplified language format, and it is often easy to use the exact policy wording. Some definitions must be paraphrased because of their length, but this can be done without altering the meaning or intent of the provisions.

An example of a company to company policy comparison is reproduced in Figure 13.2 at the end of this chapter.

From this comparison, you may conclude that ABC Company's strengths (as compared to DEF Company) are in provisions 3 (definition of total disability and 5e (return to work provision). Company DEF's advantages are in provision 2 (renewability) and the overall residual disability benefit area, despite the presence of provision 5f, the relation of earnings to insurance clause.

Figure 13.1

A Policy Benefit Analysis For: _____

Date: _____

Policy Feature	Company A (Identify Product)	Company B (Identify Product)
1. $3,000/month, 90 day E.P. to age 65 B.P., with GOI and COL rider. Male, age 40, non-smoker		
2. Renewability		
3. Definition of Total Disability		
4. Physician Care Requirement		
5. Residual Disability Definition		
5a. Definition of Prior Earnings		
5b. Minimum Residual Benefit		
5c. Significant Loss of Earnings		
5d. Qualification Period		
5e. Return to Work		
5f. Relation of Earnings		
6. Presumptive Total Disability		
7. Rehabilitation		
8. Waiver of Premium		
9. Automatic Benefit Increase		
10. Mental & Nervous Disorder Limit		
11. Optional Benefits (List)		

Can you say that one policy is better than the other? There are those who swear by the definition of total disability that ABC Company has, despite the lack of a noncancelable provision. Others point to the residual disability approach as making more sense for the majority of income earners. This is what, they argue, disability income products are supposed to do: replace lost income, not render someone better off than they were prior to disability.

These arguments have been going on for two decades and will continue into the foreseeable future. Get used to this type of comparison since it will be the most common in the future.

The proper answer to the question of which contract is better is: it depends. It is here that disability income agents will have to be at their sharpest in the future. Since both these approaches will likely become the norm, identifying which suits your client better is a challenging task. Residual disability benefits will probably fit more clients than the total disability approach, yet there will be some for whom the measurement of total disability is more important than an income approach. A company employee who may return to work part-time after a disability and not receive any cut in pay will find residual benefits not very useful.

Policy premiums are likely to be quite different depending on the approach. While total and residual disability are both addressed in ABC's contract, the guaranteed renewable provision helps to lower the total cost. DEF's noncancelable provision brings the overall premium up considerably but there will be no further increases in premium until age 65, a measure of security that ABC doesn't offer.

Once the agent understands which policy definitions best suit the client, the premium can be addressed. It must fit comfortably within the client's budget or the job is only half done. It may be necessary to adjust policy parameters such as the monthly benefit, the elimination period, or the benefit period to arrive at the right number. This is as important as the proper policy selection since affordable coverage is more likely to be kept to provide the protection the client needs should disability strike.

Figure 13.2

A Policy Benefit Analysis For: J. A. Bullwinkle, M.D.		
Date: May 1, 1995		
Policy Feature	ABC Life Insurance Company Policy Form R2D2	DEF Life Insurance Company Policy Form 6-PRIS
1. $10,000/month, 90 day E.P. to age 65 B.P., with GOI rider. Female, age 40, non-smoker	Annual Premium $5,713.20	Annual Premium $5,354.65
2. Renewability	Guaranteed Renewable to age 65.	Non-cancelable and Guaranteed Renewable to age 65 at guaranteed premium rates.

Figure 13.2 (continued)

Policy Feature	ABC Life Insurance Company Policy Form R2D2	DEF Life Insurance Company Policy Form 6-PRIS
	Renewable for life if employed full-time.	Renewable for life if employed full-time.
3. Definition of Total Disability	Insured will be considered totally disabled if, due to injury or sickness, is unable to do the substantial and material duties of regular occupation.	Insured will be considered disabled when, due to injury or sickness, he or she has a restricted ability to work at any reasonable occupation.
4. Physician Care Requirement	To qualify for benefits under this policy, insured must be under a doctor's care. This requirement is waived if future treatment would be of no benefit to the insured.	To qualify for benefits under this policy, insured must be under a doctor's care. This requirement is waived if medical care would be of no benefit to the insured.
5. Residual Disability Definition	Residual disability means that, due to injury or sickness, the insured is: a) able to perform one or more of the important duties of regular occupation, or b) is able to perform these duties but not for as much time as was done prior to disability, and c) earnings loss is at least 20% of prior earnings.	Residual disability means that, due to injury or sickness, earnings are reduced by at least 20% of prior earnings.
5a. Definition of Prior Earnings	Prior earnings is the greater of: a) 12 month average just prior to disability, or b) for the fiscal year with the highest earnings level of the last two fiscal years just prior to disability.	Prior earnings is the greater of: a) 12 month average just prior to disability, or b) best 24 consecutive months in the 60 month period just prior to disability.

Figure 13.2 (continued)

Policy Feature	ABC Life Insurance Company Policy Form R2D2	DEF Life Insurance Company Policy Form 6-PRIS
5b. Minimum Residual Benefit	No provision.	In the first six months, at least 50% of the total disability benefit will be paid if insured has at least 20% earnings loss.
5c. Significant Loss of Earnings	No provision.	If loss of income is 80% or higher, the full total disability benefit will be paid.
5d. Qualification	Insured may be either totally or residually disabled or any combination of the two to qualify for benefits.	An earnings loss of 20% on any day will ocunt as a day of disability in qualifying for benefits.
5e. Return to Work	For the first 4 months the insured resumes full-time work, only a loss of at least 20% of prior earnings is required before benefits cease.	For the first 12 months the insured resumes full-time work, only a loss of at least 20% of prior earnings is required before benefits cease.
5f. Relation of Earnings to Insurance	No provision.	Insured's earnings and other income sources, including disability insurance, cannot exceed 100% of prior earnings.
6. Presumptive Total Disability	If the insured, due to injury or sickness, loses sight, speech, or hearing or use of two limbs, total disability will be presumed to exist and no further tests of total disability will be taken. Benefits will be paid from the date of loss.	No provision.
7. Rehabilitation	If the insured enters a company-approved rehabilitation program, the costs of the program will be reimbursed in in addition to a continuation of the monthly total disability benefit.	If a medical determination indicates that a program of rehabilitation would assist in a return to work, the company will participate in the costs of such program in addition to continuing to pay the monthly disability benefit.

Figure 13.2 (continued)

Policy Feature	ABC Life Insurance Company Policy Form R2D2	DEF Life Insurance Company Policy Form 6-PRIS
8. Waiver of Premium	If insured has been disabled for 90 days, future premiums coming due will be waived and any money paid during the initial 90 day period will be refunded.	If insured has been disabled for 90 days, future premiums coming due will be waived and any money paid during the initial 90 day period will be refunded.
9. Automatice Benefit Increases (may be an optional benefit)	Automatically increases the policy monthly benefit by 4% each year based on the CPI change. No medical evidence is ever required and only financial evidence is needed after 5 such increases to renew an additional 5 increases.	Automatically increases the policy monthly benefit by between 3 and 7% each year based on the CPI. change. No medical evidence is ever required and only financial evidence is needed after 5 such increases to renew an additional 5 increases.
10. Mental & Nervous Disorder Limit (Only on payroll deduction cases)	No limitation.	Restricts the benefit to 24 months if claim is for a specified mental or nervous disorder.
11. Guarantee of Insurability Option	Allows insured to add more benefits at specified option dates without any medical evidence of insurability. Total increases can equal up to 2 times the policy monthly benefit amount.	Allows insured to add more benefits at specified option dates without any medical evidence of insurability. Total increases can equal up to 1 1/2 times the policy monthly benefit amount.

Disability Income

■ *Chapter 14*

PERSONAL DISABILITY POLICIES: WHAT THE CONTRACTUAL LANGUAGE REALLY MEANS

Knowing how to do a disability income policy analysis is a promising start that will lead to a successful finish if you understand what the specific policy provisions mean to the insured at claim time.

So much has changed in product availability in a short period of time that the agent's ability to absorb and interpret these modifications is being severely tested. There are substantial alterations taking place today that haven't entirely shaken out yet, but this chapter captures the current changes and the spirit of future ones.

The better you comprehend the origin and purpose of a contractual definition, the more assistance you can offer to your client in a product evaluation. This does not mean that you must cover every policy provision in detail during a sales interview. As you have seen in Chapter 4, The Basic Sales Presentation, you can close a sale for disability income without ever mentioning one clause from the policy.

This is homework time. What you review and study here you may never have the opportunity to fully explain to the client. But when disability income is purchased, it is done so by the client on the basis of your recommendation. There is an underlying trust on the part of the client that you have researched this market and identified the best possible contract for his occupation and compensation situation.

This chapter will discuss the various common policy provisions that are prevalent in personal disability income contracts today.

RENEWABILITY

Renewability is one of the more important features of a disability income policy. This provision will offer several viable choices for the future, based on the company's claims experience. The issuer of disability coverage can be subject to increasing risk and subsequent heavy losses since even a single long-term claim for a sizable monthly benefit amount can add up to a great deal of money. It has not been possible to completely predict the total payout potential for disability income contracts containing a lifetime benefit period. Companies, therefore, must be careful about the sort of renewal guarantees they incorporate into a policy and to whom they market the more liberal provisions.

There are two major types of renewal provisions that have emerged in the individual disability income business. In addition, a third type can be used in some payroll deduction or franchise situations where the occupational class is of a higher risk.

Noncancelable

This is the most generous of the disability income renewal provisions and is offered primarily to the higher income, more stable occupational risks. Formerly representing the primary renewal provision of most individual disability income carriers, noncancelability is now being withdrawn or at least re-evaluated by a number of leading disability insurers.

This provision "locks in" the premium rate for the policy until age 65. No matter what the claims experience on the individual policy or the collective product line, the rate is *guaranteed*. The company cannot change it. Further, the policy provisions are guaranteed and cannot be changed during the same period of time.

Noncancelable disability income policies are one of the few types of insurance where guarantees are solid. It is a unilateral contract with the client in the power position.

This inability to make any rate changes after the policy is issued forces the insurer to price the policy accurately to begin with since this is the only chance the company gets until age 65. At 65, the rates are subject to increase if the insured decides to further renew the policy which can be done if the insured is employed full-time. The insured will have to agree to a higher rate and continue to pay the renewal premium for as long as the coverage is needed and as long as the insured is actively at work up to a certain age, usually age 75.

Lately, these guarantees have been difficult for insurers to manage. Mounting claims losses due, largely, to other liberal policy definitions and an easing of underwriting requirements have placed the noncancelable provision on the "endangered species" list. In addition, many state insurance departments are now using the NAIC (National Association of Insurance Commissioners) risk-based capital formula for evaluating an insurer's financial strength. The noncancelable disability product carries an unusually high risk factor, making it more difficult for the carrier to comply with the regulatory guidelines.

Another factor is important here. The guarantees associated with noncancelability have come with a much higher premium cost recently than in prior years. In many cases, the premium (due to having only the one opportunity to get it right) is not affordable for the average, middle income earner. Since there were few alternatives to noncancelability, a number of potential clients passed up the chance to purchase the coverage. This helped no one.

Companies will continue to offer noncancelability for as long as they feel it is a marketing necessity. If enough companies decide to keep this feature, it will remain available. If most decide to use another renewal feature, it's unlikely there will remain any holdouts.

Companies may continue to monitor who can purchase noncancelability and with which *definitions* it will be offered. (See the discussion of total disability definitions later in this chapter.) For now, agents should present it as an option for a client who wants to pay a higher price for the solid premium guarantee.

Guaranteed Renewable

Once a feature only for higher risk occupations, guaranteed renewability has re-emerged from the long shadows cast by the noncancelable provision. It is almost identical to the noncancelable provision with one "fallback" exception that may help the insurance carrier. With guaranteed renewability, the company does have the right to *increase* the premium.

However, this increase cannot be made on an individual basis. There must be a rate increase justification filed with the state insurance department showing the reasons for the increase to a specific policy type, specific occupational class, or specific gender. In other words, the rates will be increased for all policyholders who fall within a certain category.

This type of "out" for the insurers is probably necessary for policies that contain the most liberal definitions of total disability since this is where claims can pile up at an alarmingly quick rate. A guaranteed renewable provision may take anywhere from 15 to 30% off the overall cost for the policy, a welcome decrease for many previously priced out of the noncancelable product.

The rate increases are not an annual event. Many carriers go several years before finding the need to increase premiums. Having the alternative open to disability insurers is important right now. Having a policy providing solid protection that is also affordable for many prospects is equally important.

This winning combination is sure to boost sales of policies featuring this provision. It may be the only type of renewal provision you can buy in conjunction with the most liberal of policy total disability definitions. It is certainly a provision that many agents will want to show their clients as an option and represents another way of staying within the discretionary budget of the client. This alone makes it a more important feature than it has been over the last thirty years.

Conditionally Renewable

Offered less frequently, but still common with higher risk occupations, is the conditionally renewable provision. Under this provision, certain qualifications must be met for the insured to renew the policy. These qualifications most often have to do with employment. Full-time employment is the usual stipulation that must be met to continue the product. In some franchise or association plans, the insured must also belong to a certain association to continue to qualify for coverage.

Rate increases are also possible under this kind of provision. However, as long as the insured meets the conditional qualifications and pays the required premium on time, the company will not cancel the plan.

This provision is not as widely used as either noncancelability or guaranteed renewability, but there is the possibility of seeing it occasionally. There are also a few cancelable contracts on the market, under which an insurer could refuse to renew the policy on a premium renewal date. Such a policy may be terminated individually or the insurer may cancel all policies in a state where experience is poor. Watch for this renewal provision in group or association type coverages.

DEFINITIONS OF INJURY AND SICKNESS

Since disability policies do cover both injury (or accident) and sickness, these terms must be defined in the contract.

Injury or accident is usually defined as accidental bodily injury sustained while the policy is in force. Such a definition encompasses virtually all types of accidents and does not often specify that the injury must be sustained through accidental means.

Accidental-means wording would allow the insurer to deny a claim where the insured was injured while knowingly engaged in the endeavor that caused the injury. For example, an individual who lifts a piano and throws his back out would not ordinarily be disabled under accidental means-wording since the individual intended to lift the piano.

Sickness is defined as illness or disease which first manifests itself (makes itself known) to the insured while the policy is in force. Sicknesses are not subject to the aforementioned "means" type of wording. The definition of sickness covers both physical *and* mental illness unless otherwise specified.

DISABILITY DEFINITIONS

The key feature in any disability contract is how it defines disability for the purposes of qualifying for benefits. This is the provision every insured is most interested in since it lays down the ground rules for collecting benefits under the policy.

Today's policies may diverge based on the types of disability for which policy benefits will be paid. You will find total disability policies only, policies which cover a loss of earnings only (following an injury or sickness) and policies which provide a dual definition of disability, with benefits for both total disability and a loss of earnings.

The critical definitions to review are:

- total disability and

- residual disability.

These policy provisions are the measurement of the contract: what you pay your premium dollars for in exchange for coverage. They address vastly different types of claim situations. They are intended for use with separate audiences; one for whom the total disability definition alone is the crux of the plan while the other consists of individuals whose incomes are generated based solely on their ability to work on a full-time basis.

In a dual definition approach, the basic policy includes either total or residual disability coverage with the other available to add as an optional benefit. Occasionally, both definitions are built into the same contract. This is becoming a rarer form of disability coverage as policies are developed which concentrate on covering either one or the other effectively.

Total Disability

Definitions of total disability vary considerably from contract to contract depending usually on the type of occupational risk covered by the policy. The more stable the occupation, the better the insurance risk and it is to individuals in such occupations that the more liberal type of total disability definition is made available. The best of these definitions is commonly referred to as "own occupation" coverage.

Own Occupation: Own Occupation means that the insured has to satisfy only one measure of disability: The insured must be unable to perform, due to injury or sickness, the duties of his regular occupation.

There are variations on this wording. Some provisions say "unable to perform the substantial and material duties," but the essence of the provision and how it is enforced at claim time is the same as the "unable to perform the duties" language.

If the insured meets this one test, that is, he is unable to work at his regular job, total disability benefits are payable, even if the insured could (or does) work in another occupation. (Physician care could also be required, but this issue is addressed separately later in this chapter.)

It doesn't take much imagination to see the claim potential of this definition. A disability income policy with a $5,000 a month benefit owned by a physician, for example, could generate a sizable payout based on the slightest of disabilities. For example, if the physician is a surgeon who breaks his hand, he will likely be unable to perform in his occupation if the hand doesn't heal properly or if there is residual damage to nerve endings or muscles which makes it difficult to grip the scalpel. Thus, the surgeon is unable to practice surgery and is, under this policy definition, totally disabled.

Look how the dollars pile up. If the surgeon was 40 when this incident occurred and had a policy paying benefits until age 65, the total payout would be:

$5000 x 12 months = $60,000 x 25 years = $1,500,000.00

A million and a half for a broken hand is probably not what the actuary had in mind when pricing the policy. What if the policy had a lifetime benefit period, as many of these actual claims do? There is no reason to suspect an early mortality based on a broken hand, so if the surgeon lives to age 75, add another 10 years of benefits ($60,000 x 10) or $600,000 to the claim.

If the policy was for $10,000 a month, as many are, the claim is now $3,000,000 for the age 65 and $4,200,000 for the lifetime claim if the claimant dies at age 75.

How many of these claims does it take to create havoc with a portfolio's profitability? An insurer needs a substantial premium volume, from both new and renewal business, to offset just *one* claim.

Making it more difficult for insurers to justify this provision in terms of economic need is the probability that this surgeon will pursue another occupation, earn income and still collect total disability benefits. If he made $300,000 (qualifying for $10,000 per month in benefits) as a surgeon and could earn $100,000 annually as a family practice physician where dexterity of the hands is not as critical, the physician would suffer a pure earnings loss of $80,000 a year between the $100,000 income and the $120,000 in disability income benefits ($220,000 in total). Since the $120,000 in this example would be received income tax-free, there is substantially less of a loss to the physician than $80,000.

But what if the surgeon makes $200,000 in the new field? Now $320,000 ($120,000 of it income tax-free) is covering the pre-disability taxable income of $300,000. The purpose of disability income is to help an individual maintain his standard of living during disability. The disabilities considered by insurers in pricing are more catastrophic in nature than a broken hand. Yet an injury of this type is all it would take for certain professionals to collect benefits under the contract. Is this truly disability insurance? I've heard arguments both ways.

What about a dentist with a bad back? Out of his primary occupation, he may well find a job equalizing his dentist's pay if he pursues a field that doesn't have the same overhead that dentistry generates. Bad backs are common and so, too, are dentist claims, prompting the removal of dentists from the top two occupational class levels of most companies.

Interpreting what the duties (or substantial and material duties) are that measure disability becomes important at claim time. The identification of these duties can be the key factor in determining disability. What companies mean by "the duties" or the "substantial duties and material duties" are those duties that contribute the most to an individual's income. This may or may not be directly related to the percentage of time spent performing these tasks.

For example, a trial attorney may spend only 25% of a week's time actually in the courtroom. Yet without the ability to practice in the courtroom, the consequences to the attorney's income can be devastating. After all, trial attorneys are hired on the basis of how well they perform during the trial, not how well they take depositions, or write briefs or visit with their clients. Hence, "substantial and material duties" may mean only one specific duty, but it is the key to their ability to earn an income.

The fewer duties that are used to measure disability, the more likely the chances that a disability, however small, will cause a claim under this own occupation definition. It is this "ease" at qualifying for benefits that cannot be taken away that is giving insurers second thoughts about the validity of this definition. The idea that an individual is better off disabled than healthy defeats the entire pricing mechanism surrounding the policy. Said one disability insurance executive in a recent publication, "The purpose of D.I. is to replace your income and serve as a safety net. The idea of making money off D.I. with the *own occupation* (coverage) violated the basic principles of disability insurance."[1]

Companies are at work tending their recent wounds. It is quite likely that shortly the lifetime benefit period will no longer be sold with own occupation coverage. Moreover, most companies are rethinking the combination of noncancelability and own occupation reasoning that if they offer this type of definition it should be on a guaranteed renewable basis where the company can apply premium increases to a product line whose primary definition is being utilized more than originally expected.

The own occupation definition of total disability won't disappear overnight. But controlling how and to whom it is sold is, currently, a primary goal among disability insurers.

Modified Own Occupation: This definition is the same as the above own occupation definition with the exception that the definition applies as long as the insured does not elect to return to another occupation.

This definition reads: "The insured must be unable to perform the [substantial and material] duties of his regular occupation *and* must not be working in any gainful [or reasonable] occupation."

This definition allows the insured an election at time of disability. If the individual becomes totally disabled and is unable to do the substantial and material duties of his occupation, it is the insured's election whether or not to enter another occupation. If he does *not*, total disability benefits will be payable as long as there is a continuing inability to work in his regular occupation. If that individual decides to return to another occupation, then the occupation must satisfy the additional test: that it not be a "gainful" or "reasonable" one.

The gainful or reasonable measurement is based on the insured's education, training, experience and, usually, prior income. If the job is within the scope of all these categories, then benefits either stop (in a total-disability-only contract) or the insured collects benefits based on a loss of earnings (in a dual definition approach).

Short-Term Own Occupation: Another variation of own occupation coverage is to offer the liberal definition using only the test that the insured must be unable to perform his or her regular occupation for a specified period of time. This time period could be two years, five years, ten years or based on reaching a specific age such as 55 or 60. Following this time period, a new definition of disability is introduced.

Thus, a short-term own occupation definition is divided into two parts as shown in the following example: "For the first five years of a disability, the insured must be unable to perform the [substantial and material] duties of his or her own occupation. Thereafter, the insured must be unable to work in any gainful occupation for which the insured is suited by education, training or experience and with due regard to prior earnings."

This second test is more restrictive and reviews the insured's ability to perform a number of occupations other than the regular one. It also effectively cuts down on the exposure for a long-term own occupation type claim, by cutting losses after five years. Of course, if the insured is still unable to work in a reasonable or gainful occupation, the claim continues.

The wording for this second test is slightly different from the modified own occupation language. Here, the individual's ability to perform other work will halt the claim whereas the modified definition gives the insured the choice of whether or not to work at a job. This latter language still leaves the insured in control of his or her destiny in deciding whether to return to work. The "ability" test keeps the control at the insurance claim department.

Any Gainful Work: The last and least liberal of the total disability definitions applies the second test outlined above for the entire period of disability. An example of this type of wording is: "The insured must be unable to perform the duties of any gainful [reasonable] occupation for which he or she is suited by education, training or experience [and with due regard to prior earnings]."

This definition is commonly written on the more hazardous occupations where disability is more likely to occur.

HIV Policy Language

These definitions listed above all require a physical loss to become eligible for benefits. The ability to perform at some level of work activity is the driving force behind the terminology.

The impact of testing positive for the AIDS virus has altered the wording for new contracts filed in many states. A positive HIV test may not be immediately followed by a physical loss of ability to do work-related activities. But, in the medical profession, the positive HIV test will mean the end of the ability to practice in medicine, whether the person is a nurse, doctor or other type of medical worker. There may not be an actual physical loss for some time, but there is certainly a great economic loss in having to change fields. In recognition of this, carriers are considering a positive HIV test for medical personnel to be sufficient to satisfy the definition of disability in the disability contract.

Older policies are being handled this way on an administrative basis. New policies may actually include some type of HIV wording, as required by statute in many states.

The definitions of total disability will qualify an individual for the full monthly benefit payable under the policy. This is well suited to individuals who could either work in their occupation or not and to employees of companies who would return to work at a full-time earnings level even if working only on a part-time basis. Other workers, whose presence is tied directly to income, might do better to consider a residual disability (or loss of earnings) approach to disability income.

Residual Disability

The second type of disability definition has been evolving on its own over the last twenty years. Today, many carriers are offering a loss of earnings (or income replacement) coverage often called residual disability. It pays benefits based on an economic loss following a physical disability event, either an accident or sickness. The key factor here is how much income is lost. The answer to this question dictates the benefits that will be paid.

This type of coverage evolved through actual claims statistics kept by a number of companies. These statistics revealed the high frequency of a claimant's return to his regular occupation on a part-time (or residual) basis following a disability. The reluctance of workers to leave the field in which they have trained and worked for a significant amount of time is more the rule than the exception.

Residual disability, either on a stand-alone policy basis as a loss of earnings plan or as the second half of a dual definition approach (paired with total disability), has recently been the benchmark by which the policy has been competitively assessed. Since the loss of earnings type of policy may soon be the only plan that still carries the noncancelable renewal feature, the importance of this type of definition will only be further increased.

It wasn't always this way. In its infancy, residual disability was a controversial, under-appreciated benefit which had more to do with how it was introduced than the quality of the feature itself.

In the early to mid-1970's, companies offering disability coverage were starting to experience deteriorating claims results due to the own occupation definition of disability. More and more individuals were utilizing this benefit much as they are today, only on a lesser scale. As a result, several major carriers phased out their policies that offered own occupation coverage and replaced them with a more restrictive definition of total disability coupled with a new provision — residual disability.

From an agent (and to a lesser extent, a consumer) standpoint, it appeared that total disability benefits were being taken away and that residual (or a portion of total disability benefits) was being substituted.

This was not technically correct. Residual disability actually provided a benefit where none was payable in the past: for a return to one's own occupation. Under total disability-only definitions, if an individual went back to his own job, benefits were no longer payable. The residual disability provision paid benefits based on earnings loss after this return to work.

A number of company studies have shown that the large majority (90 to 95 percent) of disabled people return to their original work. Why would they give their profession up if they did not have to? Most professionals have a substantial amount of education behind them and, until recently, have been reluctant to abandon it just to collect total disability benefits.

Over time, companies that abandoned their own occupation definition eventually restored it and sold it in conjunction with the new residual disability benefit, creating the dual definition approach to paying disability benefits. Under a pure dual approach, the individual received:

- a total disability benefit for being unable to work in his regular occupation even if working in another job; and

- residual disability benefits if a return was made to the regular occupation on a reduced income basis.

Today, these definitions are being separated again by a number of carriers.

To understand how residual disability works at claim time, there are several important definitions and provisions one must know. These provisions are:

1. Definition of Residual Disability

2. Qualification Period

3. Pre-disability Earnings

4. Earnings During A Residual Disability

5. Loss of Earnings

6. Significant Loss of Earnings

7. Minimum Residual Benefit in the First Six Months

8. Return to Work (Recovery) Benefits

9. Relation of Earnings to Insurance

Definition of Residual Disability. To be considered residually disabled, the insured must suffer an injury or sickness that reduces income. Some companies require physician care, as discussed in more detail later, and a reduction in either the insured's ability to perform all of the duties or the time it takes to perform such tasks.

There are two common types of residual disability definitions: those that measure earnings loss only and those that measure earnings loss and require additional loss of the ability to work. Examples of these are shown in Figure 14.1.

Figure 14.1

Earnings Loss and Loss of Time or Duties	Residual disability means, as a result of injury or sickness, you are able to do some but not all of the substantial and material duties of your regular occupation, or you are able to do all of the substantial and material duties of your regular occupation but for less than full-time, and earnings loss is at least 20% of pre-disability earnings.
Earnings Loss Only	Residual disability means, as a result of injury or sickness, earnings loss is at least 20% of pre-disability earnings.

The second definition is less complicated (and often more desirable) than the first.

If the insured satisfies the definition of residual disability, a qualification period is sometimes required before the insured becomes eligible to receive benefits.

Qualification Period. The insured must, of course, satisfy the elimination period before any benefits are payable, as discussed in more detail later. In addition, a qualification period may also be established. A qualification period is generally defined by the industry as the number of days the insured must be *totally* disabled first before becoming eligible for residual benefits. In other words, total disability of a certain length of time such as 30, 60, or 90 days must precede any return to work and eligibility for residual benefits.

For many occupational classes, judged to be the company's best in terms of claims experience, there is almost always *no* qualification period required, or no total disability that must happen first. Check in the policy schedule page under residual disability to see if any qualification period exists for a specific policy.

The definition of residual disability and the qualification period are how an insured becomes eligible for benefits. Now, how are residual benefits calculated?

The calculation is based on a loss of earnings formula made up of the following provisions.

Pre-disability (or Prior) Earnings. To determine the amount of income loss due to a disability, the amount of income earned while the insured was healthy must first be established. This figure should accurately represent the earnings power of the insured immediately prior to becoming disabled.

Usually, the insured has a choice of earnings periods prior to disability to be used in determining this figure.

The first choice is usually the monthly average for the 12 month period (sometimes six months) immediately preceding disability. Generally, the insured's highest earnings level is reached during his most recent year's efforts.

If this is not the case, a second choice is offered. This can take any of several forms, the most common of which is the highest average monthly earnings for any 24 consecutive months in the 60 months prior to disability. Under this option, the insured can go back five years for a higher income average. Variations on the 60-month look-back account for other differences in this policy definition from contract to contract.

The insured will be allowed to use the highest figure in arriving at the final number for this portion of the residual benefit calculation formula. The higher the pre-disability earnings figure, the better for the insured. It is against this number that current earnings after returning to work will be measured and an income loss determined.

Generally, the last 12 months average is the higher figure, but a poor earnings year just prior to disability may not be an accurate reflection of the insured's income. This is entirely possible for self-employed individuals whose earnings tend to fluctuate regularly from year to year. Having the choice to review a number of months prior to disability eliminates the potential inaccuracy a poor earnings year would have upon this figure.

If a claim lasts several years, an adjustment should be made to the pre-disability earnings figure to prevent inflation from gradually eroding this amount. Most companies offer an indexing feature and generally make the first adjustment 365 days after the start of disability. The adjustment is made annually and is often based on the Consumer Price Index for the most recent year. Some companies use a set percentage increase such as 5 percent; others use numbers set as guaranteed minimum increases without regard to the CPI, but may go higher if the CPI measurement is higher.

These adjustments will be made for the duration of the claim. Thus, inflation will not have the effect of reducing the value of the prior earnings figure.

Earnings During a Residual Disability. The second key factor in determining the amount of income loss from the residual disability is the amount that the insured is earning after returning to work.

Companies usually define earnings as compensation for work the insured has done, such as salary, wages, commissions, or fees. Importantly, earnings *do not include* (1) dividends, interest, rent, royalties, or other investment income; (2) income from any annuity, pension, or deferred compensation plan; or 3) amounts deductible from gross income as a business expense for federal income tax purposes.

There are two methods of accounting for income earned after a return to work. The accrual method credits earnings during the period in which they were earned rather than the period they were actually received. This eliminates from consideration any money earned prior to disability but not paid until after the insured has returned to work. The one drawback is that counting income while it is earned measures only the insured's physical ability to work, not financial status. The insured can only spend amounts actually received not amounts which have only been billed.

The cash method of accounting measures amounts received. Some companies do not count any money earned prior to disability. Thus, it is only income that is earned after a return to work following a disability that is actually measured. This measures income as it is actually received, rather than when it is billed.

Loss of Earnings. Current earnings measured against pre-disability earnings produces an income loss percentage. For example, if pre-disability earnings is set at $5,000 a month and current earnings is calculated at $2,000, the insured is earning 40 percent of pre-disability earnings and suffering a 60 percent earnings loss. The earnings loss percentage, 60 percent, is the number needed for the calculation.

The actual residual disability benefit paid is a portion of the total disability monthly benefit. An insured who is totally disabled under the policy would receive a total disability monthly benefit. Logically, an insured who is residually (partially) disabled would receive only a part of the full total disability benefit. That part would depend upon the extent of the residual disability earnings loss.

To determine the residual benefit, the earnings loss percentage is multiplied by the total disability monthly benefit. The final formula for calculation is shown in Figure 14.2.

Figure 14.2

Monthly Pre-disability Earnings	Monthly Current Earnings	% Income Loss	x	Total Disability Monthly Benefit	=	Residual Disability Monthly Benefit
$5,000	$2,000	60%	x	$3,000	=	$1,800

The residual benefit is calculated each month utilizing the same formula. The percentage of income lost is subject to minimums and maximums when being used to determine the residual benefit.

Significant Loss of Earnings. If the insured's income loss is high enough, he will be considered totally disabled for the purposes of the policy. This would set the income loss percentage at 100 percent. In the formula example in Figure 14.2, a high loss would generate payment of $3,000, the actual total disability monthly benefit.

The level at which the income loss is assumed to be 100 percent varies considerably, but a 75 percent or 80 percent loss is the most common.

Minimum Residual Benefit in the First Six Months. Under this provision, in the first six months of a residual disability, the insured would receive the *greater* of 50 percent of the total disability monthly benefit or the actual benefit based on the percentage calculation. Therefore, the *minimum* residual *benefit* an insured would receive for the first six months of a residual disability would be 50 percent of the total disability benefit.

These last two policy provisions can be summarized by the table reproduced in Figure 14.3.

Figure 14.3

% of Loss of Earnings	Residual Benefit Payable in First Six Months	Residual Benefit Payable After Six Months
0-19%	-0-	-0-
20-50%	50% of total disability benefit	20-50% of total disability benefit
51-75 or 80%	51-75 or 80% of total disability benefit	51-75 or 80% of total disability benefit
76 or 81-100%	Full total disability benefit	Full total disability benefit

In the residual benefit calculation formula, these two provisions would directly affect the percentage loss of earnings figure and, of course, indirectly, the residual disability monthly benefit paid.

Residual disability benefits are payable as long as the insured is residually disabled for the maximum benefit period specified in the contract. Benefits are not usually payable beyond age 65. Naturally, benefits payable during a total disability are also part of the maximum benefit period.

As an example, consider an insured who was totally disabled for six months and residually disabled thereafter. The elimination period under the policy is 60 days and the maximum benefit period is five years. No benefits are payable for the first two months. Total disability benefits are payable for the next four months. Residual benefits are payable from that point and will be payable for 56 months or up to age 65, if earlier.

Return to Work (Recovery) Benefits. Also called a recovery benefit, this policy provision limits the number of months during which the insured can be back working full time and suffering an earnings loss of 20 percent or more while still collecting residual benefits. There is some recognition that a full-time return to work may not mean an instant return to 80 percent or more of pre-disability earnings. However, this provision limits how long the residual calculation will be made under these circumstances.

The limitation ranges from three months to twenty-four months while some companies do not have this provision at all. Others offer it as an optional benefit where their definition of residual disability includes a requirement that a loss of either time or duties accompany an income loss of at least 20%.

Relation of Earnings to Insurance. Another of the checks and balances being re-introduced into disability income contracts is the relation of earnings to insurance clause. Here, the total of all income sources, including disability benefits, cannot exceed 100 percent of prior earnings. If it does, the monthly benefit payable under either residual or total disability will be cut back accordingly.

The purpose of this provision is to ensure that the individual claimant is not better off disabled than working. It was part of disability contracts a few years ago but was discontinued for competitive purposes. It is a leaner time today, though, and the return of this policy provision underscores the insurers' determination to put the contract back in the arena of common sense.

Partial Disability Benefits

Prior to the introduction of residual disability (the long-term approach to partial disability) in the 1970's, a partial disability benefit was sold and continues to be marketed, especially for higher risk occupations.

This benefit is simplified greatly from the residual approach. Partial disability is defined as the inability to do some of the duties of a job or profession. The definition does not usually refer to loss of time as a measurement of disability.

To qualify for benefits, the insured usually has to experience a period of total disability first. The period of total disability required is often linked to the number of days in the elimination period.

Income loss is not a factor in determining the benefit. The benefit payable is 50 percent of the benefit that would be paid for total disability. As long as the insured has met the required period of total disability and is able to perform only some of the occupational duties, this benefit will be paid.

The benefit period for this provision, however, is usually limited to either three or six months although some companies market a twelve month version of this option.

This benefit can be identified as short-term partial while residual disability carries the long-term implication.

REGULAR CARE AND ATTENDANCE OF A PHYSICIAN

As part of the requirement for meeting the definition of disability under a contract, the insured generally must be under the care of a legally qualified physician. This provision may be waived if future treatment would be of no benefit to the insured.

For example, if an individual suffers multiple traumas to the back after a skiing accident, the problems may eventually no longer require the regular care and attendance of a physician, yet the back problems will continue to cause work loss and the insured may never be normal again. The doctor is caring for the claimant regularly, but it is understood that this isn't necessary to substantiate this rather serious disability.

This completes the requirements for qualifying for either total or residual disability.

SATISFYING THE ELIMINATION PERIOD

If the contract includes a dual definition approach to disability by including both total and residual benefits, each type of disability can usually be used interchangeably to satisfy the policy elimination period. The exception to this would be the presence of a qualification period stipulating a time of total disability first. The elimination period, you will recall, is the number of days of disability required prior to being eligible to receive any disability benefits.

Following are three examples of how the elimination period can be met.

Example One — 90 Day Elimination Period

Insured suffers a broken leg, and misses work for ten days before returning on a part-time basis for the next four weeks (28 days). The broken leg fails to heal properly, an infection results and the insured is out for another two months. The elimination period consists of 10 days of total disability plus 28 days of residual disability plus 52 more days of total disability for a total of 90 days.

Thus, the elimination period is satisfied and the insured is eligible for total disability benefits on the 91st day. If the insured subsequently returns to work, he will be eligible for residual benefits if income loss is greater than 20 percent of earnings prior to the broken leg.

Example Two — 180 Day Elimination Period

The insured suffers a heart attack and is away from work for 57 days. The insured returns slowly on a part-time basis for the next several months. The elimination period consist of 57 days of total disability plus 123 days of residual disability for a total of 180 days.

Thus, the elimination period is satisfied and the insured is eligible for residual benefits on the 181st day and will receive them for as long as the residual disability lasts up to age 65 (or maximum benefit period, if less). If the insured should suffer a relapse into total disability, total disability benefits will immediately become payable.

Example Three — 60 Day Elimination Period

The insured is in a car accident. He returns to work the next day. Within a week, the insured is experiencing headaches and fatigue and, though able to continue working for the next several weeks, suffers a loss of income since he is no longer able to spend the same amount of time at his job. The insured, after 17 weeks of these difficulties, finally consults a doctor and is operated on for a brain tumor within two days. The insured is out of work completely and will never be able to return to his occupation. The elimination period consists of 60 days of residual disability.

Thus, the elimination period is satisfied and the insured is eligible and receives residual benefits until the operation. Total benefits are then payable which continue for the duration of the policy benefit period.

OTHER COMMON POLICY PROVISIONS

Presumptive Total Disability. Disability of a catastrophic nature will remove some of the basic total disability requirements and total disability will be presumed. These types of losses, caused by an injury or sickness, are the loss of sight in both eyes, or hearing in both ears, or loss of speech, or loss of the use of both hands, or loss of use of both feet, or use of one hand and one foot.

If the insured suffers one of these losses, benefits are automatically payable from the date of loss. The elimination period is waived.

Benefits will continue for as long as the loss lasts, usually up to the end of the policy maximum benefit period. All further requirements of total disability are waived.

Even if the insured is able to return to his own occupation in some capacity, there is no reduction of the payment of benefits, as long as the loss continues.

Automatic Benefit Indexing. This provision provides small increases to the total disability monthly benefit annually to keep pace with the CPI, without evidence of insurability. It is fully explained in Chapter 15, Personalizing The Disability Plan With Optional Benefits.

Mental and Nervous Disorder Limitation. Used in payroll deduction cases, this option restricts the benefit period for most mental and nervous disorders to 24 months and reduces the policy premium accordingly. It is fully explained in Chapter 15, Personalizing The Disability Plan With Optional Benefits.

Rehabilitation Benefit. Once a forgotten policy feature, rehabilitation has emerged as a major component of today's disability contracts. Rehabilitation programs are far more prominent today than ever before. Advancements in medical technology can mean that, after undergoing the rehabilitation process, an individual formerly unlikely to return to his regular occupation will now be able to do so.

Any encouragement to return an individual to the occupation performed prior to disability is in the insurance company's best interest since it may eventually lead to the end of claim. This is the key to the heavy support being placed behind the use of this provision. Even if the insured can change a claim from total disability to residual disability, a substantial amount of dollars can be saved.

While the wording of this provision is purposely vague, the extent of help from the disability carriers is unprecedented in the individual field.

Claims managers will now entertain almost any type of program and reimbursement. From reimbursing actual training expenses to paying for the first six months of a new office's rent to providing consultants to help set up the books and train in a new career, the rehabilitation provision has expanded beyond the initial forecast and is now providing insurers and claimants with real options at the time of claim.

The investment of rehabilitation benefits can pay big returns over the long haul. Here is a claims example of what would ordinarily have been a total disability own occupation claim for the entire benefit period in the past, but with some rehabilitation investment, instead has turned into a residual claim.

The insured has a total disability monthly benefit of $5,000. Following a total disability of several months the insured has, with insurer assistance, entered a rehabilitation program. In addition to this re-training investment, the company has agreed to help the insured start over by paying for the first four months of office rent and secretarial costs to help minimize overhead as the insured works back into his job.

In the first year, the insured is out for most of the time, finally returning to work in the tenth month of disability and starting to earn a small income. For the first year, the full $5,000 total disability monthly benefit is payable each month, for a total of $60,000 in benefits paid. Figure 14.4 illustrates the residual claim in the second year, as the $5,000 monthly benefit is eventually reduced.

Figure 14.4

		2nd year			
Month	Prior Earnings	Current Earnings	% Loss	Total Benefit	Residual Benefit
1	$8,000	$1,000	87.5	$5,000	$5,000
2	8,000	1,200	85.0	5,000	5,000
3	8,000	1,300	83.75	5,000	5,000
4	8,000	2,200	72.5	5,000	3,625
5	8,000	2,800	65.0	5,000	3,250
6	8,000	3,100	61.25	5,000	3,063
7	8,000	2,700	66.25	5,000	3,313
8	8,000	3,500	56.25	5,000	2,813
9	8,000	3,200	60.0	5,000	3,000
10	8,000	3,300	58.75	5,000	2,938
11	8,000	3,000	62.5	5,000	3,125
12	8,000	3,400	57.5	5,000	2,875
					TOTAL: $43,002

Already, the rehabilitation investment has started to pay dividends as the claim has moved from a steady $5,000 a month to a reduced residual benefit. For the insured, the residual benefit is an enticing option because there is always more money for the claimant under a residual benefit between the benefit itself and the income earned. In month 12 above, the insured collects a reduced benefit of $2,875 in addition to $3,400 in earnings for a total of $6,275 versus $5,000 for total disability. It's a win-win situation for both the insured and the company which may explain the willingness of both participants in this process.

In the third year of this example, the insured earns more money, further reducing residual benefits as shown in Figure 14.5

Figure 14.5

Month	Prior Earnings	Current Earnings	% Loss	Total Benefit	Residual Benefit
1	$8,000	$3,600	55.0	$5,000	$2,750
2	8,000	3,500	56.25	5,000	2,813
3	8,000	4,100	48.75	5,000	2,438
4	8,000	3,700	53.75	5,000	2,688
5	8,000	3,900	51.25	5,000	2,563
6	8,000	4,300	46.25	5,000	2,313
7	8,000	4,700	41.25	5,000	2,063
8	8,000	5,100	36.25	5,000	1,813
9	8,000	4,600	42.5	5,000	2,125
10	8,000	4,400	45.0	5,000	2,250
11	8,000	4,700	41.25	5,000	2,063
12	8,000	4,400	45.0	5,000	2,250
				TOTAL:	**$28,129**

The third year resulted in more savings to the insurer and continued the situation for the insured where more money is coming in on a residual basis between benefit and income than would have been payable under total disability.

To understand the net savings involved, which includes actual rehabilitation reimbursement, and to view how much savings has been achieved to date versus a pure own occupation claim, review Figure 14.6.

This rehabilitation claim has already cost the company nearly $15,000 and the bulk of rehabilitation costs have *already* been paid. This potential dollar savings is what has created the current enthusiasm for this benefit. There is a significant possibility that rehabilitation benefits will be designed more elaborately in the future. Whatever attention this policy provision receives, it is a return to the common sense disability approach of helping the insured get back on his or her feet in a way that benefits both client and company.

Figure 14.6

Effects of Rehabilitation on an otherwise Own Occupation Claim		
	Total Annual Benefits	Rehabilitation Costs Paid by Co.
First Year	$60,000	$18,000
Second Year	$43,001	$15,000
Third Year	$28,129	$1,000
TOTALS:	$131,130	$34,000

Residual claim: benefits plus rehabilitation costs equal $165,130

vs.

Total claim: 5,000 x 12 months x 3 years = $180,000

Waiver of Premium. This provision, unlike its counterpart in a life insurance contract, is built into the policy. If the insured has been disabled for 90 days, future premiums coming due will be waived for as long as the disability lasts.

In addition, if any premiums were paid in the initial 90 day period, this money will be refunded to the insured once the 90 day period is reached.

Some carriers use the policy elimination period as the point where waiver of premium is triggered. Since this point is most often 90 days today, there is not much difference between this and the standard 90 day waiver provision.

Where a dual definition of disability is used, either total or residual or some combination of the two can be used to satisfy the time period.

Recurrent Disability. When an individual is no longer totally or residually disabled, a period of disability is considered over. If the total or residual disability starts again within six months from the date the previous disability ended and results from the same or a related injury or sickness, the current disability period will be considered a *continuation* of the prior period. Therefore, the new period of disability will be continued at the exact point the previous one ceased.

If more than six months separates the current total or residual disability from the earlier one, it will be considered a new disability and a new elimination and benefit period will be established.

Companies often use this wording in both continuing benefit payments already begun or in satisfying the elimination period.

Remember, however, that if the policy has a qualification period, total disability may have to come first again for the stated time frame before residual benefit payments can resume.

Treatment of Injuries. This provision pays benefits in lieu of normal disability payments for the policy. If injuries require treatment prescribed by a licensed physician, expenses for this treatment will be paid.

There is a dollar limit to this benefit, usually one-third to one-half of the total disability monthly benefit.

Exclusions. Very few exclusions are listed for a disability income policy. The most common are war, or act of war (declared or not declared), and normal pregnancy, although complications resulting from a pregnancy, including a Caesarean section, are covered.

Occasionally, there is an exclusion for self-inflicted injuries or attempted suicide.

Pre-existing conditions are usually excluded from coverage for the first 24 months of the policy. These conditions are defined as those that include symptoms which would cause an ordinarily prudent person to seek medical care.

Some companies place a time limit on how long a condition is considered pre-existing before the policy takes effect. Two years prior to the policy effective date is the most common time period.

This wording is only to protect the insurance carrier from paying claims on medical conditions which were not disclosed on the application. If a medical condition was disclosed, the company cannot deny a claim based on this condition, unless it was excluded from coverage originally.

These are the most common policy provisions under a personal disability income contract. It is important to know and understand them to be truly comfortable making the disability income sale.

Insurers will likely make more product changes in the future, some of which are outlined in Chapter 19, Future Trends In Disability Income. The difference between total and residual disability coverage will continue to be explored by carriers looking for ways to offer quality benefits at an affordable cost to both insured and insurer.

CHAPTER NOTES

1. "Treating Disability", *Life Association News*, April, 1995, p. 52.

■ *Chapter 15*

Personalizing The Disability Plan With Optional Benefits

Today, disability insurance companies recognize that the middle income prospects ($25-75,000) that they desire to sell to will have varied amounts of discretionary income to spend on disability income policies. Some individuals will be able to afford only the basic coverage while others who are in better financial positions may have an interest in expanding their coverage accordingly.

To accommodate both extremes (and other prospects in between), companies are offering a variety of optional benefits which can enhance the basic coverage. The base policy will contain the total disability or loss of earnings definition, rehabilitation and several other features. Some companies may even offer the loss of earnings (residual disability benefit) portion as an addition to the base coverage. There are employees of companies whose earnings would not be modified if they returned to work in any capacity; in this case, the residual benefit has no applicability and the important definition is that of total disability. Why, then, pay for the residual benefit if it is not needed? Making it an optional benefit answers this concern.

Chapter 14, Personal Disability Income Policies: What The Contractual Language Really Means, dealt with residual disability coverage in depth, so it will not be reviewed again here as an optional benefit. Instead, this chapter focuses on the more common optional benefits such as guarantee of insurability, cost of living and return of premium, among others. It is important to note that while these benefits enhance the overall protection, the basic disability income policy is normally sufficient in accomplishing the fundamental task of providing income while an insured is sick or hurt and cannot work.

INFLATION PROTECTION

Inflation has an effect on numerous items in our economy and a disability income policy is no exception. The amount of coverage that can be purchased is tied directly to income. The more an individual makes, the more monthly benefit he can buy, up to the insurer's maximum issue and participation limit. After purchasing a basic policy, there is every reason to expect that one's income will continue to increase over time. As it does, it is important to be sure the policy monthly benefit also keeps up to date. Otherwise, the policy will not cover the percentage of income that was called for in one's financial planning objective.

There are three primary inflation consequences to address:

1. *Covering routine salary increases.* From year to year, a worker may receive raises in pay based on the Consumer Price Index and merit. As these increases happen, will the agent be servicing the policy regularly enough to keep track of them and adjust the policy accordingly?

2. *Covering larger salary/compensation jumps.* Possibly, there will be situations where an individual will need to make larger increases to the basic disability policy. Or, if the individual disability policy is serving as a supplement to an individual's group disability plan and he leaves the employer, the group coverage is lost, overall benefits drop drastically and a large increase in the benefits provided by the individual basic policy is needed. Will the individual be able to qualify medically for these large increases?

3. *Receiving level claim check benefits.* Once an insured is disabled, and the disability appears to be one of a long-term nature, what will be the purchasing power of the claim check ten years from today? Twenty years?

There are three distinct optional benefits that address these inflation concerns: the automatic benefit increase, the guarantee of insurability (GOI) rider, and the cost of living rider.

Automatic Benefit Increases

Some insurers build this into their basic policies, while others allow the insured to add it for a small extra premium. This feature addresses inflation problem number one, as noted above.

Many employees receive annual increases in pay tied to the Consumer Price Index (CPI) and, possibly, a merit raise. These increases have been modest, on the average, in recent years. For example, someone who earned $32,000 last year, may receive a 5.3 percent increase this year, bringing total compensation to $33,696. The $32,000 income was used to buy a disability income policy with a total monthly benefit of $1,950. The increase in pay might qualify the insured for an additional $100/month in benefits, or a new total of $2,050.

However, many companies will not consider an increase this small through the usual application process. A $100/month policy does not make much economic sense to issue. The question is how to adjust the policy monthly benefit to stay apace of income?

As the name implies, the automatic benefit increase option will update the policy monthly benefit on a regular basis with no paperwork involved. While versions of this benefit vary from insurer to insurer, this option generally works as follows:

1. The policy monthly benefit is adjusted automatically each year by either a stipulated amount (three to seven percent) or by the change in the CPI. This increase will have an effect on the premium payment since adding more coverage will increase the cost of the policy. However, the increases are small and the premiums increase minor.

2. The option may be refused by any insured who does not wish to pay the extra premium and add the coverage. Usually, several refusals will mean no future adjustments will be made.

3. Adjustments are made without any type of evidence of insurability, medical or financial. In fact no paperwork is involved at all. The insurance company notifies the insured of the increase amount and new premium by sending a new policy schedule page detailing the benefit changes. If the insured does not want the increase, he simply informs the carrier. Otherwise, the increase will be built into the regular premium payment.

4. These adjustments occur for a stipulated period of time, usually five years. At the end of this time, the insurer will request evidence of financial insurability to renew the increases for an additional five years. The insurer is merely trying to verify that income has gone up sufficiently to warrant the first five increases. If it has, the provision is renewed for another five year period. If it has not, the insured keeps the increased monthly benefit, but no further automatic increases will be made.

The automatic increase benefit option is a convenient way to keep a policy up to date without having to do anything except pay the new premium amount. It is a popular benefit; many insureds take advantage of this paper-free method of battling inflation erosion.

Guarantee of Insurability (GOI) Rider

One of the most important optional features in disability income is the guarantee of insurability (GOI) rider. As the need for increases larger than those handled by the automatic benefit increase option arises, the importance of this provision becomes apparent.

The key feature of this optional benefit is that the insured can add more coverage in substantial amounts and is asked to provide only financial evidence of income to qualify for the increase. Medical questions are not asked.

How important is this protection? Disability income is one of the most strictly underwritten forms of insurance coverage sold today. The simple facts are that disability can and does occur in multiple instances during the working years. Advances in medicine may have had positive effects on mortality by increasing life spans, but those people being kept alive are now, more frequently, disabled for a long period of time. Depending upon his occupation, the health of the insured could be quite fragile and easily cross the line between ability and disability.

In addition, bad health that prevents the insured from increasing coverage in accordance with income increases, may cause the benefits to fall far short of the amount needed to maintain the family's standard of living if the poor health results in a lengthy disability.

An individual who purchases a disability policy without the GOI rider may have no difficulty, initially, in obtaining standard coverage. However, assume that two years later this same individual, who has experienced a significant increase in earnings, applies for benefits to cover this additional increase and that, during this two year period, he experienced a low back strain. Although the strain is not severe enough to cause any missed work, it acts up every now and then. When the new policy is issued, it may carry an exclusion for the lower back, meaning that there is no new coverage for disability caused by this condition. It does not affect the initial policy.

Under the same circumstances, an individual with the GOI rider on the policy would have been issued a new policy *without* the back rider because no medical evidence was needed to purchase the additional coverage. The only information taken into consideration in issuing the policy would have been the new financial data justifying the increased benefit.

The importance of this rider is obvious. Once a policy has been issued on a standard basis, the GOI rider "locks in" this standard issue on subsequent applications for increases under this provision. This is one of the most meaningful guarantees an insured can have.

An agent that I worked with on a case had sold her client on the idea of disability protection but could not convince him of the importance of the GOI rider. I advised her to have the policy issued with the rider and said I would go along to help place the case.

The premium was approximately nine percent higher because of the addition of the GOI rider. The client balked, stating that he was only 29, not sure about how the business he was starting was going to do, or if he would ever need to apply for any additional coverage. We pointed out that he had a substantial number of years left in the work force and this meant a significant period of time in which medical problems could surface and prevent future purchases of standard coverage.

He finally decided to keep the rider on his policy but did not seem particularly enthusiastic about it. He paid a quarterly premium and I advised the agent to monitor the business carefully to ensure it stayed in force.

Nearly nine months later, I received a call from the agent. The client had called her a day earlier to ask if it was too late to add the GOI rider. She explained to him that he already had the benefit and he remembered, then, that he had indeed accepted it when the policy was delivered. When the agent asked why he wanted to add the rider now, he replied that he his physician had just told he that had a malignant tumor in his neck that required immediate surgery. We must have made an impression on him. He remembered enough to call to see if he could obtain the benefit because he knew that he would have difficulty purchasing more coverage. His business had taken off and his income was increasing rapidly.

His operation was successful; he added more coverage at his one year anniversary through his GOI rider and he has exercised the option twice since then. He has had no recurrence of the cancer and, it is hoped, this will continue to be the case.

The GOI rider allows increases to the basic monthly benefit on specified option dates. These dates vary from company to company as does the maximum age at which an option to increase coverage can be exercised. Many companies allow an increase on the first anniversary; others on the second anniversary. Usually an increase can be made every two or three years after the initial one. Maximum ages range from 49 to 63.

Officially, the insurance carrier sends out a notice of option along with a short-form application or card to the client or agent about 60 days before the option date. The insured has that time to complete the application, indicate current earnings, sign, and return the paperwork to the insurance company for approval.

After approval is given, a new policy schedule page updating the monthly benefit and premium numbers is sent out. The new premium will be reflected in future billings as in the case of automatic benefit increases.

Generally, the insured does not have to exercise the option every time it comes up, but may have to exercise one increase over a certain period of time in order to maintain the benefit.

This option can help an agent keep pace with a client's increasing earnings and can easily be worked into a policy review. Staying on top of the client's coverage needs is an effective way to prevent policy benefits from falling short of what they were designed to do: insure a large portion of a client's earnings.

I recommend that the agent quote this rider automatically as if it were not an option. It is *that* important to protect the client's insurability. Having to explain that the insured cannot purchase standard coverage, or possibly cannot purchase any coverage again, means the agent has not done the proper financial planning necessary to keep the client and his family secure.

Cost of Living Rider

When the General Motors-United Auto Workers contract was signed in May, 1948, it recognized a problem few people knew was here to stay — inflation. That contract provided an across-the-board increase to help restore workers' wages to their pre-World War II level *and* tied any future increases to the Consumer Price Index (CPI).

The third part of the optional benefits inflation fighter program also provides for across-the-board increases to disability benefits annually as they are paid out. Otherwise, yesterday's dollars will be buying today's goods and services to help a family maintain its standard of living during a period of disability.

The CPI has been raging on since 1948, dropping only in 1949 and 1955. All other years have resulted in an increase to this market basket of goods. In the late 1970's, the increases came in double digit fashion, severely reducing the purchasing power of the working individual and making it virtually impossible to increase wages quickly enough to keep pace.

The point is that over time (five, ten, fifteen years) inflation will have a significant effect on a long-term claim if the monthly benefit remains level. A disability payment of $3,000 a month will certainly not be worth as much in ten years as it is today. Yet clients will need to purchase goods based on then current prices, not on the cost of items at the inception of disability.

For the marketers of disability income products, this is an important story to tell. The healthy wage-earner can strive to attain increases in pay to help offset decreasing purchasing power. For the disabled individual, the ability to attain these increases has been abruptly removed. If this individual has been fortunate enough to have purchased disability income coverage, he faces the prospect of having to make ends meet on a level claim check. A prolonged disability could make it impossible to live on only the fixed claim check.

The disability income industry's solution is to purchase and add the cost of living rider to the basic policy. This optional benefit provides increases every year after the first to compensate for inflation.

The cost of living (COL) rider has been available for sale for more than 20 years, but remains one of the industry's more controversial benefits. The source of this controversy is the price of this rider, often 25 to 50 percent of the basic policy premium. What makes this cost seem unusually high is the likelihood of use. Nearly 98 percent of all claims show recovery within the first year of disability. The COL rider does not apply its first increase until *after* 365 days of a disability. Why then, the high price?

The substantial extra monthly benefits that can result from COL rider increases is the driving force behind the price of this rider. Once the increases are applied, meaning the insured has reached the 365th day of a disability, the recovery rate is remarkably low. After an insured has reached the first anniversary of a disability the likelihood that he will come off claim anytime soon is remote. Hence, the few people who do use the COL rider may increase the claims liability for the company substantially.

The example in Figure 15.1 compares a level benefit with a benefit under a COL rider that increases on a compound basis tied to the actual change in the Consumer Price Index.

Figure 15.1

Year	CPI Increase	Level Benefit	Benefit with COL
1	1.3%	3,000	3,000 *
2	3.6%	3,000	3,108
3	4.5%	3,000	3,247
4	4.0%	3,000	3,376
5	4.7%	3,000	3,535
6	5.4%	3,000	3,726
7	3.7%	3,000	3,864
8	3.0%	3,000	3,979
9	2.6%	3,000	4,083
10	2.8%	3,000	4,197

*Increases not applied until after 365 days of disability.

In the first year, both contracts paid the same amount because COL increases are not applied until the insured has been disabled for 365 days. In the second year, the level claim check paid $3,000 a month, or $36,000 for the year, while the COL benefit increased by 3.6 percent to $3,108 a month, or $37,296, a difference of $1,296.

In the third year, the level benefit stayed at $3,000 a month while the COL benefit increased another 4.5 percent on top of the $3,108 a month to $3,247, generating an annual difference of $2,964 and a cumulative difference in payout of $4,260. The difference continues until, in the tenth year of the example, the COL monthly benefit is $4,197 compared to the $3,000 level benefit, an annual payout difference now of $14,364.

Over ten years, the difference in payout is $73,380. The premium paid for the level benefit, in this example, was about 30 percent less than the level benefit plus the COL rider, but that is of little consequence after a ten year claim. There was not $73,380 more in premium paid.

One does not need an actuarial degree to see the pricing problem the COL rider creates. Yes, the chances of utilizing it are relatively small. Yet it hasn't taken but a handful of claims to have an impact on insurers' bottom lines. When the COL benefit happens, it happens big. While the chances of being disabled beyond one year aren't necessarily high, the low chance of recovery beyond that point makes it an almost certain thing to see multiple cost of living increases made to claim checks each year.

Thus, the cost of this optional benefit should be weighed against the potential benefit increases in assessing its true value. If spending an extra $300 annually for a potential extra $73,380 in the first ten years of a claim makes sense to your client, then the COL rider should be added. In most cases, if the client can afford the extra premium for the rider, add it; it is crucial in a long-term claim situation.

The key features of the COL rider are:

1. percentage increase and if it is tied to CPI

2. what benefits can be increased by the COL factor

3. compounded or simple increases

4. any cap on increases

5. is there a buy-back option?

The example illustrated in Figure 15.1 demonstrated how the COL rider works to increase the monthly benefit during a *claim*. This rider does not increase any benefits prior to a claim.

1. The percentage increase is either guaranteed or tied in some way to the Consumer Price Index (CPI). If tied to the CPI, it normally has a minimum increase such as four or five percent that is used if the CPI is less than this (which has been the case in recent years).

2. Total disability benefits are always affected by the cost of living rider. In addition, residual disability benefits are indirectly affected by the rider, as discussed in more detail later. Presumptive total disability benefits are usually subject to the increase as is the Social Security offset rider (see Chapter 5, The Art of Programming Benefits, in addition to the description given later in this chapter).

3. Increases will either be compounded annually or made on a simple basis. Compounded increases make more sense and increase the benefit more rapidly. Insurers, however, are reconsidering offering the increases on this basis because of the resulting substantial increase in liability during the course of a claim. A simple increase uses the original monthly benefit to measure each increase and, accordingly, is less expensive than the compound version.

4. Some companies cap the amount of increase each year and/or limit the total amount of increased benefit. An example of the former approach is keeping the annual increases to no more than seven percent. The latter type of limit is accomplished by limiting the monthly benefit to no more than two or three times the original amount.

5. The buy-back option allows an insured who recovers from a long-term claim to purchase (and add to the existing policy) the amount of benefit increased by the COL rider. Using numbers from the example in Figure 15.1, if the insured recovers after five years of disability, four COL increases would have been made, increasing the monthly benefit to $3,535. The insured could then purchase the additional $535 a month to add to the original $3,000 so that if another claim should occur, either a claim arising from a different origin or a related claim beginning after 6 months of full recovery, the benefit level would start at $3,535 instead of the original $3,000. Again, this is all part of keeping the claim check (the benefits) in step with the current inflation rate.

During a residual disability, the COL increase will work twice. Two of the most important variables used in determining the amount of the residual benefit are (1) the pre-disability earnings figure, and (2) the total disability monthly benefit amount. The increases are applied each year to *both* of these variables, as follows:

1. The pre-disability earnings figure is established at the time of disability. The insured has the choice of the greater of the 12 month income average immediately prior to disability or the best consecutive 24 month period out of the 60 months immediately prior to the disability. Once established, this figure is used during the first claim year. During the second and subsequent years, this figure

is increased by the COL percentage. This helps to protect this important income figure from inflation, since the income the individual earned at time of disability will not have the same purchasing power in the years that follow.

2. The income the disabled individual actually earns upon return to work part-time is measured against the pre-disability earnings figure each month to determine the percentage of income loss. The policy *total* disability monthly benefit is multiplied by *this percentage* each month to determine the amount of residual benefit to be paid. In the first year of disability, the policy total disability monthly benefit is the same as would be paid for total disability. During the second and subsequent claim years, this total disability benefit is *also* increased by the COL factor. Thus the percentage of income loss is being applied to an increasing total disability benefit.

How this double indexing works during a claim is shown in the following example using a guaranteed four percent compounded rider that is not tied to any index.

Insured is totally disabled at age 50; he subsequently returns to his own occupation at a reduced income. His income earned after returning to work increases in varied amounts each year just as normal salary increases would. His policy has a $3,000/month to-age-65 benefit and a 90 day elimination period with the COL rider. His pre-disability earnings figure is established at $51,000 ($4,250/month). His initial earnings when he returns to work are $20,000 ($1,667/month). The chart in Figure 15.2 illustrates the ten year duration of the claim.

Figure 15.2

Year Of Disability	Predisability Earnings[1]	Income Earned During Residual[2]	% Lost	Total Disability Benefit[3]	Residual Benefit
1	$4,250	$1,667	61%	$3,000	$1,830
2	4,420	1,717	61%	3,120	1,903
3	4,596	1,405	59%	3,244	1,913
4	4,779	1,802	61%	3,373	2,057
5	4,970	1,852	62%	3,507	2,174
6	5,168	1,898	61%	3,647	2,224
7	5,374	1,992	60%	3,792	2,275
8	5,588	2,131	61%	3,943	2,405
9	5,811	2,192	61%	4,100	2,501
10	6,043	2,354	61%	4,264	2,601

1 Figure indexed annually on a 4% compounded basis.
2 Income reflects annual fluctuations between 2 and 7%.
3 Basic total disability monthly benefit increased annually on a 4% compound basis.

In the first year, the income earned by the disabled insured after return to work is $1,667 per month. When applied to the $4,250 of pre-disability earnings, the percentage income loss is 61 percent. This 61 percent income loss is multiplied by the monthly total disability benefit to determine the amount of the residual benefit: $1,830 per month.

In the second year, the *increases* take effect. The pre-disability earnings figure is increased 4 percent to $4,420 per month. The disabled insured's earnings averaged $1,717 per month, sustaining an income loss of 61 percent again. This percentage is now multiplied by an increased total disability monthly benefit, up 4 percent to $3,120. The resulting residual benefit ($3,120 x 61 percent) equals $1,903 per month, $73 more a month even though the insured is earning at a higher rate.

In the third year, the pre-disability earnings figure is $4,596 ($4,420 increased by 4 percent); residual income earned is $1,802, for an income loss of 59 percent. This 59 percent is multiplied by $3,244 ($3,120 increased by 4 percent), for a residual benefit of $1,913 a month.

Figure 15.2, using the same calculations, illustrates the next seven years.

There are many promotional features about COL riders that feature the term "double indexing." The example in Figure 15.2 shows exactly what this means: two increases in the same calculation of monthly benefits.

To summarize this discussion of the effect of inflation, there are three distinct optional benefits with each providing its own hedge against inflation's effect on a disability policy. Does one need all three features? It's the agent's duty to propose them but only the client can be sure of what he wants. The guarantee of insurability (GOI) rider is a top priority; the others are available if the client can afford them.

THE RETURN OF PREMIUM RIDER

Disability income coverage, unlike cash value life insurance, offers no tangible value for those who do not become disabled and collect benefits under the policy. The importance of being covered, for peace of mind and safety for the family during the working years, is not enough for some of us. Of course, the majority of policyowners would prefer not to become disabled just to see some return on the policy.

The lack of equity is one drawback to the average disability income contract. Many do not believe they will ever be disabled. They face an interesting choice: forego the policy completely and take a chance that they are right, or buy the policy and pay in premium dollars they are convinced they will not get back.

Statistically, there is a less than one in ten chance of sustaining a long-term disability. But can you or anyone else afford to take the chance that you will not be the one? Is it not wiser to put $3.00 or $4.00 a day into a disability policy than to risk the thousands of dollars that are at stake if you become disabled?

The return of premium rider was created to answer some of the policy critics who argue that the contract does not build equity or that the chances of using it are very minute.

For those who never use the policy, or use it to an extent less than the money invested, this rider provides a return of all or a portion of this money. For those skeptics, this rider is "insurance against never being disabled." They will get their money back when it is over.

The other side of the return of premium rider has supporters pointing to the excellent return on the dollar — *if* the policy is not used. That big *if* is what sours most of the consumer publications on this rider's value. Many look at it as a good deal for the insurer and thus advise against it.

While it's wrong to portray the return of premium as an investment, this is not really the point. Return of premium is an up-front hedge (requiring a sizable investment) that the policy will never be utilized. If the insured is right, an attractive cash payback is waiting down the line. If the insured is wrong, benefits are still being received well in excess of both premium and income provided by other sources. Given this scenario, the return of premium rider remains an option to look into regardless of the final outcome. The high premium will discourage most from playing the game; the majority who have opted for it in the past swear by its value.

There are two types of return of premium riders being marketed today. The first uses a "cash value" approach where value in the policy starts to build after the first two or three years and continues to grow until at age 65 it reaches 100 percent of premium paid. The older the insured is when he purchases this benefit, the faster his equity will build in the shorter span to age 65.

The second type of rider returns a substantial portion of premium at specified ages or intervals. These riders can return 50 to 80 percent of money paid in after five years, ten or twenty years, or at age 55, 59½, 62, or 65. The payouts can happen more than once during the lifetime of the policy.

Both riders make their payouts net of any claims paid. If claims incurred by the insured are high, then the rider will have little or no value, but the individual will obviously have coverage from a policy that may not have been purchased if the return of premium rider was not attached.

Let's examine these *optional* riders more closely:

Equity Builder Return of Premium

For a substantial extra premium (25 to 100 percent above the total policy cost), the insured becomes entitled, beginning in the third policy year, to the return of an increasing percentage of money *less* any claims paid. Thus, if the individual surrenders the policy at any time after three years, a calculation will be made to determine if a refund is available. The calculation calls for premiums paid to be multiplied by the percentage less any claims paid. At age 65, the percentage in this formula is 100 percent and the rider expires. If an individual goes to age 65 without incurring any claims all of the money paid in is returned.

Illustrated in Figure 15.3 is a sample chart showing some specific ages at policy issue and the type of equity build-up possible over the policy years.

Figure 15.3

RETURN OF PREMIUM EQUITY BUILD-UP									
POLICY	ISSUE AGE								
YEAR	35	36	37	38	39	40	41	42	43	44
3	5%	5%	5%	5%	5%	5%	5%	5%	5%	5%
4	6%	6%	6%	6%	6%	6%	6%	6%	7%	7%
5	8%	8%	8%	8%	9%	9%	9%	10%	10%	10%
6	10%	11%	11%	11%	12%	12%	13%	13%	14%	15%
7	13%	14%	14%	15%	16%	16%	17%	18%	19%	20%
8	17%	17%	18%	19%	19%	20%	21%	22%	23%	25%
9	20%	21%	22%	23%	24%	25%	26%	27%	29%	30%
10	24%	25%	25%	27%	28%	29%	30%	32%	34%	36%
11	27%	28%	29%	31%	32%	34%	35%	37%	39%	41%
12	31%	32%	33%	35%	36%	38%	40%	42%	44%	47%
13	35%	36%	37%	39%	41%	43%	45%	47%	50%	53%
14	38%	40%	41%	43%	45%	47%	50%	52%	55%	59%
15	42%	44%	46%	48%	50%	52%	55%	58%	61%	64%
16	46%	48%	50%	52%	54%	57%	60%	63%	66%	70%
17	50%	52%	54%	56%	59%	62%	65%	68%	72%	76%
18	53%	56%	58%	61%	63%	66%	70%	73%	78%	82%
19	57%	60%	62%	65%	68%	71%	75%	79%	83%	88%
20	61%	64%	66%	69%	72%	76%	80%	84%	89%	94%
21	65%	68%	70%	74%	77%	81%	85%	89%	94%	100%
22	69%	72%	75%	78%	82%	86%	90%	95%	100%	
23	73%	76%	79%	82%	86%	90%	95%	100%		
24	77%	80%	83%	87%	91%	95%	100%			
25	81%	84%	87%	91%	95%	100%				
26	84%	88%	92%	96%	100%					
27	88%	92%	96%	100%						
28	92%	96%	100%							
29	96%	100%								
30	100%									

Is it a good deal? Would the insured be better off by placing the extra premium in an interest-earning side fund? That depends. If the insured incurs a few claims, the refund may be zero for all of that extra premium paid in. A side fund investment alone gives no disability coverage especially for a long-term claim. Thus, a return of premium rider is not an investment and an investment is not a disability policy. People that buy this option do so simply because they do not believe they will use the policy. For these individuals, speculation about the types of potential payouts that await is important.[1]

Let's look at an example of the equity builder return.

Insured, age 35, buys a policy that will pay $3,500 a month, with a 90 day elimination period, and a to-age-65 benefit period. The annual premium cost of the base policy is $1,358.44. The return of premium rider costs is $421.12 (31 percent more premium) for a total annual premium of $1,779.56.

After 20 years, the insured takes early retirement and decides to surrender the policy. Over the 20 year period the extra premium paid in is $8,422.20 ($421.12 x 20). The total premium paid is $35,591.20 ($1,779.56 x 20). Based on a return of premium percentage of 61 after 20 years (see Figure 15.3), the return of premium amount would be $21,710.63 if no claims were paid in the 20 year period.

The 20 year gain would be $13,288.23 ($21,710.63 return less $8,422.40 extra paid for the rider). If insured had put this $421.12 into a side fund each year, a net interest rate of 8.35 percent over the 20 year period would have to be realized to achieve the same result, assuming the refund is merely a return of capital and there is no tax liability to the insured. In a 28 percent tax bracket, this is a before tax average of 11.6 percent over a 20 year period.

It is important to remember that the percentages shown in the chart in Figure 15.3 are multiplied by the *total* premium paid and not only by the amount of extra premium paid for the return of premium option.

Return of Premium at Specified Periods

If there is a disadvantage to the equity builder approach, it is the low return in the early policy years. The true pay-off (in dollars) does not take place for at least 15 to 20 years. It's a long-term deal, and the rider's assumption is that the policy will be retained for some time.

To offer a short-term return alternative, other versions of the return of premium option offer money back much earlier, at five years, at seven years, at ten years, giving the individual more incentive to buy the rider for the quicker payoff. Those that buy the option do so to hedge their bet against a disability. If they cannot see themselves being disabled over a 25 or 30 year period of time, 5 and 10 year return potentials will feel like a sure thing. This explains the popularity of this specific version of the option.

For example, one version of this type of return of premium option is designed to return 80 percent of total premiums paid *less* any claims after ten years. What's more, there is no need to surrender the policy to obtain the equity. The insured can still *keep* the protection. Money coming out in 10 years may well provide dollars for a child's education, for a home acquisition or to add a screened-in patio to the house. As long as the insured views this return as he would winning the lottery, there's no problem with using the plan this way. If there are claims, the return will be diminished, but the coverage will be doing what it is supposed to do.

In the past, those holding this rider have used their 10 year return to prepay the disability policy for another ten years *with* the return of premium rider still attached, saving ten years of premium payments. If the insured incurs few or no claims and continues to prepay premium with the return, the first 10 years may be the only time frame during which the insured has to use his money.

The return works like this:

Figure 15.4

Basic DI premium:	$1,409.55
Return of premium cost: (55% above policy premium)	780.64
Total premium paid:	$2,190.19
Total premium paid in 10 years:	$21,901.90
10 year return percentage	80%
Return (assuming no claims):	$17,521.52
Total rider premium in 10 years:	$ 7,806.40
Rate of return over 10 years:	14.31%

The return is even higher if no claims are paid than the equity builder example shown earlier. However, the premium is also higher, this time costing 55 percent more than the policy itself. It is a substantial sum to come up with to hedge a disability bet. For those with the fortitude — and the cash — the rewards may well outweigh the risks.

Insurers sometimes charge an administrative fee to calculate and pay the refund, so be sure to read the fine print of the optional rider to see if this requirement is indicated.

Consider the return of premium option only after the purchase of the proper amount of benefits and coverage to provide the maximum protection available.

THE SOCIAL SECURITY OFFSET RIDER

The amount of coverage one individual can purchase from a carrier is determined, in part, by how much would be available from the Social Security system in the form of disability retirement benefits. What companies do offer to write on an individual is usually reduced by an estimated Social Security benefit average to prevent the possibility of over insurance (i.e., insuring more than 100 percent of earned income) if a disabled individual collected from both the private insurance policy and the Social Security system.

Because of the high percentage of Social Security rejections, however, it became unreasonable to assume that the disabled insured would also automatically qualify for Social Security or other types of federal, state or local disability benefits. This led to the creation of an optional rider to be added under which the insured would receive benefits if Social Security denied the claim. (For more on Social Security, see Chapter 5, The Art of Programming Benefits.)

The purpose of the rider is to help provide the insured with the maximum benefit protection available and take the guess work out of whether or not the application for Social Security benefits will be approved.

There are several versions of this rider available for sale. Some riders offset only with Social Security benefits (and are often referred to as a Social Security offset rider). Others offset benefits with sources in addition to Social Security and are more commonly known as "social insurance" offset riders.

This option's cost is less than the calculation for base policy benefits which are guaranteed to pay regardless of what Social Security does. But as part of the effort to help a family stay with its budget, the Social Security offset rider (in all of its various forms) can save the insured money.

An example of each type of definition of social insurance benefits is illustrated below.

Social Security Offset Rider

Social security benefits means benefits paid under the Social Security Act of the United States or any similar law of any other country to the insured or to any member of the insured's family on the insured's behalf in the case of family disability benefits.

Social Insurance Offset Rider

Social insurance means benefits paid under:

1. the federal Old Age, Survivors and Disability Insurance Act (Social Security);

2. the Railroad Retirement Act;

3. Civil Service Retirement program; or

4. any like program covering federal, state or local government employees.

Another alternative is a "catch-all" social insurance definition which states that social insurance benefits are disability payments:

1. under any federal Social Security act or any similar federal, state or local government law, or any similar law of any other country. This includes primary or family disability benefits as well as any payment under optional Social Security retirement benefits.

2. under any workers compensation or occupational disease, employer's liability or similar law in any of the states or territories of the United States, or a similar act or law of any other country. This also includes insurance which provides benefits under any such law.

3. under any compulsory state nonoccupational disability benefit law.

4. under any federal, state, county, municipal or any other governmental subdivision retirement and disability fund. This includes amounts for dependents as well as any payment resulting from elective retirement.

5. under the Railroad Retirement Act as amended. This includes primary or family disability benefits as well as any payment resulting from the retirement option.

How Benefits Are Paid

There are three methods of payment under a Social Security or social insurance offset rider:

(1) dollar for dollar offset;

(2) all or nothing;

(3) a percentage based on the type of social insurance benefit received.

1. *Dollar for dollar offset.* This has become the most common of the offset riders and makes the most economic sense. If the insured buys a $700 Social insurance rider and collects $400 from various governmental sources during a disability, this amount would be subtracted from the $700 and the rider would pay $300. Thus, between the two the total $700 benefit remains intact.

2. *All or nothing.* To receive benefits under this rider, the insured must not receive any money from Social Security or, if applicable, other governmental sources. If no benefits are payable, the insured receives the entire amount. If, as in the example above, the insured receives benefits, even if less than the rider amount, *no* benefits are payable under the rider. If the insured had a $700 rider and $400 was paid by other governmental sources, this rider would pay nothing.

3. *The percentage approach.* Here, a formula is used to determine benefits. Usually, there are two levels of benefits payable. If the insured qualifies for either the primary insurance amount (PIA) or only one social insurance benefit, the amount payable under the rider is reduced by a stated percentage such as 30 to 40 percent. If the maximum family benefit is payable or if the insured qualifies for two or more social insurance benefits, the rider will pay no benefits. In most circumstances, the insured will not collect less than the rider amount regardless of whether the rider pays all, a portion or nothing. Between other benefits received and the rider payment, the insured is generally covered for what was purchased.

Insurers tend to offer an extensive amount of assistance in helping the insured to file claims with the appropriate administrative agencies. Many riders offer some reimbursement of attorney's fees for reconsideration and appeal of a social insurance benefit denial.

If the insured is approved for Social Security benefits and the rider either reduces benefits or stops paying entirely, this doesn't mean that circumstances cannot change. Social Security has a system of Continuing Disability Reviews (CDRs) to ensure that people who no longer meet the definition of disability under Social Security law are removed from the benefit rolls.[2] If this should happen, the rider will kick back in at the appropriate level, providing the insured meets the policy definition of disability and the benefit period under the policy has not expired.

The Social Security offset rider is usually effective with the same elimination period as the base policy, but it could also be written with a supplemental rider that provides coverage of the same amount, *without* the offsets in the first year of disability. In this case, the rider would be effective at the conclusion of the supplemental benefit payments, usually on the 366th day of disability. (See Chapter 5, The Art of Programming Benefits.)

The social insurance rider is also used in the calculation of both residual and cost of living rider benefits. The fact that the cost of this rider is lower than base policy coverage makes it an attractive optional benefit for many insureds.

PARTIAL DISABILITY BENEFIT

An abbreviated version of the residual disability benefit is the partial disability option. Here, the insured must still meet the definitions of residual disability (loss of time or duties), but the benefits payable are level at 50 percent of the total disability monthly benefit *and* paid for a shorter time frame (generally 6 to 12 months).

This benefit is intended for use with a base policy that has total disability coverage only where the insured does not wish to add the residual benefit due to cost or probable lack of need for a long-term type of residual benefit.

This option is also used with more hazardous occupations in place of the residual disability benefit.

MENTAL AND NERVOUS DISORDER OPTION

Because of the growing number and increasing size of claims for mental and nervous disorder conditions, the price of the base policy has continued to increase as companies battle to keep their bottom lines intact on their disability income portfolios. For many groups, this has priced them beyond what they can afford for reasonable coverage.

For list bill situations, where two or more employees of the same employer are buying coverage on an individual basis, a new option is available for consideration that can reduce the overall cost of the policy. The mental and nervous disorder option will place a maximum benefit period of 24 months for any disability payments for these types of conditions. The only exception is for continuous confinement as an inpatient in a mental hospital or institution in which case benefits will be paid in accordance with the regular policy benefit period.

This two year limitation, similar to the one used in group disability insurance, can reduce the premium by five to ten percent and sometimes more. In a time where we are all trying to fit insurance coverage into our budgets, opportunities to reduce the premium should be carefully considered. Mental and nervous disorder claims are not necessarily frequent in nature for a company, but they tend to be sizably larger in amounts paid out than virtually any other type of condition for which benefits under the policy are payable. Thus, insurers are willing to trade a discount against the base policy in return for a lower liability for these conditions.

ANNUITY/RETIREMENT OPTIONS

With many carriers no longer offering lifetime benefit periods, the emergence of a new type of optional benefit has growing appeal. With this option, rather than extend the monthly benefit beyond age 65 (or age 70), insurers put aside an extra amount of benefits for each month of disability that can be utilized once the benefit period (or policy) expires.

For example, for every month of disability benefits payable, the insurer puts aside a specified amount, such as $300, into a side fund account or an annuity. This money is maintained, earning interest, and held in account for the insured until distribution at age 65 or 70, whenever the policy or benefit period (if on claim) expires. The insured will then have a supplement to retirement benefits in place of the old lifetime benefit period.

The insured may be disabled for fifteen months and then recover. If the insurer had been putting aside $300 per month into a side fund, the amount invested would be up to $4,500 by the time the claim is over. This money would then continue to grow in the account and even if the insured never used the policy, there will be a sum of money available at policy expiration time.

While some people feel this program does not replace the loss of the lifetime benefit period, it can add some important dollars to an individual's retirement program, which may have been hurt by the disability suffered. At a time when individuals are being forced to assume more fiscal responsibility for their own retirement, this benefit may be worth consideration.

SUMMARY

Wrapped around the basic disability income coverage, these optional benefits help to package the *total* protection plan the insured is interested in, representing the most flexible and effective way to protect earnings from unexpected injury or sickness. Selecting only the benefits the prospect deems necessary and affordable can help the agent package this important protection within the individual's budget constraints. Insurers will likely continue to streamline the basic disability policy and make more items available on an optional basis to ensure that the person considering coverage is paying only for the type of coverage he considers most beneficial.

CHAPTER NOTES

1. "Why Money Back Disability Insurance is a Gamble", *Kiplinger's Personal Finance Magazine*, August, 1993, p. 30.

2. "Review of Continuing Disability at the SSA", *The Disability Newsletter*, October, 1994, p. 1.

■ *Chapter 16*

THE BUSINESS OVERHEAD EXPENSE POLICY

For most agents who work only occasionally in the disability market, insuring an individual's income has become synonymous with writing a personal disability income policy. With the changes to the personal disability income products and underwriting guidelines for the professional market, the Business Overhead Expense (BOE) policy may take a more prominent position in the agent's arsenal of products displayed to fill specific needs.

While many professional practices have begun banding together to share in the costs of running a business, the need for the Business Overhead Expense policy is still great. Many firms are not aware that coverage for business expenses is available, yet the loss of an owner or partner could place a financial burden on both the disabled individual and the business.

Moreover, this country has hundreds of thousands of small businesses. The income of the business is not necessarily the income taken home by the business owner. There are numerous business expenses to pay before money can be drawn for personal use. Yet little coverage, if any, is written to protect one's ability to pay these *business* expenses.

A personal disability income policy covers only the take home portion of income. This may leave a sizable amount of actual earnings uncovered. For example:

Monthly Gross earnings $10,000

Business expenses 6,000

Take home pay 4,000

The personal disability income policy will reflect coverage on the take home pay. At 60 percent coverage, this will provide a $2,400 monthly benefit. Even though the disability income is tax-free (if purchased with after tax dollars), this amount is far short of the $10,000 the individual actually earns each month. It will not cover even half of the business expenses the individual incurs. Most individuals will try to use the $2,400 in benefits to cover the critical bills of both, but will fall far short of maintaining both home and business.

Yet, many agents, after completing the personal disability income sale, go home thinking they have fought the good fight. A personal sale is made; the insured is protected.

In this common scenario the job is only partially done. Business owners may feel that the $2,400 in monthly coverage is adequate, but only because they are unaware that business expenses can be protected in the same manner. A disability leaves the owner in the unenviable position of possibly having to sell the business if expenses cannot be paid.

Professional clients like physicians and attorneys may look to a Business Overhead Expense (BOE) policy for additional protection when their personal disability income limits have been reached. Fringe benefits paid for by the business, that might normally have been used to increase compensation figures for the purposes of obtaining more personal disability income coverage, are often overhead expenses items. As such, they can be insured under a business overhead expense plan rather than used in the purchase of a personal disability income policy.

For example, let's say a physician had $15,000/month of personal disability coverage and was unable to purchase any more due to the industry's new, lower issue limits. The income his company paid him was ample in qualifying for this $15,000/month. The company also pays for an automobile needed by the doctor to reach three separate offices and four hospitals. The payment is $500/month. In the past, that $6,000 annually may have been added to the personal income level to increase the amount of coverage that could be bought, an option no longer available to this physician since he cannot qualify for more. Instead, this car payment can now be added to other business expense items like mortgage (or rent), payroll taxes, malpractice insurance premiums and other expenses.

Business expenses are important to cover. Like personal expenditures, business expenses are not going to stop when an individual becomes disabled. Rent (or mortgage) payments on the business premises will continue to come due. So will the utility, phone bills and insurance premiums. What about the payroll for the employee(s)? Will the insured be forced to let them go?

Because the recovery rate is extremely high in the first year of disability, the best alternative would be to keep the doors of the business open so that the disabled individual can return to a business that still exists. Even without the owner's presence, the business' clients will be more likely to continue to trade if the business appears to be a going concern. Once the doors are closed, a return to work may mean starting over again — a situation that can be avoided.

In our previous example, where the firm's gross monthly revenue is $10,000 and business expenses are $6,000, a policy can be purchased to protect the $6,000 of business expenses. Many agents and business owners are not aware of the plan's existence, although more insurers are taking pains to promote this type of coverage today. This product would reimburse the insured for expenses incurred on a month to month basis following a claim.

In many cases, 100 percent of the monthly average expenses can be insured. If a $6,000 Business Overhead Expense policy were written on the individual in our example, total coverage would be for $8,400 of the $10,000 instead of just $2,400. With both policies, the business owner has sufficient coverage of monthly gross earnings.

Business overhead expense coverage protects that portion of total income earmarked for continuing business expenses. With business expenses being paid, the income demands of the firm are decidedly less, giving the insured the opportunity to return to a business without a major debt and work back to the income level earned prior to disability.

The market for business overhead expense coverage is wide open. It is a new idea to bring up with a business owner, whether the business is a sole proprietorship or a multi-life practice. These individuals may not have been approached about this subject, and thus, may find it a refreshing change from the repetition of insurance concepts they frequently hear. Moreover, the premium paid for a Business Overhead Expense policy is tax-deductible — for *any* business, as discussed in more detail later. All considered, this is a product that may see substantial utilization over the next few years.

REIMBURSABLE CONTRACT

The Business Overhead Expense policy does differ from the personal disability contract in more ways than just the need it fills. Personal disability income contracts are paid on a specific indemnity basis; if a $2,000 a month policy is purchased and the insured is totally disabled, $2,000 a month will be paid as benefits.

Business overhead expense coverage is not as specific. A monthly benefit will be paid only if the insured has incurred business expenses while disabled that are reimbursable under the policy during a given month. Whereas a personal disability contract pays a level benefit during each month of total disability (excluding cost of living increases), the BOE monthly coverage may be $800 one month, $2,000 the next and $1,300 the month after that. This is the reimbursable method of disability income payments and is how the BOE contract works. This method of actual reimbursement will be detailed shortly during a discussion of how benefits are paid.

ELIMINATION PERIODS, BENEFIT PERIODS

Elimination periods are usually short in length. Some companies still offer a 30 day elimination period, although 60 and 90 day periods are more common today — and more affordable. 180 days is also an option. This is the type of coverage that needs to start relatively quickly unless the business has a large amount of receivables that can carry the burden of paying expenses for a time.

Benefit periods are also, in a word, short, since the business owner should know within a few months of disability whether it will be feasible to return to the business. While this is not a decision to rush, it should not take forever to reach a conclusion based on the progress of the individual's recovery. Accordingly, the benefit periods available are of short duration — 12, 15, 18 and 24 months being the most common. Possibly there will be 6, 30, and 36 month benefit periods for sale, too.

The purpose of the BOE policy is to eliminate the business debts entirely, or at least keep them to a minimum, after an insured's disability. After a few weeks or (even) months, the insured will make the decision to return to work or to sell the business if a return is not possible. Without being saddled with additional debt as a result of the disability and with the BOE contract still taking care of expenses, the insured can take some time to find the right buyer. More important, the insured does not have to settle for an offer that is far below what the business is worth. This has happened far too often to business owners in the past who did not possess BOE coverage.

BENEFIT PERIOD AND OVERHEAD MAXIMUM

Since the BOE contract pays benefits on a direct reimbursement basis, the term *benefit period* does not necessarily indicate a finite period of time. Actually, a benefit period selection is used to determine the *overhead maximum* — that is, the *total* amount of dollars that could be payable for any one claim under the BOE contract.

For example, if the benefit period selected is 15 months and the monthly overhead expense benefit is $3,000, the overhead maximum would be $45,000 ($3,000/month x 15 months). Since benefits are paid on a reimbursable basis, which could result in monthly benefits being paid at a rate of less than $3,000/month, the full $45,000 may not be used by the time the fifteenth benefit month is concluded. Since there is still more benefit available, the claim will continue as long as the insured is disabled, until the overhead maximum is exhausted.

Most companies call this feature an *open-ended benefit period*. Even though 15 months is the selected time frame, the claim may go on for 17, 18,

20 months or longer if some of the $45,000 remains to be paid out and the insured continues to meet the definition of disability under the policy.

Thus, rather than establishing the maximum *time* that overhead expense benefits are paid out, the benefit period is utilized instead to establish the maximum amount that could be paid out.

This will be important to remember when analyzing how a claim is actually paid later in this chapter.

RENEWABILITY

Most business overhead expense contracts are noncancelable to age 65. This may change since many insurers are removing the noncancelable provision and replacing it with a guaranteed renewable definition which allows the carriers to raise premiums on a class basis, if necessary.

Since the BOE coverage is of short duration, insurance companies may decide to keep the noncancelable feature, adding to the appeal of this product. Or, this renewability provision could be optionally available for purchase at a cost of 15 to 20 percent more than the guaranteed renewable language.

DEFINITION OF TOTAL DISABILITY

A professional's or business owner's covered overhead expenses are reimbursed during total disability. An insured will be considered totally disabled if unable to do the substantial and material duties of his regular occupation. Regular occupation is the insured's usual work prior to the total disability.

Some companies do not specify *substantial and material* but refer only to the insured's inability to perform the duties of his regular occupation. While this definition is recognizable as the *own occupation* type of language that the insurance companies are moving away from, it should not present much of an extra risk with the BOE product because the open-ended benefit period length is still relatively short.

This definition may be modified to add language concerning HIV positive results for medical personnel. If an individual is diagnosed as being HIV positive and works in the medical profession, it will be assumed that total disability exists even though a physical loss is not yet present. For example, if a physician is diagnosed as HIV positive he will not be able to practice even though physical disability will not present itself for some time. Thus, he will be considered totally disabled. While a return to his profession is not possible, the BOE policy will reimburse expenses until the physician can sell the practice.

RESIDUAL OR PARTIAL DISABILITY COVERAGE

There are a number of methods by which a return to work in a reduced capacity is handled by various insurance carriers in the overhead expense policy:

1. *Not at all.* Once the insured returns to the job in any form, no payment for business expenses is made.

2. *A short-term partial benefit.* If the insured is unable to perform some but not all of the duties, or can perform the duties but for less time than prior to disability, expenses are still reimbursed but at 50 percent of the amount for which they would have been reimbursed during total disability. The period of time this benefit is payable is generally limited to three to six months as long as the insured remains partially disabled.

3. *Residual benefit.* This reimbursement works as a residual benefit does in a personal disability contract. Prior earnings are calculated by a set formula; current earnings are applied against this formula to determine a percentage of income loss. This percentage is applied to what would normally be paid if the insured were totally disabled. For example, in the case of a 60 percent earnings loss, a $4,200/month benefit would pay $2,520 for covered overhead expenses (.60 x $4,200).

4. *Dollar for dollar coverage.* This return to work benefit takes the actual gross income the disabled insured earns after he returns to work and subtracts it from the amount of actual covered expenses incurred. For example, assume that an insured earns $2,500 of gross income in one month and his business expenses total $5,600. The actual benefit paid is $3,100 ($5,600 - $2,500). A new calculation is done each month as it is in the example in 3 above.

5. *All or nothing.* Once an individual returns to his own occupation and is unable to earn more than 50 percent of prior income, the benefit normally payable for total disability will continue to be paid. Once earnings reach 51 percent or more of prior income, no benefit will be paid. For example, a $5,000/month overhead expense monthly benefit would pay a benefit of $5,000 in the case of an earnings loss of 65 percent. However, if the earnings loss were 40 percent, no benefit would be paid.

Under some of the methods outlined above, a definition of pre-disability earnings is necessary as well as earned income and the other residual disability definitions discussed in Chapter 14, Personal Disability Income Policies: What The Contractual Language Really Means.

COVERED EXPENSES

Before reviewing how benefits are calculated and paid, it is appropriate to review exactly which business expenses the policy will cover and which it will not.

The percentage of overhead expenses that can be insured ranges from 80 to 100 percent depending on the company and its guidelines. Some carriers like to keep the "gap" between benefits and actual expenses as an incentive for the insured to return to work. Still other carriers base their payouts so closely on actual expenses that they prefer to cover them at 100 percent.

Covered expenses include (but are not necessarily limited to):

1. regular monthly mortgage or lease payments on business property;

2. electricity;

3. telephone;

4. heat;

5. water;

6. installment costs of furniture and equipment;

7. taxes on business property;

8. compensation of employees including payroll taxes and contributions for benefits;

9. malpractice, property and liability insurance premiums;

10. janitorial, maintenance, and laundry services;

11. postage;

12. accounting, legal, billing and collection fees;

13. miscellaneous supplies;

14. professional and trade dues and subscriptions.

This is a comprehensive list and includes most items that need to be paid whether the insured is present at the business nor not. These are also expenses that much of the insured's personal effort goes toward paying.

A word about coverage of principal of a mortgage payment. This has only recently been accepted by most carriers as a covered business expense. Some companies may still cover only interest and taxes which may be the larger portion of the payment, anyway.

A checklist is reproduced in Figure 16.1 for use during a sales interview:

Figure 16.1

Eligible Monthly Expenses of the Business

Rent or mortgage payments (including principal, interest and taxes) or

Depreciation—if greater than principal payments $_____

Utilities (electricity, heat, telephone and water) $_____

Leasing costs or installment payments $_____

Laundry and maintenance $_____

Accounting, billing and collection service fees $_____

Business insurance premiums $_____

Other regular monthly expenses $_____

(except for cost of goods sold)—itemize

_____ $_____

_____ $_____

_____ $_____

Salary Expenses should be listed and included ONLY for businesses or professional practices which are purely service in nature and where business revenue is generated directly by the services of the insured.

Do not include the salaries of any member of the insured's profession.

Employee Name	Job Title	Salary
_____	_____	$_____
_____	_____	$_____
_____	_____	$_____
_____	_____	$_____
_____	_____	$_____
	Total Salaries	$_____
	Total Expenses	$_____

Your share of these expenses is _____%

EXPENSES NOT COVERED

The list of expenses not covered is short, but there are common-sense reasons why they are omitted.

1. Expenses which do not require cash payment such as depreciation or insurance premiums which are waived. Since there is no dollar outlay actually made by the insured, there is no reason to pay a cash benefit under the policy.

2. Insured's salary. This is meant to be protected under a personal disability income policy.

3. Compensation of anyone employed in the insured's business that does the same type of work. (For example, another chiropractor in a chiropractor's office.) The theory here is that these people in the same profession should be able to generate enough revenue to cover their own salaries.

4. Compensation of anyone hired to replace the insured during a disability. The same theory as in 3 applies here with the exception that it may take a short period of time for the replacement to begin generating revenue. This is covered under a "Substitute Salary Expense" rider which is discussed in a later part of this chapter.

5. Compensation of anyone in insured's immediate family who was not a full-time employee of the business for at least 60 days (and sometimes longer) before disability began. This time requirement lends a legitimacy to the family member as employee. Some companies exclude family members without qualification, yet there are many situations where working family members are valid employees. To exclude them completely is unfair to the insured business owner.

6. Some carriers do not cover the cost of any goods sold or used in the business.

HOW BENEFITS ARE CALCULATED

Now that you understand what expenses are covered during a disability and which ones are not, you can see that the key to the sale of this product is in the benefit payment.

Unlike personal disability income coverage which is fixed at a level amount, the BOE policy must be more flexible in meeting the fluctuating costs of running a business. Some expenses, such as the mortgage payment or employee salaries, will be fixed each month while other expenses, such as an annual malpractice premiums paid in a single month, can cause either high or low expense months.

Under the BOE policy, there must be actual expenses to generate a benefit payment. Until the expenses occur, the policy will not pay. Each month, the amount of covered expenses is totalled and submitted for claim payment.

There are three methods of payout under a business overhead expense contract. These methods are illustrated in the examples that follow, using a policy with a $4,000/month benefit, a 30 day elimination period, and a 12 month benefit period. The policy provides an overhead maximum of $48,000 (12 x $4,000).

Method One

Under this method, as illustrated in Figure 16.2, each month the insured receives the lesser of the actual expenses or the monthly benefit amount. Unreimbursed expenses may be carried forward to be paid out at the conclusion of the benefit period.

Figure 16.2

Month of Disability	Monthly Policy Benefit	Actual Expenses	Monthly Benefit Paid	Carry-Over Account (paid at end of 12 months if insured still disabled and maximum overhead is still available)
1	EP=30 Days	nonreimbursable	-0-	-0-
2	4,000	6,100	4,000	2,100
3	4,000	3,700	3,700	2,100
4	4,000	4,650	4,000	2,750
5	4,000	4,800	4,000	3,550
6	4,000	3,250	3,250	3,550
7	4,000	3,600	3,600	3,550
8	4,000	5,200	4,000	4,750
9	4,000	5,000	4,000	5,750
10	4,000	3,100	3,100	5,750
11	4,000	4,300	4,000	6,050
12	4,000	3,900	3,900	6,050
13	4,000	4,500	4,000	6,550
	48,000	52,100	45,550	

After a full 12 months of benefit payments, $2,450 of the overhead maximum remains which could be paid out in the next month if the insured is still disabled under the contract. Since there are $6,550 of unreimbursed benefits in the account, the insured need not incur any additional expenses to receive the $2,450.

The first method accumulates a substantial amount of unreimbursed business expenses that the insured must find a way to pay to keep the creditors away. The second method of benefit payment tries to keep that balance at a reasonable level.

Method Two

The second method of payment is illustrated in Figure 16.3, using the same facts as under the first method. This method creates an account balance, a vehicle used to carry forward unused benefits in a month when business expenses are less than the monthly benefit and pay them out in a month when business expenses are higher than the monthly policy benefit.

Figure 16.3

	A	B	C	D	E
Month of Disability	Monthly Policy Benefit	Actual Expenses	Monthly Benefit Paid	Unpaid Benefit Amount	Expenses Carried Forward
1	EP=30 Days	nonreimbursable	-0-	-0-	-0-
2	4,000	6,100	4,000	-0-	2,100
3	4,000	3,700	4,000*	-0-	1,800
4	4,000	4,650	4,000	-0-	2,450
5	4,000	4,800	4,000	-0-	3,250
6	4,000	3,250	4,000	-0-	2,500
7	4,000	3,600	4,000	-0-	2,100
8	4,000	5,200	4,000	-0-	3,300
9	4,000	5,000	4,000	-0-	4,300
10	4,000	3,100	4,000	-0-	3,400
11	4,000	4,300	4,000	-0-	3,700
12	4,000	3,900	4,000	-0-	3,600
13	4,000	4,500	4,000	-0-	4,100
	48,000	52,100	48,000		

* 3,700 plus 300 from expenses carried forward.

Each month the insured receives the lesser of

1. the amount of actual expenses that month (column B), or

2. the total amount in the account balance (the monthly policy benefit in column A plus the unused benefit amount not paid in previous months in column D); plus

3. an amount of any unreimbursed expenses carried forward from a prior month(s) (column E) that will make up any difference between the amount found above and the monthly policy benefit (column A).

Using this method of calculation, the insured can make immediate use of unused benefits (where the full $4,000, in our example, is not paid in any month) and receive it in a month where expenses are higher than the monthly policy benefit.

In addition, carrying forward expenses that are not reimbursed because of a low account balance, allows them to be reimbursed when the account balance grows as a result of smaller expense months.

This method improves somewhat on the results shown using the first method by paying the overhead maximum out in full in the 12 month period.

The theory behind the account balance is quite plausible with one exception, illustrated in the example. If, in the first month of a claim, expenses run higher than the monthly benefit, there is no account balance to draw from since there has been no time to build up with months of lower expenses. The result is that, as in this example, the insured starts behind in a claim, having to come up with $2,100 in expenses from some source in the second month.

Method Three

The third method of payment is identical to the second with one major exception. During the elimination period, the account balance is credited with one month's benefit. Figure 16.4 illustrates how this affects the claims scenario.

Figure 16.4

Month of Disability	A Monthly Policy Benefit	B Actual Expenses	A&D Account Balance	C Monthly Benefit Payable	D Unpaid Benefit Amount	E Expenses Carried Forward
1	EP=30 Days	nonreim- bursable	4,000	-0-	4,000	-0-
2	4,000	6,100	8,000	6,100	1,900	-0-
3	4,000	3,700	5,900	3,700	2,200	-0-
4	4,000	4,650	6,200	4,650	1,550	-0-
5	4,000	4,800	5,550	4,800	750	-0-
6	4,000	3,250	4,750	3,250	1,500	-0-
7	4,000	3,600	5,500	3,600	1,900	-0-
8	4,000	5,200	5,900	5,200	700	-0-
9	4,000	5,000	4,700	4,700	-0-	300
10	4,000	3,100	4,000	3,400	600	-0-
11	4,000	4,300	4,600	4,300	300	-0-
12	4,000	3,900	4,300	3,900	400	-0-
13	4,000	4,500	4,400	400*	-0-	3,900
	48,000	52,100		48,000		

* The 48,000 overhead maximum has been reached.

The amount of the monthly benefit payable (column C) will be equal to the lesser of

1. the amount of covered expenses during a given month (column B) plus any unreimbursed covered expenses carried forward from a prior month (column E), or

2. the amount of the account balance (columns A + D).

The account balance is the monthly total disability benefit (column A) plus any unpaid monthly benefit amount from the prior month's account (column D). During the elimination period, the account balance will be credited with an amount equal to one monthly total disability benefit.

There is only one month where there was a shortage of $300 that was immediately made up in the following month. This method is a more realistic treatment of the fluctuation in actual expenses.

The only deficit of any size occurred when the overhead maximum expired and benefits under the claim ceased. A longer benefit period would have continued the claim. In this example, the overhead maximum was nearly paid out in 11 months instead of 12.

REGULAR CARE AND ATTENDANCE OF A PHYSICIAN

As part of the requirement for meeting the definition of disability under a contract, the insured generally must be under the care of a legally qualified physician. Most companies stipulate this condition without modification.

As with the personal disability income policy, though, some carriers state that if it can be shown that the insured has reached a maximum point of recovery but remains disabled under the contract, the physician care requirement is waived.

PRESUMPTIVE TOTAL DISABILITY

On certain disabilities of a catastrophic nature, some of the basic total disability requirements are dropped and total disability will be presumed. A presumed loss is one caused by an injury or sickness that results in the loss of sight in both eyes, or hearing in both ears, or loss of speech, or loss of use of both hands, or loss of use of both feet, or use of one hand and one foot.

If the insured suffers one of these losses, benefits are automatically payable from the date of loss. The elimination period is usually waived, as well as the other standard total disability requirements.

This provision is similar to the one described in the personal disability contractual features in Chapter 14, Personal Disability Income Policies: What The Contractual Language Really Means.

CONVERSION PRIVILEGE

The BOE policy is sold with a specific situation in mind: to reimburse a business owner for covered business expenses during a disability. If the insured ceases to have responsibility for continuing overhead expenses, the policy has no value since benefits are paid only if he has expenses.

If this happens, the insured has the option to convert the BOE policy to a personal disability income plan which will, of course, protect his ability to earn an income. The personal policy available for purchase will be any policy available at that time for that particular occupation class. The new coverage must fall within the following guidelines:

Amount: The monthly benefit amount of the BOE policy up to a specified maximum and within the issue and participation limits then in effect at date of conversion.

Elimination Period: Minimum of 30 days.

Benefit Period: Same as in BOE policy or, if greater, the shortest benefit period in effect at time of exchange.

Premiums: Some carriers specify that the premium will be at the rates in effect at the *attained* age at time of conversion. More competitive is the stipulation by other carriers that *original* issue age will be used with rates then in effect at date of conversion.

BENEFIT IF INSURED DIES WHILE DISABLED

If the insured dies and has been receiving benefits under the BOE policy, a benefit will be paid for the next one or two months to a specified beneficiary. The benefit will be calculated based on actual expenses incurred and paid as if the insured had remained alive and totally disabled during the additional month(s).

This gives the insured's family time to sell the business at a fair price without concern over increasing indebtedness.

WAIVER OF PREMIUM

If the insured has been disabled for 90 days (or, for some companies, the elimination period, if shorter), future premiums coming due will be waived for as long as the disability lasts.

In addition, if any premiums were paid in the initial specified period, this money will be refunded to the insured once satisfaction of the period by disability has been completed.

EXCLUSIONS AND PRE-EXISTING CONDITIONS

Exclusions under a BOE policy are the same as those listed for the personal disability policy. Refer to Chapter 14, Personal Disability Income Policies: What The Contractual Language Really Means, for a discussion of these limitations.

TAX DEDUCTIBLE PREMIUM

Whether the insured is a sole proprietor, a partner, or an owner in a corporation, premiums paid by the insured (or the corporation owning the policy) responsible for business expenses for a plan designed specifically to reimburse business expenses during a disability are deductible as a business expense. (See Revenue Ruling 55-264, 1955-1 CB 11.)

The deductibility of the premium makes this policy an even more attractive sale. As is true with any disability policy, a premium deductible up front means taxation of benefits on the receiving end. However, these benefit payments are used to pay actual business expenses, a deductible item. Thus, the beneficiary's income tax return will show benefit payments as income, but expenses paid as deductions, thus canceling out the effect of the taxable event.

OPTIONAL BENEFITS

The three most common optional benefits that may be packaged with the BOE policy are guarantee of insurability, return of premium, and the substitute salary expense benefit rider.

Guarantee of Insurability

This benefit will work in a fashion similar to that described in Chapter 15, Personalizing The Disability Plan With Optional Benefits. Here, though, the evidence to justify an increase to the policy monthly benefit will be based on increased business expenses.

Return of Premium

This rider has been described in detail in Chapter 15, Personalizing The Disability Plan With Optional Benefits. Some of the same versions can be packaged with the BOE policy. The premium is still substantial in relation to the total policy premium, but is more affordable here since the BOE premiums are low due to the short benefit periods. This lower dollar cost makes the rider a tempting buy. The cost for the rider should be split out from the regular BOE policy premium since it is not deductible. The rest of the premium is — and should be taken as such. By not including the return of premium cost in the deductible amount, the insured can receive the return, if eligible, on an income tax-free basis.

The Substitute Salary Expense Benefit Rider

During a prolonged disability, it may be necessary for the disabled insured to hire a replacement to maintain the business as closely as possible to pre-disability conditions.

As discussed above under "Expenses Not Covered," the salary of a replacement for the insured is not a covered expense since the substitute would, one hopes, generate enough business to at least cover the salary expense. Realistically, it will probably take a short time to realize any income from the replacement's production. There is an optional benefit to assist in this situation.

The Substitute Salary Expense Benefit rider will pay a monthly benefit for the monthly wage expenses the insured actually incurs to assist in paying this substitute during the insured's period of disability. The substitute can be anyone in the insured's profession excluding the insured's spouse, or any member of either the insured's or his spouse's family.

The amount of the benefit will be requested at time of policy issue. The maximum benefit that can be purchased is usually the lesser of 50 percent of the basic overhead expense monthly benefit or 80 percent of the insured's monthly salary.

The benefit will commence during the insured's disability on the later of the first day following the elimination period or the date the expense is first incurred. Payment of this benefit can be made for up to six or twelve months but not beyond the expiration of the policy benefit period.

Malpractice Protection Benefit Rider

While the BOE contract itself will reimburse the insured for the basic costs of his malpractice premium, this rider provides additional coverage in the event the insured has a claims-made type malpractice contract.

Under a claims-made policy, the contract must be in force as of the date the claim was filed, not necessarily when the services in question were performed.

If the insured is disabled during the period the claim is filed, this could present a problem. It is hoped the basic contract here reimbursed the insured to keep the malpractice policy in force, as it is a usual and customary business expense. Under a claims-made policy, however, if the insured becomes disabled, an extended reporting period premium could be required.

This rider provides an additional lump-sum benefit amount to help pay all or a portion of this premium. It pays during the insured's total disability usually after six or twelve months, in a lump-sum generally up to $100,000. The benefit paid is a percentage (80 percent to 100 percent) of the extended reporting period premium and helps to supplement the basic premium reimbursement provided under the basic BOE policy itself.

Summary

These optional benefits should be packaged and sold in accordance with the insured's needs. When written together with the base policy, though, these features provide some outstanding protection for replacement of the insured's business expenses during a disability.

■ *Chapter 17*

THE DISABILITY BUY-SELL POLICY

Life insurance is sold frequently to fund a buy-out agreement between business owners. The purpose is to provide cash to the business or a partner to buy out the deceased owner's interest in the business.[1] Quite often, the buy-out (or buy-sell) agreement is a precondition to obtaining bank financing or a bonding agreement. The concern about premature death runs high and the buy-out agreement stipulates the specifics of the ownership interest transfer in the event of the death of one of the owners.

But what about a catastrophic, long term disability of the owner? Will the disabled person be any more productive for the business than one who has died? Could some of these situations develop as a result of disability?

• The disabled business owner continues to collect a salary and share in the profits without being an active contributor. A replacement is hired, creating twice the cash drain on the business.

• The disabled owner needs money to try to maintain his pre-disability standard of living and decides to sell the business interest to an outsider. The disabled owner does not realize the full value of the interest owned since he must agree to a bargain sale in order to obtain cash quickly.

• A new owner with no experience in the business becomes a co-owner with the remaining owner(s) who continue to struggle from the financial losses incurred as a result of the disability of one of the firm's key people.

Is this fall-out from the disability much different from what would happen if the insured died? A disability presents many of the same problems and potentially creates even more financial trouble than death because the disabled owner expects to continue to draw cash from the business while alive and an active owner.[2]

THREE SCENARIOS

The agent is confronted with one of three possibilities when talking with small business owners about the disability buy-sell concept. The majority of business owners have not adequately planned for the sale of their businesses due to death, disability or retirement. A recent study indicates that only 17% of small businesses have addressed this problem.

The three possibilities are:

- no buy-sell agreement at all

- a buy-sell agreement with no mention of disability

- a buy-sell agreement that contains a disability provision.

In the first circumstance, the agent must discuss the importance of planning in advance for the formal transfer of ownership interest if an individual can no longer be an active partner due to premature death, disability or retirement. In the second situation, the buy-sell agreement has been created but ignores the possibility that a catastrophic disability could result. If it does, with no formal agreement in place to govern the situation, chaos will likely ensue. Finally, the third scenario has produced a substantial unfunded liability since either the remaining owners(s) or the firm have agreed to buy out a disabled owner's interest. Where will the money come from? If life insurance has been used to fund the premature death liability, it is not a long leap to understanding the concept of disability buy-out insurance.

Quite simply, disability buy-out (DBO) policies provide the funds in the event of disability, just as life insurance furnishes the cash following the death of an owner. There is no difference in the money, only in the *type of event* that triggers the need for the dollars.

The chances of the catastrophic disability happening are significant when there are several owners in a business. Individually, the chances of disability are not as great as the possibility of one long term disability happening to one of two, three, four or more owners. It only has to happen once to a business to wreak financial havoc.

The chart below illustrates the chances of at least one disability that will last at least *12 months or longer* among a group of 2, 3 or 4 owners whose average age varies between 27 and 52.

Average Age	Number of Owners		
	2	3	4
27	26.3%	36.7%	45.7%
32	25.6%	35.8%	44.7%
37	24.5%	34.5%	43.1%
42	23.0%	32.4%	40.7%
47	20.7%	29.4%	37.1%
52	17.4%	24.9%	31.7%

For example, let's suppose you are talking to three business owners, whose average age is 42. There is about a one-in-three chance that one of them will suffer a disability lasting 12 months or longer before retiring at age 65 to 70. This is simply too much of a chance to ignore. If the odds are one-in-twenty, or maybe one-in-ten, you can gamble. But — one-in-three? Too risky!

The chart shows the probability decreasing by age, but that is only because the exposure period (the number of years until retirement) is decreasing.

As the disability statistics have previously shown, the likelihood of a disability is greater at any age than the likelihood of dying in that same year. Coupled with the numbers shown above, ignoring disability as a hazard to the business can be a grave financial mistake.

The loss of an active owner due to a disability presents many money problems:

- What would happen to the firm's income while an active owner is sidelined by a significant injury or illness, especially if that person is a strong revenue generator?

- With this impediment to cash flow, where does the money come from to buy out the disabled owner's interest?

- If the business has to borrow the money (providing a loan can be arranged under the circumstances) or pay the disabled owner in installments, how much will interest charges add to the existing financial obligation? A business could end up paying two or three times as much as the business interest is worth simply because it is the only way to pay it off.

Other difficulties that are present if a disability occurs include:

- For how long must an owner be disabled before the buy-out is effective? The period of time must be some lengthy minimum number of months, with twelve months being the most common time frame.

- How is disability defined by the agreement? What type of work restriction characterizes a disability as catastrophic? This is the definition that must be met each day to qualify for the buyout. In addition, do the disability days have to be consecutive?

- How will the dollars be paid to buy out the disabled owner's interest? Will it be on a lump sum basis? Installment payments? Or some combination of the two?

All of these questions must be addressed. The easiest way to do this is to identify the owners, value their interests and fund the liability with a disability buy-out policy. This disability product will:

- establish an elimination period (number of days before the buy-out is triggered);

- define disability;

- provide all or a substantial portion of the dollars needed to effect the buy-out; and

- stipulate how the money will be paid out.

It can be as simple as using life insurance to fund the premature death liability portion of the buy-sell agreement. The financial valuation of the owners' interests in the business will not change for the different products. As mentioned earlier, the financial liability is the same; the event that triggers the need for the buy-out is different.

Today, new life insurance products are saving firms money in premiums that can be used towards the purchase of the appropriate disability buy-out policies. In the past, with several owners, the firm may have purchased a policy on each life and paid separate premiums. Now, with *first-to-die* life insurance policies, one plan can be set up to insure several owners, with the death benefit payable at the first death which is, after all, when the money is needed to complete the buy-out. This may save enough money to buy disability buy-out policies on all individual owners.[3]

For example, one insurer illustrates the following scenario:

Business valued at $1,000,000
5 owners, ages 35, 40, 42, 45 and 47 (male, non-smokers)
20% ownership interest each
Benefits amounts: $200,000 (same for life and disability coverage)
Entity-purchase arrangement (business owns policies)

Usual funding: five life policies
total cost: $9,390
Five D.I. Buy-Out policies $3,800
Total cost: $13,190

New idea: First to Die Life policy: $5,426
D.I. Buy-Out policies: $3,800
Total cost: $9,226
or less than the total cost of the five separate life policies ($9,390)

The disability buy-out sale should not ignore the life sale. Both of these products can often be structured together as above to strengthen the effectiveness of the agreement in addition to enhancing the credibility of the agent making the recommendation for this type of coverage.

The disability buy-out policy is uniquely designed to fill the need to purchase a disabled partner's interest and the policy provisions reflect this.

RENEWABILITY

The disability buy-out has never been, in the strict sense of the word, noncancelable. There have always been a couple of provisions that could terminate a plan, unlike noncancelable coverage. First, once a buy-out is triggered and benefits paid, the policy is finished. Only one claim per plan! Since the owner is no longer affiliated with the firm (having been bought out), the policy is no longer necessary here. Second, if the insured ceased to be gainfully employed by the business for 30 hours a week or more (except if caused by disability) the coverage would also cease since the original business relationship and ownership arrangements would appear to have changed.

With the buy-out policy in the past, premiums could not be increased and policy provisions remained unchanged. Today, the policy provisions are still unchangeable by the insurer, but it is likely that the premium guarantee resembling a noncancelable clause will be removed. Therefore, renewability may be of a guaranteed renewable type (with the above noted exceptions) or companies might still offer a guaranteed premium rate for a higher cost. Either way, the renewability provisions strongly favor the insured.

DEFINITION OF TOTAL DISABILITY

Most insurers did not use the pure form of the *own occupation* definition of total disability. Rather, this definition was usually modified from the language stating, "the insured must be unable to perform the duties of his own occupation" to allow a slight alteration to the effect that "the insured must also not be working within the business organization".

To require that the individual no longer be affiliated with the business in any working capacity was a reasonable change to the *own occupation* definition. The entire reason for the disability buy-sell (DBS) (also called disability buy-out by some carriers) policy was to buy out the value of the ownership interest under the presumption that the individual will not be coming back to the business under any circumstances. This definition of total disability makes this clear.

The DBS policy does not address partial or residual disability for obvious reasons. This implies the individual has returned to work within the firm, canceling the necessity for the buy out to be triggered. Or, if the individual, unable to return to the business owned, works somewhere else instead, and still conforms to the disability definition in the contract (and buy-sell agreement), the benefits will be paid. In either event, there is no need for a definition of disability other than that already described.

ELIMINATION PERIOD

As previously mentioned, the selection of an elimination period for a DBS policy must coincide with what is considered to be a catastrophic disability. You will recall that Social Security's rather restrictive definition calls for an injury or illness lasting at least 12 months or that will likely result in death. That's pretty catastrophic!

Disability insurers generally offer a minimum elimination period of 12 months (but without the "or likely to result in death" wording). This is thought to be catastrophic in the sense that the chances of a full recovery are very remote. It says, in effect, that the insured will never again be well enough to be a productive member of the business. A firm certainly does not want to buy out an owner who has a chance of recovering and returning to the firm. Twelve months is the minimum standard of measurement to assure the possibility of return to be virtually impossible.

However, twelve months is not the only elimination period that companies offer. Also available are elimination periods of 18, 24 and 36 months. Often, a Business Overhead Expense (BOE) policy (detailed in Chapter 16, The Business Overhead Expense Policy) is set up so that the end of its benefit period (12, 18, 24 months, for example) coincides with the elimination period of the DBS contract.

For example, suppose a BOE policy was written with an 18 month benefit period. During this time frame, when the owner is disabled and out of work, the business expenses that he is responsible for are paid by this policy, keeping the business out of additional debt. At the conclusion of this 18 month period (or close to it since the BOE policy benefit period can be open-ended), the DBS policy is designed to kick in. All the business needs to do is purchase a DBS policy with an 18 month elimination period. Once the buy out is complete, there is no need for the BOE policy since the individual is no longer an owner. This prevents the policies from overlapping while maximizing the benefit potential of each.

The days in the elimination period of a DBS policy need not be consecutive. Most insurers allow days of disability to be accumulated in satisfying this definition — as long as it is done within an acceptable period of time. For example, wording here might read "if a disability due to the same or related cause recurs within six months from the end of a prior disability lasting at least 90 days, the later disability will be considered a *continuation* of the previous period".

Therefore, if an individual was out for 120 days and then attempted to return to work only to suffer a recurrence of the problem two months later, the elimination period count would not start over again. Since the recurrence from the same cause was within six months, the first day of the second period of disability would be day 121 of the elimination period. This means only eight additional months are necessary to complete the elimination period and trigger benefits rather than a full twelve months.

Insurers will vary the wording in this type of policy provision, so read the language carefully to see how it works. The selection of the elimination period is critical and should, whenever possible, be done in conjunction with the BOE policy.

TRIGGER DATE

The DBS policy does not have a benefit period as other disability contracts do. Whereas most disability contracts require a continuing need to meet the definition of disability, the DBS policy only looks to this definition during the elimination period. Once the insured reaches this point, the legality of the buy-sell agreement takes effect and a buy out is triggered. This point, one day past the required elimination period, is called the trigger date.

It is important to understand that once the period of time defined in both the agreement and the policy as to when benefits must be paid, has been reached, there is no further need to conform to the definition of disability. It is irrelevant. A recovery will not reverse the disability buy out of the owner's interest. The financial obligation to buy out the interest takes effect once the trigger date is reached and there is no going back for the business or the disabled owner. The buy out happens and the ownership interest is transferred.

HOW BENEFITS ARE PAID

Simply because the definition of disability is no longer important following the trigger date does not mean that DBS plans are not sold with benefit periods. They are! In fact, there are three possible ways to collect under DBS policies:

- In a lump sum

- Via installments over a specified period of months

- In a partial lump sum payment combined with installments over a specified period of months

Lump Sum

This is a much different way to collect benefits than either the personal disability income policy (indemnity) or the BOE plan (reimbursement). But disability benefits here can be paid out just as life insurance benefits are — in one lump sum. Considering the time value of money, the lump sum approach has more appeal than an installment type of payout. It also conforms better to the idea that the trigger date ends all need to continue to meet the standards of the disability definition. Once all the benefits are paid out, there is definitely no reason to look further at definitions.

Until and unless there is a change in the capital gains tax rate, the disabled owner may realize a substantial capital gains tax liability as a result of the buy-out. If, for example, the owner originally invested $25,000 into the business and his interest was now valued at $200,000, that $175,000 increase in basis is subject to capital gains taxation, diminishing the owner's enthusiasm for a lump sum settlement. One suggestion is to set up an interest-earning trust designed to avoid constructive receipt and have a trustee manage the funds and distribute payments to the insured accordingly. There is always an option to leave the money with the insurer and let them make payments (with interest) to the disabled owner. Most individuals want, however, to obtain their money from the insurance company when it's due.

Benefits purchased for a lump sum settlement under a DBS policy can range from a minimum of $25,000 up to $1,000,000 and possibly higher. This is quite different than the monthly benefit normally provided under a disability policy.

Installment Option

There may be several choices for the insured here. Under the lump sum arrangement just described, an option often exists to leave the money with the insurer and accept installment payments instead. This choice is actually made on or around the trigger date.

Some insurers do offer an installment contract, sold at the time of application. Here, a benefit period of 2, 3 or 5 years, or more is selected. The total amount of coverage does not change; only how it is paid out. For example, a $500,000 lump sum policy would translate to $8,333/month over a benefit period of five years ($8,333 x 60 months = $500,000).

When electing this, be sure that the policy contains a *presumptive* total disability clause. This language is different from the provision of the same name under a personal policy which presumes total disability if an insured loses his or her sight, speech, hearing or use of two limbs. In the DBS policy, it merely means that the insured is presumed disabled once the trigger date is reached. Even though benefit payments are still being paid out, there is no need to conform to the definition of total disability in the contract.

Combination Payout

This type of settlement uses both the lump sum and installment payouts. The arrangements are flexible as to what percentage of the total amount can be attributed to either method. Our $500,000 policy, for example, may be set up as $200,000 payable in a single sum as of the trigger date and $5,000/month payable for 60 months (for a total installment payout of $300,000).

This has the effect of providing a large amount of cash immediately ($200,000), while spreading out the capital gains taxation by using an installment payout for the $300,000 balance. As much as $1,500,000 (or more) can be purchased to fund a buy-sell arrangement under method of payments two and three. Insurers allow higher amounts to be purchased when an installment method is used (in whole or in part) since the insurers do not have to come up with all of the money at the trigger date. The premium payments can be reduced by electing either the installment only or the combination plan.

Of course, before selecting an amount of coverage, the value of the various ownership interests should be ascertained.

BUSINESS VALUATION

Insurance companies are not business appraisers. In establishing formulas to calculate the amount of an owner's interest in a business for DBS purposes, the carrier is merely trying to assess a reasonable dollar amount for the business in the event of a forced sale like a disability buy-out.

Many insurers will try to work with the formula(s) already set up within an established buy-sell agreement. However, since there is often *no* agreement, ready-made formulas are available for use in arriving at a dollar value for the interest. It has been my experience that many small businesses have not gone through this procedure of placing a legitimate business value on the firm. There is, then, much interest in what the numbers will be after the calculation is done. They can then say, with credence, that the value of their business is $_____.

In addition to working with the client's attorney in putting together the appropriate language for the agreement, as discussed in more detail later, the agent also will work with the firm's CPA (or comptroller) to obtain the numbers necessary to perform the calculation. What is necessary for review are two documents:

- the company's most recent balance sheet and

- one to three years of income (profit and loss) statements

These two financial statements will have the numbers necessary to arrive at a dollar figure representing the insured's ownership interest. Depending on the type of business, however, the numbers selected from these sheets may differ.

There are, in general, four types of businesses to be evaluated:

1. *Professional Service Corporations.* Here, goodwill of the owners is critical in the overall value assigned since the revenue of the firm is largely dependent on the *services* the owners can perform. Hence, the amount of the owners' salaries will be one factor used in the calculation. The other will be the net book value of the corporation. This number is the difference between assets and liabilities. It can be called net book value, net worth, owners' equity, stockholder's equity, retained earnings or any of several other terms. But, it is always the difference between assets and liabilities and can be found at the bottom of the balance sheet. Thus, the calculation will add the owners' salaries to the net book value in arriving at a value for the business. (It is important to note that some insurers use a multiple of owners' salaries such as 2x or 3x to calculate good will.) Once the total value is determined, each owner's percentage of ownership is applied to arrive at individual values. For example, if a business is valued at $300,000 and has three owners, each with a $33^{1}/_{3}$ percent interest, the individual value of each owner's portion of the company is $100,000.

2. *Professional Service Partnerships.* This type of business is valued much like the profession service corporation, discussed above, except that the good will portion is calculated by using net partnership profits rather than owners' salaries. This is done because, in a partnership, the bottom-line profits are passed directly to the partner's individual 1040 forms and, therefore, are a better representation of the income the partners receive from the firm. This number can be found on the income statement and should then be added to the net book value, ascertained from the balance sheet. (Again, there is a possibility the insurer may use a multiple of the net partnership profits, such as 2x.)

3. *CPA Firms.* The CPA's book of business is somewhat different than other service companies since a CPA has a fair amount of repeat business. To account for this, the good will value will consist of an average of two to three years of the firm's gross fees as taken from the income statement. This allows for the financial acknowledgement that a CPA will generate a fair amount of renewal business without acquiring new clients. This number is also added

to the net book value (from the balance sheet) to arrive at the total value of the business.

4. *Commercial Businesses.* This type of business entity is different from a service company. These firms may be retail companies, restaurants, wholesalers, small manufacturers and similar types of companies. Their valuation is similar to the service companies only in respect to the use of net book value as part of the calculation. Otherwise, the remainder of the equation derives from the firm's average net income over a set period of time, such as two to three years, multiplied by a capitalization rate. The capitalization rate is the number of years a business could expect similar earnings and is based on a number of factors including, but not limited to, past earnings history, the age of the firm, economic conditions and recent results. The higher the capitalization rate, the more successful and established the business. This naturally (and deservedly) creates a higher valuation of the firm.

Most insurers selling the DBS policy offer computer assistance to come up with the right numbers. Once the calculation is done and the individual values assigned, the agent can then compare the amounts needed for proper funding with the issue limits available for sale by the insurer. The longer the elimination period selected, the more coverage that can be purchased which is something to keep in mind while programming disability buy-sell benefits. Insurers will now often allow coverage to be written with more than one carrier if their limits do not allow satisfactory coverage of the actual buy-out liability.

WAIVER OF PREMIUM

The majority of DBS policies have some type of waiver of premium provision. It usually states that the insured must be totally disabled for a specified period of time, most often 90 days, before premium payments are no longer required until, and unless, the insured recovers. Any money paid during the initial disability period will be refunded. This is similar to the waiver of premium provision described in Chapter 14, Personal Disability Income Policies: What The Contractual Language Really Means.

CONVERSION PRIVILEGE

As discussed under the renewability provision, ownership responsibility may change over time. If so, the need for the DBS policy may vanish if ownership is relinquished at some time before the usual expiration of the policy. Rather than completely dispose of the coverage, the insured will have the option to convert to a more useful version of disability protection.

To convert to a personal disability income policy, some requirements must be satisfied. The conversion need must occur prior to age 60, the insured must be working at the time of conversion, and the insured must be earning a minimum income to qualify. Other personal disability income coverage must be disclosed to prevent a conversion from creating a situation of over-insurance.

The new policy will come from the insurer's disability income portfolio then in effect. The other key parameters are:

- *Monthly Benefit*: based on insurer's issue and participation limits then in effect at time of conversion.

- *Benefit Period*: 24 months is usually the shortest period the insurer has available since there is not a benefit period in a DBS policy for lump sum settlements. If it is an installment contract, the insurer may allow conversion to the exact monthly benefit period of the installment-type DBS policy.

- *Elimination Period*: At least 30 days, but more likely 90 days.

- *Premium*: Generally, the insured's original age is used to calculate the premium based on the rates in effect at time of conversion. Some carriers use attained age in computing the premium amount due.

- *Evidence of Insurability*: Only financial evidence is required. No medical evidence is necessary to qualify. This can be an important consideration, especially if the insured is over 50.

TAXATION

Federal income taxation principles applying to disability buy-sell plans are relatively simple. Regardless of the type of business entity or arrangement for payment of the proceeds, the premium payments are *not* deductible. The benefits under the contract, therefore, are paid on an income-tax free basis.

The insured, however, may be subject to capital gains taxation, as previously mentioned. If the buy-sell agreement is between related parties, there may be gift tax consequences. If the business receives the proceeds to pay out, it may affect the alternative minimum tax calculation.[4]

All of these possibilities should be referred to the firm's CPA or comptroller. The insurance agent should not dispense specific tax advice, only the general guidelines of the appropriate sections of the Internal Revenue Code.

PROTOTYPE BUY-SELL AGREEMENT

Most insurance companies do not require a copy of the buy-sell agreement in order to issue policies. The business will have to send the agreement in to the carrier at some later point in time, however, if it is not available at time of issue. The insurer must be sure that a legal agreement to buy out an ownership interest does, in fact, exist, before it pays out any policy benefits. This must all happen *before* any claim takes place.

There are two types of buy-sell agreements: entity and cross-purchase arrangements. Under the entity purchase, the business owns the policies on the principal owners. The business pays the premium and is the beneficiary of the proceeds, which are then used to buy out the disabled owner's interest. When there are more than two owners in the business, this type of arrangement is generally preferred.

Under a cross-purchase plan, each owner possesses a policy on the other's life. This is more suited to two person firms; otherwise, the number of policies required can be prohibitive. For two people, each owns a policy on the other, receiving the proceeds personally with which to buy out the other. Only two DBS policies are needed here. If there were three owners, each would have to own two policies each, one on each of the other owners, for a total of six policies altogether. If the three owners elected the entity purchase method instead, the number of policies needed would be three instead of six, a more practical and manageable arrangement.

To assist you in suggesting language appropriate for a disability buy-sell situation, a prototype agreement is included In Figure 17.1 for your convenience.[5]

Figure 17.1

(This Agreement is intended for use by policyholders' counsel and is not intended as legal advice. The policyholders must rely on their own advisors for legal and tax advice.)

DISABILITY BUY-SELL AGREEMENT

The Information and Elections below Shall be Part of this Agreement.

1. Name of Business Organization:_____

2. Address of Business Organization:_____

3. Business Owners and Percentage of Ownership:_____

Owner	Percentage of Ownership
_____	_____
_____	_____
_____	_____
_____	_____

Figure 17.1 (continued)

4. Type of Buy-Sell (elect one)

( )   Entity Purchase:

The Business Organization hereinafter Purchaser shall purchase the complete ownership interest of a totally disabled Business Owner hereinafter Seller for the value of such interest hereinafter Business Value and the Seller shall sell all such interest to the Purchaser. Such interest shall be determined as of the time the Seller's total disability commences.

( )   Cross-Purchase:

The non-disabled Business Owner hereinafter Purchaser shall purchase the complete ownership interest of a totally disabled Business Owner hereinafter Seller for the value of such interest hereinafter Business Value.

If more than one Purchaser exists, each Purchaser shall purchase that portion of the Seller's interest as such Purchaser's interest would be if the Seller's interest did not exist. The Seller shall sell all such interest to the Purchaser(s). The purchase and sale shall be in accordance with the terms and conditions of this agreement.

5. Business Value (elect one)

( )   Stated Value:

Unless and until changed as set forth herein, the total Business Value of the entire Business Organization shall be $_____. The Seller's percentage of ownership, determined as of the time the Seller's total disability commenced, shall be applied to this value to determine the price to be paid by the Purchaser.

On or about the first day of the month of _____ in each succeeding year the Business Owners or Business Organization will in writing either reaffirm the Business Value in effect or agree upon a new Business Value. Copies of this reaffirmation or revision shall be given to all Business Owners and shall be part of this Agreement.

If the Business Owners do not reaffirm or agree upon a new value, this failure to do so will not void this Agreement. However, the value set forth above, or the last value agreed upon by the parties, in writing, shall be fully binding upon them, except that if the Business Owners do not so reaffirm or agree for (3) three consecutive years, the value shall be determined by the independent Certified Public Accountant regularly retained by the Business Organization. If no such Accountant is available, the value shall be determined by any other Certified Public Accountant selected by the mutual agreement of the parties and his compensation shall be charged equally, based on ownership percentage, to each of the parties.

( )   Formulas (insert formula)

Figure 17.1 (continued)

The Business Value under either the Stated Value or Formula above shall be determined as of: (elect one)

( )   fiscal year nearest the date of Seller's disability

( )   fiscal year preceding the date of Seller's disability

( )   12 month period ending in the month preceding the date of the Seller's disability which caused this purchase to take place.

6. Disability Defined and Commencement Date of Buy-Sell

The Purchaser shall purchase the Seller's entire ownership interest in the Business Organization when the Seller has been totally disabled as determined by Life Insurance Company under policy number(s) #_____, #_____, #_____, #_____, #_____, #_____, #_____, #_____.

The first day following the period of total disability required under the policy is considered to be the Commencement Date. This time period shall include any period of recurrent or subsequent disability that is considered one period of disability in the Disability Buy-Sell Policy(ies) used to fund this Agreement.

7. Transfer of Business Interest:

Within 30 days of the receipt of the insurance proceeds from the Disability Buy-Sell policy(ies) used to fund this Agreement, the Purchaser(s) shall deliver the payment for the Seller's business interest to the Seller and the Seller shall transfer full and complete title of said interest to the Purchaser(s).

8. Delivery of Payment:

Delivery of payment shall be accomplished through: (elect one)

( )   Full payment of Purchase Price:

The Purchaser(s) shall deliver to the Seller the full and complete amount of the Business Value in cash, or by cashier's check.

( )   Installment Purchase:

The Purchaser(s) shall deliver to the Seller an initial payment equal to _____% of the Seller's portion of the Business Value. The balance of the purchase price shall be paid in _____(#) of equal quarterly, semi-annual, annual (elect one) installments. The Purchaser(s) shall deliver to the Seller a series of promissory notes bearing interest at the rate of _____% compounded annually. The first note shall fall due _____(#) months after the Commencement Date. The notes shall contain a provision that, in the event of default in payment of any note for a period of 90 days, all notes of the series shall become due and payable at the election of the holder.

9. Disposition of Life Insurance Policies:

If a Buy-Sell Agreement for purposes of purchasing a deceased owner's interest exists, funded by life insurance, the Seller shall have the right to purchase such policies insuring the Seller's life from the Purchaser.

The purchase price shall be equal to the cash value of such policies including dividends if any on the date of purchase by the Seller. The value shall be as determined by the insurance company issuing the policies less any indebtedness secured by the cash value.

Figure 17.1 (continued)

This right must be exercised within _____(#) days of: (elect one)

( )   A.   Delivery of payment for Disability Buy-Sell.

( )   B.   Date of payment of last installment in Disability Buy-Sell.

10. Death During Installment Period:

If this Agreement contains a provision for the delivery of payment through the installment purchase method, and the disposition of the life insurance policies referred to in Section 9 is elected as Option "B" (Seller's right to purchase insurance after last installment) then the death of the Seller during the installment period shall cause all unpaid notes relating to this Agreement to become due within 30 days of the receipt of the life insurance proceeds by the Purchaser(s).

If no life insurance proceeds are available, then the installments shall continue as scheduled in Section 8, Installment Purchase Option.

11. Control of Business Organization During Disability:

In the event a Business Owner is totally disabled for a continuous period of six (6) months as defined in the Disability Buy-Sell policies used to fund this Agreement he shall: (elect one)

( )   Relinquish all control over the operation of the Business Organization to the remaining owners(s). They shall then exercise complete control of the Business Organization, in accordance with their percentage of ownership therein calculated as if the Ownership interest of the disabled Business Owner did not exist, until such time as the disabled owner recovers as defined in the Disability Buy-Sell policies used to fund this agreement or the Commencement Date of this Agreement.

( )   Retain complete control over the operation of the Business Organization in accordance with his ownership interest until the Commencement Date of this Agreement.

12. Endorsement of Stock Certificates:

Simultaneously with the execution of this Agreement, the Stockholders shall surrender the Stock certificates subject hereto to the Corporation and the following endorsement shall be placed on the face of each certificate:

"The sale, encumbrance or other transfer of this certificate is restricted. The Corporation will furnish to any share-holder upon request and without charge a full statement of such restrictions."

After such endorsement, the certificates shall be returned to their respective owners who shall be entitled, subject to the terms hereof, to exercise all rights and interest therein. All Stock hereafter issued shall bear the same endorsement. Upon the termination of this Agreement, such certificates shall be surrendered to the Corporation and new certificates without the foregoing endorsement shall be issued in lieu thereof.

13. Invalid Provision:

The invalidity or unenforceability of a particular provision of this Agreement shall not affect the other provisions hereof, and the Agreement shall be construed in all respects as if such invalid or unenforceable provisions were omitted.

Figure 17.1 (continued)

14. Insurance Company not a Party to this Agreement:

    The insurance company which has issued policies to fund this Agreement is not a party to this Agreement, nor is it responsible for its validity. The payment or other performance of the Company's contractual obligations in accordance with the terms of its insurance policies shall completely discharge the Company from all claims, suits and demands whatsoever.

15. Binding on all Parties:

    This Agreement shall be binding on the Parties, their heirs, legal representatives, successors and assignees.

16. Termination or Amendment to Agreement:

    This Agreement may be terminated or amended by written agreement of all Parties hereto. It shall terminate automatically upon the dissolution or bankruptcy of the Business Organization or when there remains only one Party to this Agreement.

17. State Law Governs:

    This Agreement shall be governed by the law of the State/Commonwealth of _____.
    In witness whereof the Parties hereto have executed this Agreement on this _____ day of _____, 19____.

_____
Business Organization

_____
Authorized Signature

_____	_____
Witness	Business Owner Spouse
_____	_____
Witness	Business Owner Spouse
_____	_____
Witness	Business Owner Spouse
_____	_____
Witness	Business Owner Spouse

Note: Business organization's signature needed only if an entity purchase.

CHAPTER NOTES

1. "The Importance of Buy-Sell Agreements", *Nation's Business*, March, 1995, p. 57.

2. "Complete the Buy-Sell Plan With Disability", *Onward*, September, 1994, p. 16.

3. "No-Cost Disability Buy-Out Insurance", *Onward*, July/August, 1994, p. 17.

4. Taxation information is from Internal Revenue Code Sections 104, 105, 106, 213 and 265.

5. This prototype was written by the author and Robert Boyd, Esquire.

■ *Chapter 18*

KEY PERSON DISABILITY INSURANCE

Key person disability income fills a special need. Personal disability income protection replaces income for personal living expenses after an injury or sickness. Business overhead expense insurance reimburses the business owner for business expenses until recovery from his disability can generate revenues again. The disability buy-sell policy provides dollars to the business or specified owner(s) with which to buy out a disabled owner's interest.

However, these solutions do not answer the question the business owner often asks about the loss of a key employee and the resulting impact that such a loss may have on business revenue. To cover the employee with personal coverage is fine; the monthly claim check goes to the insured and relieves the business of paying a salary out of revenue to someone not working. However, these dollars do not go directly to the business.

If the disabled employee is also an owner and has a business overhead expense policy, the business will receive money to help cover this individual's portion of the overhead. However, a key person may have little or no ownership interest.

What if this person's talent and ability contributed heavily to the bottom line? The smaller the business, the more likely it is that a single individual is responsible for the business' success. Losing this person for a period of time could cause business income to drop considerably and, possibly, even force the firm to close its doors.

So what does the employer do? Very likely, if the disability will be lengthy (more than two or three months), the employer will begin a search for a replacement. The cost to do this may be high including fees for a recruiting agency, newspaper advertisements, relocation expenses, perhaps an initial bonus to attract a top-notch person. A new salary has been added, along with the cost of benefits, office space, and training.

Will the replacement be effective immediately? Probably not. More than likely, it will take several weeks, or even several months for the business to adjust and profitability to return to its pre-disability level.

The problem facing the employer is how to pay the price to find a replacement and, at the same time, restore lost revenue. The solution is a disability income policy on the key person that indemnifies the *business* during the loss of this individual' services.

Also, it is important to look at the situation from the disabled key employee's standpoint. Will there be a business left to go back to? Personal disability income coverage is paying the bills while the disability lasts, but who pays after recovery if there is no business to which this person can return?

Key person disability coverage is not new to the disability insurance industry, but there are very few product vehicles available for sale. There are two primary reasons for this:

1. This is a limited market in comparison with those for other disability products and many carriers will not spend time and money on a product that will achieve modest sales at best.

2. Identifying who is a key person for purposes of providing this coverage requires solid, experienced underwriting that the majority of carriers do not have in this particular market.

However, it is being sold and underwritten by the more seasoned disability insurance companies. This chapter will review the underwriting specifics and contractual provisions of this product.

WHO IS A KEY PERSON?

In writing this coverage, the key employee's vital importance to the business must be firmly established. An underwriting manager once said to me, "Is there really any one person whom the business can't do without, other than a sole proprietor, in whose case personal disability income can handle the problem?" I think it was a rhetorical question but, historically, the thinking has been that proof of a key employee's value is not easy to pinpoint.

Questions to ask include:

*   Does the key person use specific skills that no other employee in the business has?

*   Are these specific skills difficult to replace?

*   Is the key person's occupation stable now and for the foreseeable future?

*   Is the key person highly motivated, keeping the business bottom line at the forefront of the work performed?

*   And, the critical query, will the business lose income if the key person is disabled?

If all five questions are answered "yes," a key employee situation exists for which key person coverage is indicated.

The companies underwriting this risk now ask a further question: does the key person have any ownership in the business? And, if so, how much? Usually the key person must have less than 50 percent ownership (and preferably none). Business overhead and disability buy-sell funds can be used for the owners, whereas key person coverage is provided to replace business revenue and to find a replacement in the absence of any other income source.

As an agent, be prepared to justify the selection of your client as a key person. Specific details regarding the firm and its gross revenue, the duties and income of the key person, other individuals who perform the same duties and their incomes provide useful data to the underwriter who must render a decision regarding qualification for the policy.

More often than not, the key person is an individual who attracts new clients to the business or is heavily involved in the sales or technological end of the business.

More than one person from a business could be insured as key employees but careful justification will be needed in writing multiple employees.

The business should be of small to medium size and in business for at least two to three years. The key employee should also demonstrate some longevity with the firm, being with it from the start or at least for several years. Large corporations are usually excluded because the financial impact of a loss of a key employee is less.

Family member employees of a family owned business are not eligible for key person coverage.

HOW MUCH COVERAGE CAN BE PURCHASED?

The value of a key employee goes beyond his basic compensation. That, after all, is the point of this type of policy. If a key employee earning $50,000 a year becomes disabled and could seriously jeopardize the bottom line of a $500,000 gross revenue business, this individual is obviously worth more than the basic salary.

Companies place a key person's top value for insurance purposes at twice his salary level. The basic salary will be covered by the personal disability policy and paid directly to the insured, saving the business from having to replace that amount. This means, for key person coverage, up to 100 percent of a key individual's salary can be covered up to a stated top limit, usually $10,000 a month.

The effect is to replace twice the insured's salary. For example, if the insured earned $5,000 a month in income, a personal disability policy will replace a substantial portion of the $5,000. The key person policy can be written for $5,000 a month to be paid directly to the business. This represents a total of $10,000 a month for the business to replace that key employee (i.e., $5,000 savings on salary and $5,000 to replace lost business revenue and begin the search for a replacement).

Some carriers may write less than 100 percent of salary in direct proportion to the key employee's ownership in the business.

It is important to remember that key person coverage is separate from personal disability coverage; one amount is directed to the insured and the other to the business.

ELIMINATION PERIOD AND BENEFIT PERIOD

The typical key person program is similar to the business overhead expense plan in that it meets a short-term income need. It will be apparent early in the disability whether a return to work is in the immediate future. The hiring and training of a replacement is an involved process but once done, can return the business to pre-disability revenue numbers within a few months.

The benefit periods available are 6, 12 and 18 months in keeping with the short-term nature of the need. Elimination periods are 30, 60 and 90 days, with the occasional carrier offering a 180 day elimination period.

KEY POLICY PROVISIONS

Renewability

Renewing a key person disability income policy is similar to renewing disability buy-sell; that is, the policy is noncancelable with some qualification.

In order for the business to meet the noncancelable renewal requirements (the guarantee of premiums and policy provisions to age 65), the following conditions are required:

- the insured must continue to be employed full-time (30 hours per week) by the business unless, of course, totally disabled; and

- the key employee's ownership interest must remain below a certain level, usually 50 percent.

These conditions, like the buy-sell conditions, are within employer and employee control and not that of the insurer, which will live up to its noncancelable obligation if these conditions continue to be met.

Definition of Total Disability

The insured must be unable to perform the usual duties of his occupation due to injury or sickness. This is the only test of disability and will be familiar as the *own occupation* definition of total disability. The true need for this product is to replace lost revenue to a business because a key worker is unable to work — at his job. The *own occupation* definition lends itself perfectly to filling that need.

While companies are applying more stringent language to personal total disability definitions, the *own occupation* exposure here is short-term, just as it is in business overhead expense policies, and as such, does not represent much risk to the company.

This definition may be modified to add language concerning HIV positive results for medical personnel. If an individual is diagnosed as being HIV positive and works in the medical profession, it will be assumed that total disability exists even though a physical loss is not yet present. For example, a dentist who employs another dentist to help with the practice and depends on this individual to help cover a second office location, would likely lose revenue if the employee was diagnosed as HIV positive and could no longer practice dentistry. A key person disability policy would replace some of this lost revenue until someone new could be brought in to assume the duties of the employee-dentist.

There is no provision for residual disability, nor is one necessary. An individual eligible for residual disability will have *returned to work* and be generating some income again for the business.

Waiver of Premium

If the insured is totally disabled for a period of 90 days, future premiums will be waived as they come due and any premium paid during the initial 90 day period will be refunded.

Conversion Privilege

A key person may cease to be a "key" person at any time after the policy is issued. Usually this happens when an individual leaves the company or increases his ownership interest beyond the acceptable limit. If so, the key person situation is no longer valid but coverage needs may dictate preserving insurability by converting the plan to a personal disability income policy. The new policy can be issued up to a stated monthly benefit (usually $1,000 to $2,000/month) and must be in line with the company's issue and participation limits in effect at the time of exchange.

The premium may be based on either the original issue age when the key person policy was written or the attained age at time of the exchange. In either event, the rates will be those in effect when the conversion takes place.

Personnel Replacement Expense

As an optional benefit, several carriers will write a personnel replacement expense benefit that is designed to reimburse the business for specific costs associated with securing a permanent replacement for the insured.

Among the costs that may be reimbursed are:

- the salary of the replacement for a period of time, usually three months;

- the placement fee of an employment agency or executive search firm;

- advertising;

- moving expenses;

- any expenses paid to a candidate for the position for travel, food and lodging.

This benefit is a reimbursing one, similar to business overhead expense. The costs must be incurred and submitted to the company for payment. A lump-sum amount can be purchased between a minimum of $1,000 to $5,000 and a maximum of $50,000. The business has a set period of time in which to incur these expenses, such as 12 months.

There is also a required minimum total disability time (usually six months) that the key employee must be out before these benefits are payable.

TAXATION

The business purchases the policy on the key employee. The premium paid for the policy is not deductible. The benefits, when paid to the business following the insured's disability, are received income-tax free.[1]

The key person policy provides tax-free benefits to the employer at a critical time in the life of the business. Without these dollars, the firm may close, becoming another small business fatality.

This policy helps the business ride out the key person's loss, maintain a reasonable profitability level, and begin to build for the future.

CHAPTER NOTES

1. Internal Revenue Code sections 104, 105, 106, 213, and 265.

■ *Chapter 19*

FUTURE TRENDS IN DISABILITY INCOME

When I entered the disability income marketplace in 1975, the maximum issue limit for disability income was $3,500 a month; own occupation claims experience was poor; residual disability income contracts were being introduced to an apathetic industry; cost of living and Social Security offset riders were in their infancy; and medical examinations were necessary if coverage exceeded $1,000 a month.

Less than ten years later, own occupation coverage was back in favor; individual issue limits were without limits. Companies were issuing as much as $50-60,000 a month in coverage; many carriers used a one-page application form; and examinations were not necessary unless coverage applied for exceeded $10-15,000 a month.

Now, the industry has come full circle. Its profits are in a state of free fall and have been for some time. Own occupation coverage is in serious jeopardy and issue limits are returning to some degree of normalcy at a $10-15,000/month maximum. Applications for insurance are extensive and require tax returns to substantiate income levels. Companies are responding not only from an underwriting standpoint, but from a marketing standpoint as well. For example, some companies have withdrawn from writing business in various states, Florida and California in particular, and other companies have modified their definition of physician occupations to parallel that of the lower income, gray collar worker.

So, what is the future for disability income? Will there be a period of retrenchment similar to the one that occurred in the late 1970's? Will the industry return to the abundant profit margin experienced in the early 1980's? Will the horrific claims experience of 1993 and 1994 repeat itself in the foreseeable future? Will the disability income market survive at all?

Naturally, disability income can survive this latest turmoil. But it must do so on an entirely different basis than it did when it shrugged off the losses in the 1970's.[1] The losses experienced during the late 1980's and early 1990's ran much deeper, were prolonged, and were more serious than the downturn in profitability of the 1970's. In addition, the traditional stronghold of individual disability income coverage — the physician marketplace — has changed dramatically and no longer represents the refuge it once was for premiums and positive returns. The traditional buyer of disability income coverage has aged and is now in the market for long term care insurance.

In a way, this is good. The losses of the past few years are fading and positive changes in product and premium direction are taking place. These changes have also forced disability insurers to look at a new wave of prospects for their products; individuals who have, in the past, been priced out of the noncancelable market. Today, these individuals may represent the "last best hope" for the disability industry.[2]

THE 1980'S

The blame for these current problems lies with all parties to the disability insurance agreement from the company to the agent to the insured. The industry, traditionally, has always over-reacted in good times and in bad. What remains is to learn something from our mistakes and identify the best course of action for the future.

Lower Rates and Improved Products

Ordinarily, this would not happen in the disability income industry. If products are improved, generally, rates tend to *increase* not decrease. Moreover, morbidity experience deteriorated in the 20 year period from 1960 to 1979 as medical advances kept people alive. Rates needed to be balanced with product enhancements that were introduced in the early 1980's.

However, disability insurers wanted a larger share of what was then the lucrative disability income market. In 1980, profit margins soared to 12.1 percent (see Figure 19.1) and everybody wanted a piece of the action. The approach taken by insurance companies was to take already liberally-constructed products for the traditional disability income buyer (professionals, physicians, attorneys, CPAs) and make then even more attractive. Fierce competition backed insurers into marketing corners from which the only escape was to cave in to demands for bigger and better programs.[3] Lifetime own occupation coverage was issued in substantial amounts. The question one had to ask was: at what point does collecting a $50,000 a month disability income benefit look better than actually working?

Figure 19.1

Non-Can DI: 1993 Financial Experience

TABLE 3A
9 COMPANIES EXPERIENCE, 1980-1986

Item	1980	1981	1982	1983	1984	1985	1986
New Sales Growth							17.0%
Earned Premium	$395.2	$454.7	$527.4	$611.4	$714.4	$836.0	$962.9
Premium Growth	NA	15.1%	16.0%	15.9%	16.8%	17.0%	15.2%
Incurred Claims	43.5%	44.2%	46.5%	46.9%	48.1%	50.3%	56.5%
Reserve Increases	17.1%	16.8%	15.0%	12.9%	13.3%	9.9%	11.4%
Benefits and Reserve Increases	60.6%	61.0%	61.5%	59.8%	61.4%	60.2%	67.9%
Commissions	22.2%	23.3%	24.0%	24.2%	24.9%	26.0%	26.4%
Expenses	22.7%	24.0%	25.7%	26.6%	27.4%	26.8%	27.8%
Taxes, Licenses, and Fees	3.3%	3.4%	3.5%	3.4%	3.6%	3.6%	3.6%
Commissions, Expenses, and Taxes	48.2%	50.7%	53.2%	54.2%	55.9%	56.4%	57.8%
Net Investment Income	20.9%	21.4%	21.1%	21.8%	23.1%	24.4%	23.6%
Margin	12.1%	9.7%	6.5%	7.8%	5.8%	7.8%	-2.2%
Margin/Total Revenue (Premium and Net Investment Income)	10.0%	8.0%	5.4%	6.4%	4.7%	6.3%	-1.8%

Non-Can DI: 1993 Financial Experience

TABLE 3B
9 COMPANIES EXPERIENCE, 1987-1993

Item	1987	1988	1989	1990	1991	1992	1993
New Sales Growth	12.6%	3.6%	6.3%	3.0%	3.0%	-1.3%	-8.6%
Earned Premium	$1,129.8	$1,304.6	$1,503.6	$1,762.5	$1,981.2	$2,163.6	$2,314.3
Premium Growth	17.3%	15.5%	15.3%	17.2%	12.4%	9.2%	7.0%
Incurred Claims	58.1%	64.1%	63.7%	64.7%	69.1%	77.1%	79.9%
Reserve Increases	12.3%	12.6%	11.9%	12.4%	12.3%	12.1%	13.4%
Benefits and Reserve Increases	70.4%	76.7%	75.6%	77.1%	81.3%	89.2%	93.2%
Commissions	27.1%	26.1%	25.0%	25.0%	23.7%	22.0%	22.6%
Expenses	28.0%	27.0%	27.5%	25.9%	25.0%	23.6%	21.6%
Taxes, Licenses, and Fees	3.7%	3.5%	3.4%	3.3%	3.2%	3.2%	3.2%
Commissions, Expenses, and Taxes	58.8%	56.6%	55.8%	54.3%	51.9%	48.8%	47.4%
Net Investment Income	23.6%	26.9%	27.7%	26.9%	28.7%	30.3%	32.1%
Margin	-5.5%	-6.4%	-3.7%	-4.5%	-4.5%	-7.7%	-8.5%
Margin/Total Revenue (Premium and Net Investment Income)	-4.4%	-5.0%	-2.9%	-3.5%	-3.5%	-5.9%	-6.4%

Unisex Rates

This started out as a good idea. Initially, rates were equal for males and females and were to be limited to professional occupations where there was no tangible basis for higher female rates based on the limited experience numbers available. So, one insurer priced the male rates for these occupations and set the female rates equal to these calculations.[4] It was not even a true unisex rate where the price would fall somewhere between the male and female cost. It seemed, though, that the female professional had as much of an incentive to return to work as her male counterpart. Companies introduced this change with confidence.

Needless to say, it didn't stay this way for too long. First, unisex rates were extended to other occupational classifications where the reasoning that justified this pricing in the professional market was absent. The rates here were clearly priced optimistically and the resulting experience was poor. Second, many insurers removed the one clause in their contracts where there was a one-sided claims picture: normal pregnancy. Covering normal pregnancy gave female professionals one claims advantage over the male professional and resulted in an increase in short term claims ($10-15,000) which added up quickly.

Association Programs

In an effort to attract as much of the shrinking professional market share as possible, some insurers elected to offer discounted, multi-life, guaranteed issue programs for large associations of physicians, attorneys and similar occupations. While this seems like an ideal way to add substantial premium, there were significant opportunities for adverse selection. Individuals who could not purchase disability coverage elsewhere due to poor health were given an open invitation to come on board. It was assumed that a high volume of premium would be sufficient to offset the poor claims experience.

Price Increases for Noncancelable Product

In the early part of the decade, products improved while rates declined for the professional risk. This was only partly true for the other occupational classifications. Female rates came down for other workers, but overall the substantial extra benefits for the middle income earner ($30-75,000 of income) made the policies more costly, making affordability a central issue for this key market segment. In the latter part of the decade, as experience continued to worsen, rate increases took the noncancelable product completely out of range for the middle class marketplace.[5]

Claims for AIDS and Mental and Nervous Disorders

Two conditions that barely caused a ripple in claims experience in 1980 were becoming more significant by 1990. AIDS, documented and monitored over the last several years, has averaged about three percent of all claims in the disability industry. This is significant but not alarming. While AIDS claims typically have a longer duration than other claims, the frequency of AIDS claims has not varied much since the disease first appeared in the mid-1980's.

Mental and nervous disorders, including substance abuse, illustrate a different story. These claims are averaging close to 20 percent of all claims payments and are usually of a longer duration than other claims. There are fewer claims of these types than, say, for back pain, and they surpass any other condition in terms of the sizable payments made for each claim. These claims have sky-rocketed in the professional occupations resulting in a re-evaluation of this market.[6]

Managed Care

Health care costs seem to have reached their limit and the management of these costs in an effort to bring them down has completely changed the delivery of and compensation for health care services.[7] This has impacted physicians most of all. The days of operating one's own practice are gone. Today, it's a necessity to be part of a group practice to attract insurers, large employers, HMOs and hospitals to contract for services. But the contracts no longer come risk-free. Physicians are expected to assume a larger portion of the burden for delivering health care on a low cost basis, yet keep the quality high. (Sounds like the early 1980's for disability income, doesn't it?)

As a result, many analysts feel that a number of physicians are opting to use their disability income contract as a bridge to early retirement. The lure of the higher issue limit plans with cost of living increases during a claim has proven too much for some. There is no question that the impact of the increase in claims from physicians has hurt the disability business drastically. For some carriers, physicians represent upwards of 30 percent of their total block of business. This trend has to hurt.

The 1980's are over and the decade's legacy will not soon be forgotten. The result, losses since 1986 as an industry, began bringing about changes in the latter part of the decade that have carried into the 1990's and now have been accelerated by a disastrous 1993-94 period.[8]

THE 1990's

The changes in the early part of this decade were relatively predictable given the experience of the 1980's. Certain states, chiefly California and

Florida, were the "bad boys" of claims experience. Every new restriction introduced to the rest of the nation was tried out in these two states first.

Back to Sex-Distinct Pricing

The return to sex-distinct pricing was inevitable.[9] Unfortunately, the professional female risk has lost out, too, with the poor numbers being posted for this occupational grouping as a whole.[10] Normal pregnancy has been restored as an exclusion. By now, virtually all carriers have returned to this way of pricing disability income coverage, raising premiums as much as 50 percent for the female risk. Unisex rates are still being offered by companies on multi-life payroll deduction cases and, in some instances, on business overhead expense and disability buy-sell policies. However, the individual market has put this 1980's trend to rest.

Geographic Pricing

States that have added to the bleak claims picture will be assessed higher premiums than those areas with more positive results. Residents of Florida and California, in particular, are paying 10-20 percent more for disability insurance today than are residents of any other state. A recent A.M. Best survey of 23 insurers found that 70 percent have turned to a geographical rating system. It is not as complex as health insurance where the rate varies by zip code, but it is still a significant move for the industry to isolate the high loss ratio areas and set higher rates for the same product.

Rate Increases

While the 1980's saw premium decreases for a time, the early 1990's have seen an adjustment to rate changes as often as two or three times a year in an effort to properly price the noncancelable product. Remember, a company only gets one chance to set the correct rate on a product. Once the noncancelable product is purchased no rate changes can be made until the insured reaches age 65. These rate adjustments priced the middle income earner completely out of the noncancelable market. Since many insurers offered no other alternative, these individuals went without disability protection. Considering that these income earners represent the majority of working Americans, a large share of the market was ignored. But there were very few products that an agent could sell to these individuals.

Reduced Issue Limits

Good-bye $50,000 a month sales. Hello to top issue limits of $15,000 and lower. Many professionals have already purchased far more individual disability coverage than they can qualify for today. These professionals will now be assessing their business overhead and disability buy-sell needs. Specific occupations, such as physicians and dentists, face further restriction than the published top limit, a complete reversal of the last thirty years in the individual disability income marketplace. In Florida and California these issue limits may be even lower. The majority of Americans cannot qualify for anywhere near the top issue limit, yet it remains for companies to develop and price products an agent can sell to the modest wage earner.

Mental and Nervous Disorder Limits

The trend has been to decline a high percentage of disability insurance applicants who have any history of counseling. The previously mentioned claims experience for this medical condition has much to do with these underwriting decisions. Today, more carriers are placing new limits on the length of claim for mental and nervous disorders, including substance abuse. Group disability coverage has long carried a two year limit on this type of claim and individual disability income is beginning to adapt this philosophy to its own products. Some companies have incorporated these limits in their contracts; others are experimenting with such limits as an optional provision which can reduce premiums.

Own Occupation Coverage Restrictions

In the 1970's, poor claims experience with the own occupation (total disability) definition caused a couple of large disability carriers to withdraw this coverage and replace it with residual disability coverage. It was generally thought that other sizable disability insurers would follow suit. They didn't. Instead, they offered both own occupation and residual disability coverage in the same contract and, in 1976, coined the phrase *dual definition* to market it. The companies who had withdrawn the own occupation coverage tried to stay the course and compete against this new dual definition contract with residual disability only. Battling for market share, the residual only carriers brought back the own occupation definition in the early 1980's when claims were at a low ebb and profits were high.

Own occupation coverage has run its course — for now. As a definition, it was a great concept to sell but essentially made little sense. The true purpose of disability income is to assist a person financially during a disability, not to make him better off by being out of work or by reducing his enthusiasm to return to work. Own occupation represented the danger of a long term claim that could not be reversed through rehabilitation. Once an individual could not perform his own occupation or specialty, he was not bound to reduce his claims benefits because he found other work earning an income. A $50,000/month claim produces $600,000/year in benefits. Paid out for ten years, this results in a $6,000,000 claim, which is more than some disability companies were writing in premiums in a year.

The restrictions on own occupation coverage range from complete withdrawal of the provision to selectively selling to individuals who are in occupations that are not likely to use it. Almost every carrier has taken this definition away from physicians, despite the protests of agent and insured. But the numbers don't lie and this popular policy provision is being pulled by far more carriers than in the 1970's. This time there are virtually no companies that wish to stand alone in offering this benefit in an attempt to call the industry's bluff.

Noncancelable Provision

Even more surprising than the demise of own occupation is the apparent expiration of the shelf life for the noncancelable provision. This renewability feature gave all the power to the insured. Unless the insured failed to pay the premium, the disability income policy stayed in force on the same premium and provision basis until age 65 without regard to any other factors. The pressure was entirely on the company to get it right the first time, because there was nothing they could do about it later. If own occupation experience deteriorated, too bad. If female insureds turned in a slew of normal pregnancy claims, that's the way it goes. Carriers had no options.

Insurers were becoming increasingly uncomfortable with this inflexibility when they were broad sided by two other problems. First, tax legislation in the early part of this decade produced the Deferred Acquisition Capitalization (DAC) tax, which essentially prevented insurers from taking a full deduction on the expenses incurred to add new business to their books. Instead, a 10½ year amortization schedule was substituted in place of the full deduction. Expenses were incurred and the insurer simply could not write much of them off in the year they were paid. This hurt the bottom line and increased taxes for all carriers. Efforts to pass the cost along to the insured have not proved effective and have created some difficulties for several insurers.[11]

Second, insurer insolvency problems in the early 1990's brought about new risk-based capital standards which many state insurance departments (and outside financial ratings analysts) now use to evaluate a company's financial health. There are various risk factors assigned to investments, insurance products and assets the company possesses. Noncancelable disability income carries the highest risk factor making it even less attractive for disability insurers who *specialize* in this type of product.

The willingness to give up the noncancelable renewal provision is a reasonable business decision. The industry is in a bit of turmoil over it, but time will alleviate the current tension. In truth, the noncancelable product was priced beyond the reach of the largest potential client base, so its loss will be felt only by those professional risks, many of whom can no longer buy more coverage. Incoming professionals will have to adjust to a new set of disability income programs, but since they have had little or no previous exposure to the product, it will be up to the agent to handle the transition to a product that promises a little less.

Today, changes are still occurring in many parts of the country. It will take some time to implement this overhaul of the disability product sold for the better part of three decades. But the modifications are a necessity to the insurers' survival. Since the importance of disability income protection has not decreased, agent and client must adapt to and work with the new "beast" to create the best disability income program available.

WHAT TO DO NOW

While the preceding narrative has focused primarily on rate and product, the future success of disability income lies not with what the products will look like or, and to a lesser extent, with what they will cost. Instead, the key to the future of disability income is in identifying today's best prospects and the most effective way to deliver the product. The market long overlooked by disability income carriers, the middle income worker in both white and gray collar occupations, is now the primary focus. The baby boomers and the new generation X'ers represent the clients of the future.

While Chapter 20, The Typical Prospect, and Chapter 21, The "New" Baby Boomer Market, identify these new potential clients, it is important to note that their motivations fit in well with the newest product changes. The departure of own occupation coverage has left the market to the income replacement approach known as residual disability. This type of product pays benefits based on income loss regardless of the occupation in which the insured is able to perform. This has long been the general objective of disability plans: to replace legitimate economic loss.[12]

This type of coverage also sits well with the middle income earners who are the two income families or single parents living close to the point where a disability would spell financial disaster. The money's the thing and a reduced income will hurt the individual's ability to pay bills. Disability income, used to make up the difference, can keep a person (and family) reasonably "whole" until income returns to pre-disability levels.

The elimination of noncancelability and the introduction of a guaranteed renewable product (where rates are based on class) coupled with this income replacement approach should lower rates to an affordable level for these prospects. In fact, it must! This is a key market opened to disability insurers and they must, within reason, offer quality coverage at an affordable rate.

Other changing market factors that insurers will have to address include:

1. *Dual income earners.* There may emerge some type of joint disability income coverage covering two income families at a better rate than buying two separate policies. It's a different approach than the one taken by the standard individual market, but the recognition of what two income families need to survive makes this product a

viable venture — the incentive to return to work should remain high. Disability buy-out products available on a joint basis as a "first to be disabled" plan, similar to that of life insurance's "first to die" concept, are also possibilities under a joint policy.

2. *Working at home.* The information age has opened up an enormous opportunity for people to work successfully in their homes today. A computer and a fax machine in the home office and a hook-up to the Internet puts many in business. With a substantial number of layoffs from Fortune 500 companies over the last fifteen years, intelligent, high income earners are severing corporate affiliations and striking out on their own. Traditionally, the industry has not written coverage on many who work at home. With the number of people earning good money in this situation today, it's time to rethink this philosophy. Surely, a disability policy can be developed where disability can be sufficiently substantiated to alleviate all concerns. A pure income replacement approach measures income more than physical loss and a limit on how long the residual benefit will pay when an individual is working full time eliminates the potential for adverse selection.

3. *Ease of delivery.* In this age of computers and electronics, the disability industry should be able to deliver a policy efficiently and effectively, with a minimal amount of fuss, to the applicant. With on-line applications, hard copy (and signatures) to follow, it would eliminate a substantial amount of time from the processing of the application. Today's consumer is accustomed to minimal service contact as evidence by the use of ATMs and credit card stations at the gas pump. The agent is still crucial to the sale, but technology should allow for improvement in timing of delivery and is critical in reassuring these new clients that the disability industry is serious about their needs. With benefit applications averaging in the $2-3,000/month range, the requirements to approve cases may be fewer, allowing greater speed in issuing policies.

4. *Emphasis on rehabilitation.* There is no question that the rehabilitation provision of the disability insurance policy is critical for insureds and claims departments. (See Chapter 14, Personal Disability Income Policies: What The Contractual Language Really Means.) With the own occupation obstacle out of the way, there are more reasons for the insured to be just as flexible as the insurer with regard to recovery and return to work. The rehabilitation feature gives companies the chance to be generous in paying these types of expenses since a return to work will result in a moderation

or elimination of monthly benefit payments and the lowering of overall claims costs.

There are some who doubt the disability insurance marketplace has much of a future. However, there are, as always, great opportunities that emerge within the scope of change. Disability's future lies with a new group of prospects, individuals who have not heard the story of disability income before. A lower-priced, streamlined product is tailor-made for these potential clients. Average premium may be smaller, but the number of sales opportunities is huge, allowing volume to make up for the lower average sale. As the industry moves to concentrate on this potential insured base and attempts to manage its existing block of business, the agent should educate himself about the new products available and the proper approach to use with the boomers and X'ers. New premium increases could very well match some of the numbers in the 1980's but without the same long term risks.

CHAPTER NOTES

1. "What's the Deal with D.I.?", *The Manager's Edge*, March, 1995, p. 2.

2. "D.I. Writers Try To End the Bleeding", *Best's Review*, February, 1995, p. 56.

3. "Non-Can DI: 1993 Financial Experience", *The Disability Newsletter*, June, 1994, p. 10.

4. Monarch Life Insurance Company introduced unisex rating with their disability income portfolio, *Advantage*, in April of 1992.

5. "D.I. Watchers Worry About Future Coverage", *National Underwriter*, March 6, 1995.

6. "Update: AIDS and Mental/Nervous Claims", *The Disability Newsletter*, March, 1995, p. 1.

7. "Where Does Individual Disability Go From Here?", *The Disability Newsletter*, March, 1995, p. 3.

8. "Disability Policies Shed Fixed Rates", Jane Bryant Quinn column as reprinted in the *Daytona Beach News Journal*, February, 1995.

9. "Individual D.I. Cos. Return To Sex Distinct Pricing", *National Underwriter*, March 7, 1994, p. 27.

10. "Why Women Will Pay More For Disability Insurance", *Working Woman*, August, 1994, p. 26.

11. "2 Insurers Hit With Class Action Suit on DAC Charges", *National Underwriter*, February 27, 1995, p. 1.

12. "D.I. Business Must Adopt New Rules of Survival", *National Underwriter*, March 6, 1995, p. 44.

Part III:
THE MARKET

Part 3 is designed to familiarize you with the various markets for which disability income is suited and to provide you with ideas regarding how best to work in these markets — the average prospect, the professional, the business owner, and professional and business associations.

The products that were reviewed in Part 2 have multiple applications in the markets covered in Part 3. Many of the approaches that you can use to penetrate these areas are based on a specific type of product you can sell. A knowledge of these policies and how they can be used will be helpful to any successful marketing venture.

■ *Chapter 20*

THE TYPICAL PROSPECT

To be eligible for individual disability income coverage, an individual must be working full-time, defined as a minimum of 30 hours per week, and earning an income of at least $15,000 annually. While there are exceptions to these basic requirements (primarily in the payroll deduction market, see Chapter 26, The Payroll Deduction Sale) and more specific qualifications to be satisfied depending on the insurance carrier, the work and income parameters are common hurdles in qualifying a prospect for disability income insurance.

The middle income earner ($25-$75,000 per year) has been largely ignored by companies and agents over the last two years. Even amid a flurry of product changes, the opportunities to sell disability income have never been better or greater, thanks to a changing work force tempered by a prolonged recession and the down sizing of businesses. Security is an elusive expectation today. Individual disability income can provide a financial anchor.

THE WORK FORCE

Today's demographics for the U.S. labor force reflect the change in family status that has occurred over the past three decades. Increases in the number of working women, working single parents and dual income families have opened the doors to more qualified disability income prospects than ever before.

The *Statistical Abstract of the United States* puts the number of private wage and salary workers at more than 90 million in the country.[1] The great majority of these workers will meet the minimum requirement of a 30 hour work week and at least $15,000 of annual income.

The largest segment of the work force is made up of persons in the 35 to 44 age bracket, individuals who are excellent candidates for the disability income product. In this age group, the realities of physical vulnerability are more apparent, income level is likely to be at its highest to date, and the premium and the qualification requirements for disability income coverage are still reasonable.

Being single or a single parent presents special difficulties in the event of a disability. There is simply no one to fall back on; no safety net in the form of another adult working or sharing in the family responsibilities. When disability strikes, the absence of some form of economic assistance will cause an upheaval sure to be devastating to all affected.

There is no guarantee of financial security should disability occur for a spouse who is also in the work force. If one person makes $20,000 and the other $50,000, the loss of the *higher* wage earner will be a major setback for the family. Could the $20,000 income carry them? Moreover, the disabled individual may need care from the healthy spouse, cutting down on the possibility of working extra hours to make up for some of the financial loss. If there are children, virtually the entire burden of caring for the kids will fall on the working individual, too.

Some independent financial advisers caution married couples about buying disability income insurance. In his book *Wealth Without Risk*, Charles Givens says, "Being a two-income family is the best disability protection you can possibly have."[2] As illustrated in the example above, this is not true. Agents can certainly demonstrate the fallacy of this advice.

Generally, the two income family does not save one of the incomes. The best way to identify such a family's need is to perform the financial analysis featured in Chapter 4, The Basic Sales Presentation. Add up their expenses *first* and then see how the loss of either income affects the cash flow picture. It may well be that the agent will write a different benefit amount on each based on the variance in income level. But to ignore the threat of disability completely is not sound planning.

Single workers and married working couples are two types of substantial prospect nets to which an agent can deliver the basic disability income sales presentation. However, there is a growing number of another type of worker who has come of age in this era of technology.

THE CONTINGENT WORK FORCE

Big business has been in a cutback mode for some time. Economic analysts have called this movement *down sizing, right sizing* and *reengineering*. Whatever the label, it has resulted in a decreasing need for workers at the Fortune 500 level. News of another series of layoffs runs with regularity in the business section of our local newspapers — 5,000 workers are let go here, 250 there, another 1,500 somewhere else.[3]

Have you ever wondered where these people go? Unemployment figures have not changed that dramatically in the last five years, so these laid-off workers have had to find something to do other than file an unemployment claim.

The answer is in the creation of a new kind of worker — a contingent worker. Rather than find traditional employment, this person becomes self-employed. Examples of contingent workers include a sole proprietor, following that dream of being his own boss, a member of a temporary agency, working many varied assignments in the course of a few weeks, or an independent contractor, working with several different companies on a straight fee basis. An employer may be leasing this person's services for a finite period of time. Finally, the contingent worker may have decided to work two or three part-time jobs to make up for the one just lost.

These types of workers are called *contingent* since there is nothing permanent or necessarily secure about the position. In addition, many have found themselves in this work situation accidentally due to a lay-off. This is a viable and growing work force. The latest estimates place the number of workers in this category at about 37 million. With the evolution of technology and the ability to work at almost anything from a home equipped with a computer, fax machine and modem, the growth of this working group seems inevitable.

What does this mean for the disability income agent? More prospects. With these workers that have little or no safety net a disability can mean financial disaster and the loss of the clients they have managed to retain. Not all of these individuals may satisfy the traditional disability income eligibility requirements as to hours and income, but many will. An agent's approach should be to point out the financial exposure if an extended illness or injury should occur. Disability underwriters are adjusting their positions, somewhat, on individuals who work out of their homes. With continued increases in the number of contingent workers, the chances are good for further modification of the current underwriting guidelines.

WOMEN IN THE WORK FORCE

Women have emerged as a significant part of the work force. The traditions of the past where some occupations were seen as exclusively for males have long since given way to a new culture in which women work in all professions. Income levels may not have equalized yet, but time will undoubtedly remedy this inequity.

Working mothers represent a sizable number of prospects today. Two-thirds of women with children under age 18 are working today. Typically, an appeal to purchase disability income is based on the adverse economic impact on the *family*, not merely the individual, should a disability happen. Women are more naturally protective of their children and easily grasp the position their families would be in if they were unable to work.

Statistically, in most occupations, females become disabled with greater frequency than males.[4] Thus the importance of telling the disability story to the female worker and working mother is significant. While product rates have recently increased for women due to poor claims experience, the agent can still design a competitive plan at a reasonable premium.

The fastest growing occupations today are often represented by women, primarily in the health care field. As our population continues to age, these jobs will multiply, creating more work opportunities for women — and more disability income prospects.

THE AVERAGE PROSPECT

Baby boomers will be discussed in Chapter 21, The "New" Baby Boomer Market. However, outside of the boomer market, there is a wide variety of prospects to whom the agent can relate the story of disability. The professionals whom we have relied on for disability sales in the past have grown older now. This group, termed the "post-war cohort" by *American Demographics* magazine,[5] among others, is now between 49 and 66 years old. This group is conservative and concerned about financial security. Thus, these individuals are solid disability income prospects. They enjoy feeling comfortable, secure and familiar and have accumulated substantial assets.

Today, they are still potential disability income clients, particularly at the younger part of the spectrum. More than likely they represent excellent potential long term care prospects, with assets to protect and a financial vulnerability with regard to the need for care as they age.

The younger market[6], for different reasons, is also searching for stability and a comfort level. The members of this group are in their twenties, just starting in the work force. They are the children of divorce and day care who generally feel alienated towards more recent cultural standards. Their search for stability makes them excellent prospects for disability income coverage.

While people in their twenties may normally have difficulty relating to the chances of disability, it should be remembered that this group has grown up in the environment of AIDS, teen suicide and substance abuse. They've seen, first hand, the effects of a disability and may easily understand the sensitive position their finances are in given that they have a long exposure period between today's job and tomorrow's retirement.

Younger agents coming into the insurance business who will make their initial contacts with people their age should consider opening their insurance discussions with disability income. The reception may be more positive than one might normally expect.

YOUR CONTACTS

Because of the diminishing enthusiasm insurers are exhibiting towards the professional market, individuals in the lower paid white and gray collar occupations together with a portion of the blue collar market may be better prospects for the agent to approach about disability income coverage. Start with a neighbor, a friend, a relative. Disability income is as important to the registered nurse as it is to the physician. While the size of their incomes may differ, the effects of living without it are the same.

Review your checkbook and see who you pay bills to every month. Your neighbors, friends and relatives all have the same kind of debts and can relate to the checkbook approach covered in Chapter 4, The Basic Sales Presentation. Talking about disability income as an alternative financial source during a disability is a service you are performing for these prospects with whom you may have already established a relationship.

Make your prospect list and then start calling. If you have an existing file of clients to whom you have sold life insurance, major medical coverage, or an annuity, then it makes sense to contact these clients about protecting their most valuable asset. Try out your sales presentation on people you are comfortable with first and then move on to ones you do not know.

IT CAN HAPPEN TO ANYONE

The homeless have been in the news quite often over the past fifteen years. Many people view this segment of our society with less than a sympathetic eye, labeling the homeless as individuals who do not really want to help themselves.

In Orlando, the local newspaper ran an article about a single parent who worked as a bricklayer and suffered a cervical spine injury which prevented her from working. Income stopped and the inevitable occurred. Unable to pay the mortgage, she and her son were evicted from their home and have now joined the ranks of the homeless in the city. She had no disability income coverage.

The newspaper article went on to say, "Every year thousands, some of them well-established in the Orlando area, suddenly find themselves homeless after falling prey to some mishap — an injury, sickness, job layoff or divorce."[7]

In the 1990's, working individuals are more susceptible to financial trouble than ever before. Our national savings rate is at 4.1 percent of our incomes, not enough to provide the necessary dollars during an extended disability. The fine line between living comfortably in your own home and seeking compassion from a homeless shelter can be crossed in just a few months after an injury or illness. More and more, the safety net provided by our families is shredding as everyone experiences the same tight budget and lack of a secure existence. As long as one or both income earners in a family is working, circumstances, while not ideal, aren't bad. One disability can end all that.

Disability income is a stop-gap measure that can make the difference between being homebound or homeless. Every member of the working public, from physician to registered nurse to bricklayer is a candidate for some form of disability income coverage. They need to hear your sales presentation.

CHAPTER NOTES

1. Labor force information is from the *1993 Statistical Abstract of the United States*.

2. *Wealth Without Risk*, by Charles J. Givens, as reprinted by *Probe*, January 14, 1991.

3. "The Modular Corporation", *Fortune*, February 8, 1993, p. 106.

4. 1985 CIDA update of the 1964 Commissioner's Disability Table.

5. "The Power of Cohorts", *American Demographics*, December, 1994, p. 22.

6. "The Upbeat Generation", *Fortune*, July 13, 1992, p. 42.

7. "The Poor Walk a Thin Line Between Home, Homeless", *The Orlando Sentinel*, December 12, 1988, p. B-1.

■ *Chapter 21*

THE "NEW" BABY BOOMER MARKET

New? Baby boomers?

No, not this group. The boomers have been a market force for some time. It's their attitude that's new and it represents a change that has created an opportunity to tell the disability income story to (finally) empathetic ears. It's a sensibility based on the harsh economic realities that lay ahead.

This group, since birth in the years between 1946 and 1965, has enjoyed a relatively secure economic lifestyle. In contrast, today's future holds the need to save money for their children's education and their own retirement. Add in the possibility of aging parents who need financial assistance in their last years and the boomers are facing a potential nightmare!

I have a 46 year old associate that recently became a father for the third time. He pointed out to me that he'll still be in high school gyms at age 63. At that time, he'll begin putting his third child through college. His parents, still alive and well today, will be in their late 80's and possibly have used up their retirement assets. And, (in theory), he'll be two years away from his own retirement!

His situation is not unusual. Many boomers are facing a dollar crunch that will seriously affect lifestyles — *without* factoring in a disability. An extended illness or injury will likely end all possibility of continuing the comfortable existence to which they have become accustomed.

SPEND NOW, WORRY LATER

This was the generation who settled for nothing less than instant gratification. They wanted to enjoy times as they lived them. They saw their own parents working hard and postponing their rewards until later in life. That wasn't for them.

Want that Mustang convertible? All you have to do is borrow money and buy it. The four bedroom ranch house? No problem, we can get a mortgage! The second vacation home? A second mortgage! Credit cards were maximized to further enjoy this new technology *today*, not tomorrow, since it would be antiquated by then!

The Tax Reform Act of 1986 was the beginning of the end for this lifestyle. Cash tightened, jobs were lost, deductions cut back and difficult money problems, lying dormant for so long, began to surface. Debt of all kind was eating away at the family's financial foundation. Savings accounts were essentially non-existent.

At the same time, boomers were also experiencing something new: parenthood. Having kids was not a priority for the majority of boomers but when the desire for material objects wore thin and the biological clocks started winding down, starting a family became the latest boomer fad.

But delayed parenting comes with a price. Whereas the previous generation had some fifteen to twenty years, on average, to earn money on their own after the kids moved out, boomers won't be ushering their children out into the real world until they are in their mid to late 50's and older. For a group that has a dismal savings record to date, that leaves little time to pay off educational debt and start really socking it away for retirement.

The first members of the baby boom generation will turn 50 in 1996 and, according to *American Demographics* magazine, AARP will gain a prospective new member every 8 seconds for the next 18 years.[1] Reaching the age at which disability looms as an even larger possibility, the financially strained boomers are now ready to do all they can to plan for their family's monetary future.

FINANCIAL PLANNING

Is it too late for the boomers? Are their finances beyond hope?

This is a motivated group of individuals who have changed the traditional thinking on virtually every subject in America. If that inspiration were directed towards financial planning, there is every right to believe that they can accomplish whatever economic objectives they set.

The disability income approach is only one aspect of an overall financial plan that should be utilized with this group of prospects. This is important as the boomers represent the largest group of potential clients for disability income of any other worker unit. There are 82 million boomers between the ages of 30 and 50 today, all prime candidates for a disability product.

Boomers have traditionally embraced ideas that matter to them the most. Today's focus is on the children's future education. Their children represent the latest value to them and concern over the kids' future has taken precedence over their own. Boomers remain convinced that their children will not be able to progress without a college education.

College educations do not come cheap and counting on a scholarship is not the optimum way to plan for the tuition bill that will come due. Boomers know this. Their problem is they have not been good savers in the past and they have been playing fiscal catch-up as it is by paying off the enormous amount of debt they ran up in the 1980's.

The proper approach an agent should take is one of cause and effect. The agent must clearly help to solve the first problem — the need for educational funds — before demonstrating the one thing that could jeopardize this goal — disability. Thus, life insurance, mutual funds, or some other type of investment geared to safety and saving can be used to lay the financial groundwork that will ultimately put the children through school.

To do this it is important to review income, assets, and cash flow with the boomer prospect. The strategies that surface will be based on accomplishing several goals. Boomers have an affinity for plan specifics and a successful sales presentation should break down the details of the strategies needed to get started on the path to security. An example of a financial review sheet is shown in Figure 21.1.[2]

Figure 21.1

Find Your Net Worth		Check Your Cash Flow	
Assets	**Amounts**	**Income**	**Monthly Amount**
Checking Accounts	_____	Take Home Pay	_____
Savings Accounts	_____	Overtime	_____
Home or other Real Estate	_____	Bonuses	_____
Life Insurance Cash Value	_____	Social Security	_____
Annuities	_____	Interest Dividends	_____
Retirement Equity (pension, 401(k))	_____	Other Income	_____
Stocks (market value)	_____	**Total Cash Income**	_____
Bonds (market value)	_____		
Mutual Funds (market value)	_____	**Expenses**	_____
Other Investments (collectibles)	_____	Mortgage or Rent	_____
Automobile	_____	Credit Card Payments	_____
Household Appliances	_____	Alimony, Child Support	_____
and Furnishings	_____	Insurance (auto, home, health,	
Loans Owed to You	_____	medical and so on)	_____
Other Assets	_____	Food	_____
Total Assets	_____	Utilities (heat, phone, electricity and so on)	_____
		Child Care	_____
Liabilities	_____	Personal Care (clothing, hair,	
Current Bills	_____	cosmetics and so on)	_____
Auto Loans	_____	Medical Bills Not Paid by Insurance	_____
Credit Card Balances	_____	Education Expenses	_____
Mortgage Balance	_____	Recreation	_____
Student Loans	_____	Donations	_____
Other Debts	_____	Savings	_____
Total Liabilities	_____	Gifts	_____
		Miscellaneous	_____
Your Net Worth	_____	**Total Expenses**	_____
(Assets Minus Liabilities)	_____		
		Income Surplus or Deficit	
		(Income Minus Expenses)	_____

The questions to ask involve the boomers' greatest concerns. Ask and then listen. Find out what is important to each person or couple.

There may be some shared assistance in paying for college since second and third marriages are not uncommon amongst this generation. The agent should record their comments accurately so he will be able to match their concerns with the ideas recommended.

Figure 21.2 breaks down the possible concerns the boomer will likely have in addition to the threat of disability.

Figure 21.2

Needs:	College Funding
	Retirement
	Survivor Income (for spouse and children)
Threat:	Disability
	Premature Death
Financial Concerns:	Minimizing income taxes
	Keeping pace with inflation
	Emergency cash fund
	Income from investments, savings, trusts
	Sufficient savings for financial needs

Whether it's saving for a child's education, a parent's need for a home health aide, or their own retirement, an agent's recommendations must address each problem specifically. Disability is a peril that can jeopardize any financial plan. Disability will be one of the roadblocks to the completion of any planned savings program without regard to the end objective.

The agent should not be concerned with *what* the specific desire of the prospect is but with how to solve the financial needs of the boomer first and incorporate disability income as *part* of the solution.[3] Any extended illness or injury will hurt the chances of successful fulfillment of the strategies adopted to meet financial objectives.

Since most agents do not work exclusively as a disability income salesperson, this approach to the disability sale will be a natural. Much of the solution will come in the form of other products with which the agent has a higher comfort level. Disability income will be presented in conjunction with other plans involving life insurance, annuities, mutual funds, living trusts or some other financial vehicle. At this point the agent can use any ice-breaker method to convert from a life insurance sale (or other program) to a disability income presentation as outlined in Chapter 3, Breaking Into The Disability Income Market.

What is clear is the boomers are ready to talk about financial planning. In the past, it was regarded as a subject that could wait. Faced with several significant hurdles before they can even consider their own retirement, the boomers are ready to give disability income serious consideration. If not necessarily for themselves, then for their children.

CHAPTER NOTES

1. "The Power of Cohorts", *American Demographics*, December, 1994, p. 22.

2. This asset/liability/cash flow chart, is of my own making. It incorporates many of the ideas from several balance and income sheets I have reviewed over the years.

3. The financial needs dual approach idea is part of an overall financial planning strategy program called Financial Profiles.

program is loaded you can go forward by clicking on the →command button, backward by clicking on the ←command button, terminate the program by clicking on the "Exit" command button, or jump to a specific topic by clicking on the "Topic" command button (here you can also increase or decrease the speed of the mouse). If you do not have a mouse you can advance the program by pressing the Space Bar.

Speed of the demonstration. The demonstration program has been created using DEMOquick by AMT Corporation, Panama City, Florida. The program makes extensive use of .AVI simulation files. Because of this, with only 4 MB of memory you may find that the demonstration is somewhat slow to run (6 MB or more of memory will produce a better paced demonstration). To speed up the program do the following: (1) close all applications except the Program Manager, (2) increase the speed of the cursor once you have started the demonstration by clicking on the "Topic" command button and increasing the mouse speed, and (3) if you are connected to a network boot Windows in a stand-alone mode (not from the network). NOTE: The performance of *Field Guide Proposals*™ is quite satisfactory with the minimum 2 MB of memory.

Deleting the program from your hard drive. The installation program installs the program to the directory c:\fgp2demo, unless you specify a different location. To remove the program from your hard drive use the File Manager to delete the entire directory c:\fgp2demo (or other directory you specified during setup). In the Program Manager the icon can be deleted by first clicking on the icon and then clicking on File, then clicking on Delete. Follow the same procedure to remove the program group.

Field Guide Proposals™

(version 2.0)

DEMONSTRATION PROGRAM

Thank you for your interest in *Field Guide Proposals*™. The following instructions should help you with installing and viewing the demonstration program. If you have any questions please call the following numbers:

Technical Support   1-800-544-0626

Sales Information   1-800-543-0874

Minimum requirements for demonstration program. To install this demonstration program you must have a personal computer with an 80386 or higher processor, a minimum of 4 MB of memory, Microsoft Windows™ version 3.1 or higher, and 4.5 MB of hard disk space. A mouse is recommended. NOTE: *Field Guide Proposals*™ requires a personal computer with an 80286 or higher processor, a minimum of 2 MB of memory, Microsoft Windows™ version 3.1 or higher, and 5 MB of hard disk space.

To install the demonstration program. Place the install disk in Drive A. In the Program Manager, choose Run from the file menu. Type a:\setup and press Enter.

■ *Chapter 22*

THE PROFESSIONAL DISABILITY INCOME SALE

Oh, how the mighty have fallen!

For the last three or four decades, the high income earning professional risk was the optimum sale for both insurance agents and companies. Premiums were higher because the benefit amounts written were substantial. Lapse rates were low as these insureds understood the importance of having the product and, therefore, continued to pay their premiums faithfully. Claims experience was very favorable. After all, most claimants returned to their own profession and these high earners could certainly earn more by working than by collecting disability benefits.

However, in the last few years, the competition among companies and agents vying to write the professional risk intensified. Issue limits were increased dramatically — to the point where many carriers had no published limit for the high earning prospect. Product liberalizations and rate *decreases* went hand in hand; a contradiction destined to prove fateful for many insurance companies.[1]

There are a finite number of individuals earning $75-100,000 or more in this country. The battle to insure all of them with disability income coverage came at the expense of the more plentiful middle income market and caused many carriers to make some poor marketing and underwriting decisions in the desperate battle to capture this market segment. Those decisions are partially accountable for the deteriorating claims picture of this once coveted group of risks.

As alarming as this downturn in claims experience was, companies continued writing the professional risk. Guaranteed issue programs were offered carte blanche to a number of professional association members where no underwriting was done and large amounts of benefits were written. This end stage of denial finally snapped as 1994 capped a dreadful claims run with some of the worse losses ever in the professional market.

So what happened? How did this *perfect* market turn into noncancelable disability carriers' worst nightmare? More importantly, where do we as agents go from here? Is this market dead? Is it time to cut our losses and run? Stop selling disability income altogether? Concentrate on other market segments?

There has been a number of educated guesses as to why the professional market has created financial difficulties for insurance companies. Physicians and attorneys, in particular, have been singled out. The emergence of managed care as the health delivery system of today and the future has created some troublesome moments for doctors. The shifting of more financial risk to the physician, the decreasing emphasis on specialties, the micro-management of health care to save dollars has caused many practitioners around the country to look at their $40,000 (for example) per month disability income policy and think that early retirement may not sound too bad after all. Disillusionment with the rapid changes taking place and a belief that the practice of medicine is being altered dramatically from their original perception of it has driven some physicians away from their practices and into new fields, sometimes financed by a disability income *own occupation* claim.[2]

With attorneys, analysts seem to think it's a numbers game. The state of New Jersey has twice the number of lawyers as the entire country of Japan. When the United States helped to re-install Haiti's president, one veteran writer wryly observed that there were more lawyers in Washington, D.C. than Haiti had soldiers to defend its island. The dream that a prospective attorney tends to cling to while wading through the extra school years and a bar exam or two is of a high-paying, high-powered position of importance. The glut in the market has sizably reduced the high income opportunities and, in view of current tort reform proposals, the future of the legal field appears similar to the future of the medical field. In contrast, that disability income monthly benefit payable in large amounts, among other reasons, can be much more attractive.

Finally, even high income executives, who are desirable risks for companies due to their practical inability to utilize the *own occupation* definition, reached new levels of claims filed, primarily, for mental and nervous conditions and soft tissue injuries.

The claims do not have to reach a high level of volume to have an impact. One *own occupation* claim for a modest $15,000/month generates a $180,000 claims payout each year. If this claim lasts ten years, a company is looking at a nearly $2 million claim. If there is a cost of living rider attached, the claim increases to $3 million over a ten year period. How many of these claims will it take to throw an insurer's disability income portfolio into a tailspin?

The inevitable cutbacks have occurred. As discussed in the underwriting chapters, the retrenchment process has left agents without much room to maneuver in the personal disability income sale to the professional risk. Insurers have scaled back on what they will write (or participate in writing) for a professional risk to a maximum of $10-15,000/month. This maximum is well below what many insureds already carry as coverage and, essentially, means that adding on benefits using an individual policy is nearly impossible.[3] Professional risks in possession of a noncancelable disability income policy with a greater benefit amount should certainly be advised to hang on to it.

There will certainly be new arrivals on the professional market scene; fresh faces recently out of law school or a medical residency. As they will likely have no coverage, the personal disability income policy will still remain a high priority. An agent would do well to contact local medical and bar associations to see about organizing a generic financial planning seminar for students and interns. This is a great way to introduce yourself and the concept of disability income (and other insurance ideas) without being specific and you can follow up with the attendees at a later date to discuss their own personal situations. Several will likely come up to you at the conclusion of the session to talk about making appointment, especially if spouses are present at the seminar.

But the personal disability income area is not the only disability income need to be fulfilled in the professional market. Over the years, the number of agents selling disability income to professionals has increased, but the subsequent, important follow-up sales of business overhead expense (BOE) coverage and disability buy-sell (DBS) policies are often overlooked. Most physicians have gone into group practice now and the likelihood of the need for the DBS policy has heightened even though their personal expense responsibility may have dwindled. If one of these physicians is your client, you now have the opportunity to talk to one or more additional professionals within the same group.

The reduction in the amounts of personal disability income benefits that can be issued to these risks has not carried over much to either the BOE or DBS products. There is plenty of room to add coverage to existing plans or sell a brand new policy for a professional who has not yet considered these plans.

Many agents I've talked with are quite upset over the general state of affairs in the professional disability income market. Rather than dwell on the negatives, it seems more productive to review what can be done in this market, who to approach, how to approach a prospect, and what types of coverages can be sold to these prospects. There are companies who will write these individuals on a favorable basis and there are many opportunities for the agent willing to look for them. Agents will have to adjust to researching the market each time they prepare proposals for a professional prospect.

PROSPECTING

The first step in the prospecting process is to identify what companies will continue to write disability income and what they will offer in terms of product and monthly benefits, elimination periods and benefit periods. Many carriers have lowered the occupational classification for a number of professionals, thus increasing the premium and offering a less liberal approach to insuring the risk. Some classifications have been deleted entirely from the professional ranks. Dentists, for example, have been deleted from company lists for some time due to poor claims experience. Medical specialties like anesthesiology, surgery and emergency room physicians have been downgraded almost universally. Many companies will no longer write an *own occupation* definition of total disability on many physicians. The important task for an agent is to write down every occupation that is in the top occupation class and note the limits a company will write and any product restrictions that are different today than, say, a year ago. Figure 22.1 below gives an example of this type of research. This figure is not meant to be all inclusive or a reflection of any one company's issue limits or specific guidelines. It is intended to give agents an idea of the sort of list they should be composing for easy reference when prospecting for clients.[4]

Figure 22.1

Occupation	Personal	BOE	DBS	Changes, if any
Architect	$15,000	$30,000	$750,000	Own occ rider if earning more than $75,000 and apply for a 90 day EP
Attorney	10,000	30,000	750,000	No own occ rider
Engineer	15,000	30,000	750,000	Must hold RPE degree and earn $50,000
Physician	10,000	30,000	750,000	No own occ rider. Excluded physicians, surgeons, ER and anesthesiologist
Pharmacist	15,000	30,000	750,000	Own occ rider if earning more than $75,000 and apply for a 90 day EP
CPA	15,000	30,000	750,000	90 day EP only

Virtually every professional group has an association today. These organizations are formed for many reasons, among them the chance to have a voice in both the national and local political arenas and to have access to benefits. For professional associations, one of these benefits is disability income insurance.

The association can help in several ways, not the least of which is prospecting for potential new clients. (See Chapter 24, Target Marketing In Disability Income, for more specifics on the prospecting process.) The ability to approach a large number of similar prospects has great possibilities for the agent in search of a group of prospects to hear the disability story.

If an agent is going to work in the professional market, he must stay up on the trends of his client's specific industry by subscribing to their professional trade publications. The magazine business has exploded and there are numerous journals published for specific occupational categories. A trip to the library reference desk can identify a healthy list of potential reading material for the agent.

In addition, if the agent is an Internet or on-line service user, he will have access to a wide variety of information about the occupations. For many, this will be an easier way of obtaining this type of data.

Do not underestimate the value of this extra research! The information age has made one promise: things will change rapidly in all industries. Professional prospects and clients will appreciate the agent taking the time to know and understand something about the changes affecting them specifically. People, as we know, like talking about themselves and their work. Your interest (and an ability to converse intelligently about the subject matter) will set you apart from the average agent.

Go back and review your existing client base to identify who you may not have contacted about all *three* disability needs: personal, BOE and DBS. You may have written personal disability income but forgotten about the other, almost equally, important needs.

Once you've identified your prospects, what can you sell them?

THE PRODUCTS

Each need, whether it is the protection of personal assets, the ability to continue paying business expenses or the necessity of buying out a partner's business interest, is addressed by using separate disability income policies. Each need should be carefully reviewed even though the knowledge level of this group of prospects is relatively high with respect to disability income coverage. Still, you know more than they and it never hurts to stress the *need* repeatedly.

Personal Disability Coverage

There will be a new demand for agent creativity in working with veteran clients who have already purchased to maximum individual disability income benefit available in light of the decreased limits being offered today. Many of these professionals will have far more personal disability income coverage than will be available to them in the foreseeable future. If income levels continue to increase, the client will still have a need for increased coverage.

If there is more than one person in the practice (a greater probability today), then the agent should review group disability income coverage to add on top of the previously-owned personal disability income plan(s). Group disability, while undergoing some claims deterioration, has not been as significantly impacted as individual disability and even earned a profit a year ago. It may be the only way to offer your clients an increased amount of monthly disability benefits. (Chapter 29, Combining Group And Individual Disability Income, discusses the packaging of individual and group disability together.)

Another option is using a professional association's disability income program. This coverage used to be streamlined, offering few benefits and many restrictions, but the improvement in this type of disability income program has been positive and dramatic over the last several years. Like group LTD, association coverage may not be noncancelable, but may still offer a competitive definition of disability in conjunction with a reasonable premium, little or no underwriting qualifications and, more importantly, an outlet for the agent to add additional coverage for his client. This may not even be a commissionable sale, but the service effort will be worthwhile if you can continue working with your client.

If there is room to write more individual personal disability income coverage on a client, the agent will probably not have the same benefit program to offer as the in-force coverage already owned. *Own occupation* coverage may not be available, having yielded to the more economically sound *income replacement* approach. (See Chapter 14, Personal Disability Income Policies: What The Contractual Language Really Means). The client will have to be shown the new provisions and an explanation of the differences will be important in clinching the sale. Everyone's industry is changing in some fashion, so bringing a different product to the table will not likely surprise the potential insured.

It is unlikely that an agent will recommend replacing existing coverage at this point in time. Most of the in-force coverage was updated in the late 80's and early 90's and represents a more liberal, less costly and perhaps more expansive coverage with a shorter elimination period and a longer benefit period than can be purchased today. An agent should always review the coverage personally to render an opinion, but it may be more of an exercise in identifying all of the coverages currently held than a serious attempt to substitute new coverage in place of the old.

Business Overhead Expense (BOE)

This may be an area of need previously untouched by the agent and unknown to the client or prospect. If so, this is a brand new sale in the professional market and one of the best growth opportunities in the disability income arena today. BOE is a tax-deductible business policy (see Chapter 16, The Business Overhead Expense Policy) that reimburses an individual for business expenses incurred during a disability.

While the personal sale may be off-limits for updating, this program can be added to almost any professional client, since previous market penetration with this coverage is weak. Some clients may have more coverage than they need if they bought BOE in the past as a sole practitioner and now operate within a group practice. If this has happened, reduce the monthly benefit (or lump-sum) figure accordingly. Remember, this is a reimbursement contract and the insured will only collect the stipulated monthly benefit when there are covered expenses of this amount incurred during a claim month. Thus, letting a client keep the higher amount of coverage does not make the same sense as leaving the personal disability income benefit amount in place.

The company income statement (profit and loss figures) will detail business expenses. Compare those to the covered expenses listed in the company's underwriting guide to calculate the amount of coverage. Check this amount against the company's underwriting limits to see what type of disability income product can be offered.

BOE benefits have long been an excellent supplementary sale to the personal disability income contract. Since there may be little or no room to move to increase personal disability coverage, the BOE sale may become primary in the agent's mind when revisiting an existing client's program or approaching a new prospect.

Disability Buy-Sell (DBS)

With more professionals banding together into group practices to save expenses and share expertise, the number of buy-sell agreements being drafted has risen substantially. This creates a need for both life and disability income insurance to fund the liabilities created by these legal documents.

This trend should increase the potential for DBS policies (see Chapter 17, The Disability Buy-Sell Policy) and give agents another opportunity to sell disability income in the professional market. Most insurers will write up to five owners in a disability buy-sell arrangement. Since group practices are the growing trend, especially in the health care industry, BOE and DBS policies should enjoy their finest hours to date in the disability income marketplace.

CONCLUSION

Yes, the professional market has changed considerably within a short period of time. Indications have been pointing towards this shift for some time, but many of the alterations are just now being made.

The professional market remains a viable one for the disability income insurer and agent. You should not abandon the traditional manner of prospecting or turn away from the market entirely because of the changes. If you live in a small town, chances are you know all the professionals, and may even coach their kids in little league or in the various scouting organizations. Competition for the client may not be as fierce as in urban areas, but you will still need to have that extra "something" to be able to set yourself apart from other agents.

Today, that something can be the knowledge of what type of professional risk to write in the way of disability income coverage. It will be in knowing about your clients' line of work and the challenges and obstacles they face daily. It can be the willingness to look past the personal disability income need to solving other, equally important, needs that are more directly related to your clients' businesses.

Insurers still want these risks, although on different terms. Clients still need (and want) disability income protection. The agent is the link in bringing these two parties together. Never has the agent's role been more important than it is today in the professional market.

CHAPTER NOTES

1. "Disability Policies Shed Fixed Rates", a Jane Bryant Quinn "Staying Ahead" column as published in the *Daytona Beach News Journal*.

2. "Design DI Claim Provisions For Docs", *The National Underwriter*, March 6, 1995, p. 4.

3. "DI Writers Try To End The Bleeding", *Best's Review*, February, 1995, p. 56.

4. Information for Figure 22.1 did not come from any specific insurer and any resemblance to any company's limits and guidelines is purely coincidental. Nevertheless, these are the types of rules, limits and notes that can help map out a strategy for working in the professional market.

■ *Chapter 23*

THE SMALL BUSINESS MARKET

There have been many articles written that are directed at insurance agents encouraging them to evolve from the "kitchen table" personal sale to working in the daytime arena of the business market. Many of these publications strongly suggest that this is a market for the experienced agent who has "learned the ropes" in the personal insurance area and is now ready to move up to the more complex variables associated with small businesses.

Perhaps it was because I was raised in disability income, but the small business market was always the ideal place to *start* when looking for disability income prospects. Since the product itself opened the door, it seemed easier to start with a business sale and work towards the personal sale later. Consider the approaches that an agent has for disability income in the business market:

- asking if a company has established a sick pay plan (see Chapter 25, The Salary Continuation Plan Sale)

- asking if there is a provision in the buy-sell agreement for disability

- asking a physician if he would like to have the malpractice insurance payment waived during a disability

- asking small business owners if they would be interested in a tax deductible method of protecting their ability to pay business expenses during a disability

These are quick, easy questions to ask most business owners. The answers to these questions are the basis for the start of a short sales presentation that is usually rewarded with a sale for the agent and necessary protection for the insured.

WHO ARE THE PROSPECTS?

During the 1980's, while Fortune 500 companies trimmed their work forces in large numbers, the job growth in this country was attributable to the small business market. Small business growth continues into this decade and this is good news for the insurance agent. Small businesses often do not have the back-up in personnel and finances to keep the business going should a disability strike one of the principals. The disability story, then, is a critical one for these hard working business owners.

According to the Life Insurance Marketing and Research Association (LIMRA), seven out of ten businesses do not have any business disability protection. Further, the small business market has more financial strength than usually portrayed. For example, nearly 50 percent of small business owners hold investments, other than homes of $250,000 or more, while 25 percent of this group holds $500,000 or more in investments. In addition, 75 percent of small business owners carry debt of less than $100,000. Six in ten small business owners earn $50,000 or more annually and two in ten earn $100,000 or more. Clearly, this is the type of prospect who needs disability income coverage.[1]

In the early years of a small business, the expenses incurred each month are often greater than the income the principal owner(s) earn. This elevates the importance of the business overhead expense product. Moreover, business overhead expense is tax deductible to *any* firm whether it is a sole proprietorship, partnership or corporation. With almost 500,000 new companies forming each year, often with one or two principals, business disability protection is one of the first insurance packages the new company should purchase.

This chapter outlines a few methods that have proven successful in prospecting in this market.

BUSINESS OVERHEAD EXPENSE — THE CLASSIFIEDS

Reading the newspaper is a ritual in most homes across this country. For disability income prospects,[2] check the business classifieds for businesses for sale. The following illustrates a typical classified ad:

Restaurant — Italian. 10 years old. Distress sale, owner ill. $35,000 total. Principals only: (phone number).

Convenience Store Sub Shop. High traffic area, family type business. Price reduced to $115,000. Must sell immediately due to health. Titusville area. _____ Realtors (phone number)

Restaurant — with property and living quarters. Seats 60. Beer & wine. Must sell due to illness.

Contact _____ Business Brokers (phone number)

Breakfast/Lunch — Major office complex. Net $35,000. EZ to manage. Limited menu. Health forces sale.

_____ Business Brokers (phone number)

Sub Shop — Nice Mom and Pop operation. Good location and income, low hours. 5 days a week. Turn key operation. Health forces sale. Possible terms. (phone number) after five.

Daytona Beach — 8 unit Motel. Good income. Owner finance. Must sell due to illness.

_____ Realtor (phone number)

Illustrated here are six advertisements disclosing the forced sale of a business due to a disability. Circle these advertisements and call the phone numbers listed. Obtain the address of the business and drive out to see the location.

It is too late to help the disabled owner being forced to sell. However, many of these businesses are located next to other businesses. In the world of small business, your owner-neighbors are usually "up" on what's going on around them.

Call on these surrounding businesses and ask about the business that is up for sale. Almost always, the neighboring owner is very familiar with all of the details of the health problems that have sidelined his fellow business owner and whether any disability coverage existed. While talking with them, ask the neighboring business owners if they have any provision in the insurance coverage they own that pays for the expenses of the business until they recover from a disability. Or, if recovery is not possible, if they have at least sufficient coverage to stay out of debt while trying to sell the business.

Based on surveys, seven or eight owners out of ten will reply in the negative. This is seven or eight *motivated* prospects for the agent. They have just seen what it is like to endure an illness and try to keep a business concern going without disability income and business overhead expense protection.

Following the business overhead expense sale, the agent can then move on to other disability insurance needs in addition to life and pension discussions. The important task of securing the client is over.

Faithfully reviewing the classifieds can keep you in business overhead expense prospects forever.

WAIVER OF MALPRACTICE PREMIUM

Chapter 22, The Professional Disability Income Sale, addressed the sale of disability income coverage to the professional market. With the personal disability income product in a state of flux and issue limits for professionals severely curtailed, diverting attention to the business disability product line to solve additional needs which may not have been reviewed is recommended.

Most professionals, especially physicians, may be more eager to talk about their malpractice premium payment. Even with tort reform a current issue, the premiums for liability coverage are likely to remain high for those professionals, including physicians, in extreme exposure situations. An agent's approach that suggests discussion of this subject stands a reasonable chance of resulting in a scheduled interview.

The agent can begin by telephoning or by doing a brief direct mail letter that is followed up by a phone call to secure an appointment. The line of inquiry would be, "How would you like your malpractice premiums waived during a disability?"

When the prospect replies, "How can I do that?", the agent has an opportunity to tell the story of disability income.

Your answer should be, "If you were disabled, you certainly wouldn't drop your malpractice coverage just because you were sick or hurt. Yet the premium is fairly substantial and, without income, a difficult one to pay. Wouldn't you agree?"

It is highly unlikely that the physician (or other professional) will not agree.

This leads the agent to an explanation of business overhead expense (BOE) coverage. What should help seal the sale is that this coverage of the malpractice premium can be accomplished by a tax deductible premium payment for the business overhead expense policy. Remember, any business entity is eligible for the deduction.[3] The company does not have to be a C corporation.

This approach works virtually every time. Disability is the threat and the need to keep paying for the malpractice coverage compounds that threat.

The agent's solution to the problem can immediately put him into the physician market. His client base and sales will grow from there. With bad news looming for the professional on the personal disability income front, this approach is even more significant for both client and agent.

DOES YOUR BUY-SELL AGREEMENT INCLUDE A
DISABILITY PROVISION?

One last method of obtaining an appointment or interview that has a high success rate revolves around small closely held businesses and the buy-out plan among the owners or partners.

Any lawyer or accountant will advise a closely held business to implement a buy-sell arrangement, to determine how ownership will change hands, and how the transfer would be paid for. Yet, not all of these types of businesses have such an agreement in force. In a way, it is comparable to doing a *will* for the business. Since many individuals put off doing their own personal wills, it is not unexpected that business owners will also procrastinate on this important task.

For those that actually set up the agreement, the provision which applies to the premature death of an owner is often addressed first. Many agents present, and many owners purchase, life insurance to fund a buy-sell agreement in the event of an untimely death during the working years of one of the business owners.

Buy-sell agreements,[4] funded with life insurance, accomplish the following:

- provide cash when needed;

- avoid drain on working capital;

- preserve proper value in the business for the deceased's family; and

- keep the deceased's family from becoming a new owner in the firm.

If the individual does not die, but instead suffers a catastrophic disability, what has changed? Will the business want to continue to employ an owner who is permanently disabled and not contributing? Will the disabled owner and family eventually want to cash in their interests? Will the business be able to buy out a disabled owner if working capital and borrowing power are already impaired because of the disability?

Yet, most buy-sell (or buy-out) agreements do not have a clause providing for disability. Or, if one does exist in the contract, it is unlikely that any funding for the disability contingency has been provided.

Like the malpractice waiver approach, a phone call or letter to a firm, asking the specific question, "Does your buy-sell agreement have a disability provision in it?" should generate some interest. Almost always, the answer is, "I don't know." The agent's follow-up is to review the agreement in search of that contractual clause.

If the contact person at the business advises you that the company's attorney can review it for this feature, reply that you always work with the firm's attorney if additional wording or language is necessary. However, it does not hurt to point out that a simple review by you is free but the attorney will likely send a bill for his review.

This approach can get an agent in the door of many business organizations. Ask how the disability provision is to be funded. The same question may apply to the death contingency. If life insurance policies have been purchased, however, the agent can explain that disability policies exist for funding the disability buy out just as life insurance policies are purchased to cover the obligation to buy at death. If there is no funding for either, a quick review of the firm's financial obligations because of this agreement, is in order.

Chapter 17, The Disability Buy-Sell Policy, contains a sample prototype disability buy-sell agreement that can be given to the firm's attorney as a basis for drafting any additional language necessary.

CONCLUSION

The business market, especially small businesses, can be a lucrative field for the agent. Those agents who have spent some time in the professional market and are wondering where to turn next should consider these business disability products. Further, these approaches to initiate sales presentations are all field-tested and have been successful for those agents who use them faithfully. Be familiar with the business overhead and disability buy-sell products and benefit from these sales ideas.

CHAPTER NOTES

1. LIMRA study information is from assorted surveys released from 1989 to present by the Life Insurance Marketing and Research Association, Connecticut.

2. Classified advertisements are from a Sunday edition of the *The Orlando Sentinel*.

3. "Disability Sales Approaches and Tax Treatment", by Maurice Loridon, CLU, ChFC, RHU, *Insurance Sales*, July, 1988.

4. "The Importance of Buy-Sell Agreements", *Nation's Business*, March, 1995, p. 57-58.

■ *Chapter 24*

TARGET MARKETING IN DISABILITY INCOME

This is the age of specialization. A surgeon is rarely a general surgeon; he may be a thoracic surgeon, an orthopedic surgeon, or a cardiovascular surgeon. In the insurance industry, there are pension specialists, group insurance specialists, and disability income specialists.

As individuals more narrowly define their occupations, the number of associations bringing together specialists in the same field is increasing rapidly. The list of associations and professional organizations in the Central Florida phone book, for example, now occupies more than one page.

An association is formed for a common purpose: to receive goods and services at a reduced rate and to allow its members to market more effectively as a group rather than as individuals.

One of the sub-headings under "goods and services" is a benefits package for the members of the association. One of the products that is well-suited to being marketed through an association is disability income coverage.

TARGET MARKETING

With the substantial amount of changes going on in the disability income market, this is an excellent time to pull out your company's occupational classification menu. List the occupations that have been most effected by the recent insurance industry activity. Next to each profession, write the specific change such as dropped an occupational grade or improved a grade or no longer eligible for noncancelable policies, etc.

In so doing, remember that you do not have to list only the standard professions such as CPAs, attorneys, and physicians. Actually, you would do better to note other professions who most likely have not been approached about disability coverage. Do some research at your local library to identify the fastest growing occupations in your area, using, for example, your state's *Statistical Abstract*. Computer technicians and medical occupations such as home health nurses and physical therapists are examples of occupations that are among the fastest growing in the country.

Then check your local phone directory for your Chamber of Commerce to identify specific associations that match the data on the fastest-growing jobs. Now, you're ready to go to work.

STEP ONE: Select an association. Review your company's disability portfolio (as suggested) and identify its strengths and weaknesses. For the products that have the appropriate strength, match the occupations that will most likely purchase this plan. The associations do not have to include only professionals. The blue collar market offers some of the best opportunities for disability income sales.[1] Associations that represent this type of workers should not be ignored. (See Chapter 26, The Payroll Deduction Sale, for more information.) Figure 24.1 is an example of the research you will have conducted after completing this step.

Figure 24.1

Product Strengths:
still noncancelable
loss of earnings approach
new HIV-inclusive definition of total disability
wide assortment of benefit periods
Occupations:
physician's assistants
home health care personnel
physical therapists
nurse anesthetists

Review the list of occupations you have compiled to see if there is a specific one with which you identify. The list in Figure 24.1 is slanted towards emerging occupations in the medical fields, other than physicians. Your list may reflect occupations with which you are already familiar. For example, before entering the insurance business you may have been in pharmaceutical sales. Your focus, after identifying portfolio strength, will be to see how pharmacists are treated competitively since you're already familiar with approaching these individuals.

STEP TWO: Learn as much as you can about the occupation(s) you've chosen before setting up your marketing program. A major selling point on your behalf will not only be that you are a disability income specialist, but that you work primarily with this occupation and are aware of the distinct characteristics that are associated with the profession. Be familiar with peak periods, slow periods, actual duties, governmental responsibilities, state and national legislative happenings and other occupation-specific characteristics about which you may demonstrate insider knowledge.

If you know someone in this particular profession, ask him for some help. What type of disability benefits will have the most appeal? What type of disability can cause significant difficulties? What duties bring in the most earnings?

The more you know, the more likely a member of the association will be to identify with and select benefits through you.

STEP THREE: Find out if this association has a current disability income program and what the product definitions and benefits are for its members. Obtain a copy and use the disability income policy analysis form presented in Chapter 13, Comparing Personal Disability Income Policies, to compare it to your product. Some of the key areas to review in any policy analysis with association coverage are the renewal provision, the definition of total disability, the exact specifics of any residual disability, the policy elimination and benefit periods, and the maximum amount of coverage that may be written.

STEP FOUR: Before you contact the association, plan your marketing strategy. How are you going to approach the membership? Will you try to publish some program information in the association's newsletter with your name and phone number for contact purposes? Do you want to pursue the membership on a regional basis? Would the association executive prefer that the members call the association and then the association refer the call to you?

A good marketing plan will show:

- Prospecting: how and what method will interest members in a disability income plan?

- Contact of initial qualified leads: after a member responds to the program inquiry, how will you respond and what method will you use?

- Sales presentation: What brochure(s) will you use to present this program? (You will probably want to secure the association logo and imprint it on a specific product brochure.) Applications and billing arrangements should be decided upon in advance.

- Ongoing prospect generating program: make plans to stay in touch continually with the membership through mailings, seminars, a newsletter, a booth at an association meeting, an association magazine, continuing education sponsorship or a similar vehicle. The association should be convinced that this is not a "one-shot deal," but a program that will be serviced well from the outset.

STEP FIVE: Contact the association executive. The association executive who is in charge of benefits is not usually reticent about making appointments to discuss improving the organization's benefits program. It is, of course, easier if you can work through a member who can make an introduction for you, but it is not necessary.

When meeting with the association executive, present your general idea about introducing or improving upon what they are currently offering in the way of disability income benefits. Listen to the individual's feedback on ideas in order to judge how you should proceed.

Show your analysis of their current offering (or discuss the need for disability income if they have no program). Hand out a copy of your marketing plan and discuss each point, asking the executive for suggestions as to the most successful methods of reaching the membership.

It may also be possible, depending on your insurance company's compensation structure, to pay a small override to the association for each policy that's issued. This will provide further incentive for the association to promote you and your disability income program.

Doing your homework and understanding your disability income contract are the only essential ingredients to starting a target marketing program.

TWO SUCCESSFUL PROGRAMS

Two recent examples of target marketing programs that I have seen work are for physician's assistants and home health care agencies.

Physician's Assistants

While working with a family practitioner, an agent was stopped by a physician's assistant (P.A.) who had heard that the agent was working with the doctors and asked about disability income coverage. As the agent asked questions, she discovered that she was addressing the incoming president of the local physician's assistant association. She also found out that this is a growing field and, as the emphasis in the health care industry shifts more to a managed care style of health care service delivery, the importance of the physician's assistant in functioning as a first stop for check-ups is growing, bringing more and more physician's assistants into the field.

As it turns out, this local P.A. association had no individual disability income coverage that its members could purchase through their association. The national organization had not yet endorsed a specific disability income product for its membership, so they were left to their own devices to identify and obtain coverage.

The agent discussed the new definition of disability within the disability product offered by the company she represented. Specifically, she advised about the expanded wording for health care professionals concerning qualification for disability monthly benefits upon diagnosis of a HIV-positive condition. Noting that the time between diagnosis and loss of physical ability may be years, the agent explained that this represented a shift in attitude by disability income companies. Realizing that those in the medical professional would not be able to work in their occupations after such a diagnosis, resulting in economic loss, the agent stressed that the policies will begin paying immediately based on loss of earnings.

The physician's assistant was enthusiastic about this definition, noting that one of the association's members in another county had just been diagnosed with the disease and that the extra risk associated with her field is on the minds of many. She felt that many members would respond positively to buying coverage with this type of definition in it. The physician's assistant went on to schedule an appointment for the agent with the local association secretary and the program began to unfold, resulting in the approach letter shown in Figure 24.2 being sent to 250 physician's assistants. An article in the association's bimonthly newsletter was also arranged.

Figure 24.2

NEW DISABILITY DEFINITIONS!

Dear Physician's Assistant:

The _____ Life Insurance Company, a noted disability insurance carrier, has expanded its definition of total disability to include HIV-positive individuals in the medical profession as qualifying for monthly benefits upon *diagnosis*. This means that, although a physical loss of abilities may not yet be present, clearly an economic loss will result.

While all medical fields, including your specialty, have adapted precautionary measures, there is still an exposure to be covered. This excellent individual disability income policy does exactly that.

Other key provisions include:

* coverage based on loss of earnings

* flexible starting points for coverage and benefit periods

* non-cancelability, meaning **no** rate changes, **no** provision changes, **no** termination until age 65

* pays in addition to any other benefits you receive, including Social Security

* discounts as an association member

For rates and information on your own individual program, please call _____ at _____.

Sincerely,

Home Health Care Agencies

The home health care market, now one of the fastest growing industries in the United States, consisted of only a few agencies in 1980.

An agent I know helped do an audit on one home health care agency and handled the benefits portion of the audit. The idea that the employees of a home health care or home care agency, who were nurses, aides, physical therapists, speech therapists, and even physicians, could provide medical care at home instead of at the hospital struck him as an outstanding concept to be embraced by both the patient and the insurance company. The insurance company could save thousands of dollars in benefits for the care given at home rather than in the hospital or nursing home, and the patient would much prefer the care to be administered at home rather than stay longer in a medical facility.

The agent proceeded to educate himself on how a home health care or home care agency is established and operated through a somewhat complex system of Medicare (and other payors) reimbursement systems. He began to examine how agencies could establish benefit programs for employees and where the funds would come from to pay for these coverages.

One of the pieces of the benefit puzzle was disability income. The employees of these agencies see disability all the time when taking care of patients. Motivating the individual to buy is not an elaborate process.

In analyzing the agency operations, the agent saw a system called *Paid Days Off (PDOs)* as a way to further solidify his own position as the insider who puts benefits together to meet the agency's specific needs. This program paid its employees for leave based on illness, medical appointments, maternity leave, holidays, vacations, family bereavement, taking care of a sick child, and other needs. Employees accrued this leave based on years of service.

The agent structured disability income packages with elimination periods built around years of service so that an individual with a significant number of paid days off had the ability to select a longer elimination period such as 180 or 365 days (with a lower premium) to accommodate using the PDO first (payable at 100 percent of salary) during a disability, with the individual contract starting when the majority of these days were utilized.

The number of home health care and home care agencies has increased dramatically over the last fifteen years, totaling more than 15,000 across the country today. This agent secured the national endorsement for one of the associations which has over 6,000 agencies in its fold. That's a lot of prospects!

CONCLUSION

With target marketing, you can carve out a niche for yourself with any type of product. Disability income offers you an advantage since it is not always offered by associations, especially the smaller ones. Associations want to offer their members as much as possible in the way of benefits to tie them closer. Disability income, especially if the insurance company offers a discount or some form of guaranteed issue program for associations, is an outstanding product to include.

CHAPTER NOTES

1. "Blue Collar Sales To Shape Future DI", *The National Underwriter*, February 20, 1995, p. 10.

■ *Chapter 25*

THE SALARY CONTINUATION PLAN SALE

INTRODUCTION

Insurance and tax laws. The IRS and Congress see the insurance industry as a jackpot for finding dollars to help meet budget deficits. The insurance industry cries "foul" and points to the important protection it provides privately for the consumer as its defense. The result in recent years has been nearly annual passage of a tax law affecting some form of insurance, with more changes promised for the future.

In the midst of this apparent conflict are several long-standing regulations concerning disability income that provide tax incentives for the consumer to purchase this type of insurance protection. Portions of Sections 104, 105, 106 and 162 of the Internal Revenue Code address the formality of establishing a salary continuation plan to ensure maintenance of income payments to an employee who cannot work because of injury or sickness.

The concept behind this formality is simple. An employer can deduct (as a business expense) wages paid to an employee because this individual is providing a service in return. If this same employee is out sick, the service is no longer being performed; therefore amounts paid to that individual are not deductible as wages. However, if a written plan exists outlining exactly how a disabled employees's wages will continue to be paid and the covered employee has knowledge of it, the amounts continue to be deductible — a vital financial factor for the employer. If the employee is also a stockholder, a written plan is important in order to set forth terms that establish that the stockholder is being covered *as an employee*, and not as a stockholder.[1]

Complicated? Not at all, fortunately. This chapter will review the importance of establishing a salary continuation plan, the ease of doing so and a complete sales track for approaching prospects with this tax favored idea.

WHY ESTABLISH A SALARY CONTINUATION PLAN?

Visualize this situation: an employer who owns a small business with a large number of employees has never set up specific guidelines concerning payment of wages to individuals who miss work due to an injury or sickness. This employer is blessed with many loyal and hard-working employees and is more than willing to pay them when they are forced to take the occasional day off because of illness. During a routine IRS audit of the firm's books, one examiner discovers that employees who have been recorded as "out sick" still received their paychecks in the usual amount. This examiner asks to see the company's written sick pay plan, to which the employer replies, "We don't do anything that formal here; my people have never missed more than one day here or there and I won't dock their pay for that." The examiner now declares that in order to deduct payments made to an employee who is out sick or hurt it is necessary to have a sick-pay (or salary continuation) plan in writing. The final audit eliminates the deductibility of every payment made to an employee that year under those circumstances and the employer suddenly is confronted with an unexpected tax liability.

This potential financial catastrophe is easily avoided. The employer need only formalize, in writing, the sick pay program to avoid such problems and protect the tax deductible status for those payments. *Ad hoc* payments, that is payments made on a discretionary basis, are not deductible.

Establishing a formal salary continuation plan requires two tasks:

1.   Put the plan in writing in the form of a corporate resolution adopted by the Board of Directors if the employer is a corporation, or an agreement between partners if the employer is a partnership indicating who is covered, when payments start, and how long salary will be continued.

2.   Notify the individuals covered about the plan and its benefits.

The plan does not have to be filed with the Internal Revenue Service. But the plan must be established before a disability occurs to obtain the tax deduction for the payments.

One of the advantages of this tax-favored plan is that the employer is not faced with complicated nondiscrimination requirements. He can be selective. Employers frequently use criteria based on years of service, income levels, or job classification in defining who is to be covered under the plan, so that only employees they wish to cover will qualify.

For example, an employer wishes to provide a short period of salary continuation for all employees but also wants to single out the three loyal people who have worked for the firm for years. The plan could be outlined this way:

SALARY CONTINUATION PLAN FOR EMPLOYEES

Class I: All employees will receive up to seven days of salary continuation in a year if they are unable to work due to injury or sickness.

Class II: For those employees with ten or more years of service, salary payments will continue from the eighth day up to 60 months for any one injury or sickness.

This plan design covers everyone for a week of sick pay each year and the three long-term key people for as much as five years.

A sample corporate resolution is shown in Figure 25.1 for illustrative purposes.[2]

Figure 25.1

RESOLUTION OF BOARD OF DIRECTORS

_____ then discussed the concept of establishing a formal Sick Pay Plan for certain employees of the Corporation. After due discussion and upon motion duly made, seconded and unanimously approved, the following resolution was adopted:

WHEREAS, it is the desire of the Corporation to establish a Sick Pay Plan for certain employees by providing any such employee with an income during total disability and thereby providing any such employee with an added incentive to continue his services to the Corporation, and

WHEREAS, the Internal Revenue Code in Sections 105 and 106 and under the Treasury Regulations pertaining thereto, and Revenue Ruling 58-90, offers an excellent method for accomplishing this purpose,

BE IT RESOLVED, that a Sick Pay Plan for certain employees is hereby adopted in accordance with the aforesaid sections of the Internal Revenue Code, Treasury Regulations, and Revenue Ruling, subject to the terms of the forms exhibited in the meeting, attached to these minutes, and incorporated herein:

BE IT FURTHER RESOLVED, that the appropriate officers of the Corporation be, and they hereby are, authorized and directed to execute and deliver any and all endorsements, instruments or power of attorney, and do any other things that they deem necessary in order to establish said Sick Pay Plan.

Using the above example, all employees would receive a letter from the employer advising them of the adoption of a formal salary continuation plan and that they would be covered for a period not to exceed seven days. The three key employees would be told that their salaries would be continued for five years.

A sample letter informing the employees is provided in Figure 25.2.

Figure 25.2

> Dear _____:
>
> In consideration of the valuable services you have performed for the company, the Board of Directors has approved a salary continuation plan for you that will continue your wages during a limited period of absence from work due to personal injuries or sickness.
>
> Your program will continue your wages for up to seven days in a calendar year if you are unable to work due to injury or sickness.
>
> [In place of the previous sentence, the following would be used for the three key employees: Because you have more than ten years of service with the company, your program will continue your salary for up to 60 months if you are unable to work due to any one injury or sickness.]
>
> We thank you for your support and are proud to have you as part of our team!
>
> Sincerely,

FUNDING THE PLAN

Continuing an employee's pay for several sick days should not impose a financial burden on the employer. Normally, an employee's work load can be distributed among other employees if the disabled individual will be out only a few days. It is unlikely that a temporary replacement would be brought in (creating a situation where the employer has to pay two salaries for one job).

This cannot be said for the longer term continuation to the three key employees. While it is important to formalize a plan in writing, it is equally critical for the employer to understand the liability assumed in stating that salary continuation will be maintained for five years.

The cost, if a disability happens, would be as shown in Figure 25.3.

Figure 25.3

Monthly Salary	Disability lasts:				
	1 Yr.	2 Yrs.	3 Yrs.	4 Yrs.	5 Yrs.
$1,000	$12,000	$24,000	$36,000	$48,000	$60,000
2,000	24,000	48,000	72,000	96,000	120,000
3,000	36,000	72,000	108,000	144,000	180,000
4,000	48,000	96,000	144,000	192,000	240,000
5,000	60,000	120,000	180,000	240,000	300,000
6,000	72,000	144,000	216,000	288,000	360,000
7,000	84,000	168,000	252,000	336,000	420,000
8,000	96,000	192,000	288,000	384,000	480,000
9,000	108,000	216,000	324,000	432,000	540,000
10,000	120,000	240,000	360,000	480,000	600,000

If one of the key employees suffers a long term disability and actually is out for five years, the employer's financial liability is significant, ranging from $60,000 to $600,000 in the illustration in Figure 25.3. It is likely that the key employee is going to be earning a sizable salary and promise of continuation will be an expensive undertaking for the employer.

Compounding the employer's difficulty is the unknown timing of an injury or sickness. An employer could set up a salary continuation plan today and vow to begin a "sinking fund" in the event of a long term disability from which funds could be drawn at a later date. But, if a key employee is injured permanently in an auto-accident the next day, the employer's liability starts immediately. The luxury of building up a source of salary continuation funds may not be possible. In addition, the deduction of contributions to such a fund is severely limited by the tax law.[3]

The Financial Accounting Standards Board recently threw another curve at employers wishing to self-fund their salary continuation liabilities. In adopting final accounting rules for post-employment benefits (Financial Accounting Standard Number 112), employers are required to adopt accrual accounting for benefits provided to employees after termination of employment but prior to retirement. This includes employees on sick pay.

This means that employers will have to estimate any future disability benefits they expect to pay to a disabled employee, deduct the present value of those benefits from earnings in the financial reporting period when the disabling illness or injury *occurs* and carry the value of future benefit payments as a liability. This is accrual accounting where the expected cost is subtracted from the bottom line before those costs are actually incurred.

These new rules are in effect on a fiscal year basis beginning December 15, 1993. If an executive, in a long term self-funded disability plan, becomes seriously sick or injured, several years of disability payments will have to be charged to the current fiscal year's earnings. This not only affects the bottom line, but contributions to pension plans, 401(k) programs, stockholder dividends and others.

This may be a good reason to transfer the liability associated with a long term sick pay plan to a third party such as an insurance company. The cost of self-funding these programs has become too high.[4]

INSURANCE AS THE FUNDING VEHICLE

The solution to the funding problem is insurance. Insurance is usually purchased to have funds at hand during a catastrophe no matter when it happens. Here, the employer would purchase a policy on the three key employees for whom salary continuation has been extended for five years.

This transfers the bulk of the financial liability to the insurance company and erases the worry of a disability potentially jeopardizing the future of the business because it happened before the employer was adequately prepared financially for it.

The premium paid for the policies that will pay benefits to these key employees is allowed as a business deduction to the corporation owning the policies, an added extra for providing this protection. Partners and sole proprietors are not able to realize a business expense deduction for coverage on themselves, but they do benefit from the transfer of liability if the disability occurs.

The premium deduction for the coverage means that the benefit payments are taxable to the insured (just as wages or salary would be) when (and if) received. Because of the extra tax liability on the disabled employee, the insurance carrier generally allows a higher percentage of coverage to the insured to partially offset this tax expense. For example, the insured who buys coverage and pays for it with after tax dollars (and who would receive the disability payments income-tax free) can cover about 60 to 65 percent of gross earnings with the policy. (See Chapter 9, Financial Underwriting and Chapter 13, Comparing Personal Disability Income Policies, for a more detailed discussion of the percentage of income insured.) Coverage under a policy paid for by the employer who also takes a tax deduction is increased to 70 to 80 percent of gross earnings. The intent is that, after the taxation of benefits, the insured would be close to the desired 60 to 65 percent replacement of income.

THE DISABILITY SICK PAY EXCLUSION

Prior to 1984, even if a policy premium was deducted by the employer, the disabled employee could still exclude from taxation a portion of the benefits received under the policy. This exclusion was $100 per week ($5,200 a year) for individuals earning $15,000 or less. Above $15,000 of earnings, this exclusion was phased out on a dollar for dollar basis. Every dollar earned over $15,000 meant one less dollar of the $5,200 an individual could exclude. Thus, for those earning $20,200 of income and higher, the exclusion did not exist.

With the Social Security amendments of 1983, a new credit was established for individuals retired on total disability as follows: The maximum annual credit for an individual is 15 percent of the first $5,000 in benefits, or $750.00. This exclusion is phased out by reducing this $750 by one-half of gross income above $7,500 for an individual ($9,000 of adjusted gross earnings would effectively eliminate this credit.) If both members of a couple are disabled (and they file jointly), their exclusion is 15 percent of $7,500 of benefits, or $1,125, which is phased out by one-half of adjusted gross income jointly above $10,000 ($12,250 eliminates the exclusion.) A disabled person who is married and files separately receives 15 percent credit on $3,750 of benefits ($562.50) that is phased out by half for adjusted gross income above $5,000 ($6,125 ends this exclusion).

Social Security, Railroad Retirement or Veterans Administration benefits will also reduce this credit, virtually eliminating the credit entirely for a disabled employee.

CONTRIBUTING TO THE COST

Because of the relative unavailability of the credit, it is attractive for the employee to help pay for the policy premium. This would render the portion of coverage paid for by the employee income-tax free when received. Only the portion paid for by the employer would be taxed.

Example: Assume a policy with a monthly benefit of $2,000 has an annual cost of $780. Employer pays $390. Employee pays $390. If and when received, only one-half of the $2,000 benefit would be subject to taxation because the employer paid only one-half of the premium cost. Thus, $1,000 is received income tax free and $1,000 is subject to taxation.

Another alternative payment mode that allows the employer a full tax deduction and provides the employee with benefits completely tax free is explored in depth in Chapter 28, The Executive Bonus Sale.

BENEFITS PAYABLE TO EMPLOYER

It is recommended that when the employer purchases a policy on the employee, the employee be made the beneficiary of the proceeds. This gives the employer a deduction for the premium paid for the policy. If the employer is premium payer and beneficiary, the premium paid is not tax-deductible. Benefits, when received would be income tax free to the employer. The employer would then pay the amount out as salary continuation and take the deduction for those payments.

Since the frequency of disability is unknown, the employer usually likes to enjoy the tax deduction up front by making the employee the direct beneficiary of the weekly or monthly benefit.

THE SALARY CONTINUATION SALE

The next pages demonstrate the approach one can take with an employer in reviewing the importance of a salary continuation plan. For ease of discussion, I am calling salary continuation plans by one of the tax code sections: Section 105.

Prospecting

Q. Who are Section 105 prospects?

A. Almost any business that has employees — a corporation, a professional corporation, a store, small business, a large business; in fact, almost any firm.

Given this general description, accumulating a list of names to contact should not be difficult. Any corporation, professional corporation, partnership, or sole proprietorship will, after your sales presentation, want to adopt a Section 105 plan for its employees. (Sole proprietors, partners and certain S corporation shareholder-employees are not considered employees for purposes of the tax benefits of the plan.)

Here are some basic categories of prospects to help you compile your inventory of names.

1. Existing Clients. Some of your current policyowners may be employers in their own right whom you have not approached about a Section 105 plan for their key employees. Consult your files and begin work on people you already know before proceeding to other methods of prospecting.

2. Local Phone Directory. These prospects are certainly eligible candidates, although not as qualified as your existing clients. However, the yellow pages of your phone directory is a start toward developing a list of prospects. If you are target marketing a particular profession, this source will be very helpful.

3. Checkbook Prospecting. Another method of accumulating names can be done by checkbook prospecting. Simply ask yourself the question, "Who do I write checks to when I pay bills?" Your banker, auto dealer, and grocery store owner are familiar people who share the same need for a salary continuation plan. This will result in a list of prospects that may be more qualified for you and easier to call on since you have already established some form of contact with them.

4. Direct Mail. The idea of a Section 105 plan can be communicated easily in letter form and mailed to either qualified or non-qualified prospects. Direct mail can elevate non-qualified prospects to qualified ones simply by response to your letter, giving you a common ground on which to call and make an appointment. One such direct mail letter is reprinted in Figure 25.4.

Figure 25.4

Dear_____:

As a successful business owner, you may want to be aware of the financial disaster that recently befell another successful employer in Providence, Rhode Island.

One of the firm's employee-stockholders became disabled and was out of work six months. Out of concern for this employee's well-being, the business continued to pay him throughout this period of time. During a routine I.R.S. audit, these payments were determined to have been made *ad hoc*, that is, without any formal salary continuation plan in effect. The payments were considered not deductible as salary because the employee was not working. Furthermore, the amount of money paid was considered a dividend. The company then declared a dividend for the other 125 employees, who are also shareholders in the firm.

As you can imagine, this has put the business in a financial bind and recovery has been difficult. This can be avoided simply by establishing a Section 105 disability salary continuation program in writing before an employee is disabled.

If you would like more information on the installation of this tax favored plan, please return the enclosed card today. It could save your business from financial disaster.

Sincerely,

---

5. Advertise. You may also use the local newspaper to attract prospective candidates for a Section 105 plan. A suggested advertisement could read:

Business Owners

Do you have a qualified Sick
Pay Plan in your Company?
Free information is available.
Contact:

Now that you have written up an impressive list of names, you need to obtain an appointment to discuss your Section 105 idea with a prospect. Whether you are cold calling, phoning, responding to direct mail, or answering calls regarding your advertisement, your concern is to sell the *interview*, not the plan itself.

Obtaining the Interview

Your initial call to your prospect should be handled with one thought in mind: Get the interview. You cannot make a successful Section 105 sales presentation over the phone. Even on a cold call or a call to an existing client, try to set up another time to make your presentation. Your purpose is to keep it brief but put across a key sales feature of the Section 105 plan. Here are my suggested ways to "sell" the interview.

"Mr. _____, I have an idea that I would like to discuss with you that will take only a few moments of your time. This is an idea that could be worth thousands of dollars to you and your business and yet I promise you that if you like it, and wish to take advantage of it, it will not cost you one penny. This is a service that we provide to all of our business clients. Could I have just five minutes of your time to explain this idea to you?"

OR

"Mr. _____, my name is _____ with the _____ Company. My company asked me to contact you to make you aware, at no cost to you, of an employee benefit package that you could make available to your employees. Would tomorrow morning be convenient for you; or perhaps some time later in the day would be better?"

OR (referred lead)

"Mr. _____, my name is _____ with the _____ Company. Your good friend, Mr. _____, asked me to call and make an appointment to explain the tax deductible plan he has adopted, with the understanding that if you like it, fine — if not, there is no obligation."

These are three ways to get your message to the prospect, but, more importantly, to obtain an interview.

There are two common objections or questions that may arise during the course of your attempt to obtain this interview.

The first objection (or question) might be, "What plan is this?" Your answer should be, "This plan is adapted from Sections 104, 105, and 106 of the Internal Revenue Code pertaining to salary continuation for selected key employees. However, it is against my professional ethics to interrupt your day and business people have told me that they appreciate my calling for an appointment. Now, what would be the most convenient time for you later this week?" Detailed explanations about Section 105 on the phone will not do justice to this plan's importance. Remember, sell the interview. You can make your points at the interview.

The second objection is, "Is this insurance?" Your answer should be, "That's up to you, Mr. _____. It might, but it doesn't have to be. I'd just like you to be aware of this cost-saving, important plan." *Remember*, insurance is the answer to the problem of funding the plan, but the employer has the option to self-insure if he wishes.

These are the most common interruptions to your method of obtaining the interview, but as you can see, they can be easily answered.

Not every call will achieve the goal of securing an appointment. However, you can follow up those unsuccessful calls with a letter that may yet attract enough of the employer's interest to result in a call to you. A sample letter is illustrated in Figure 25.5

Figure 25.5

Dear Mr. Employer:

Thank you for speaking with me today about the Section 105 plan. My ideas concerning this plan are based on the questions:

Would you continue to pay one of your employees who became disabled and couldn't work? How much? How long? If you can answer these questions and have decided what you will do, have you communicated this to your employees? If you intend to take care of your key people and you have not formally advised them — you could be heading for trouble with the Internal Revenue Service.

Your payments to your disabled employee probably will be disallowed as a business expense to you—unless you install a formal Section 105 plan. This plan is easy to install and could save you thousands of dollars in back taxes, interest, penalties, etc.

I would appreciate the opportunity to meet you and discuss this plan. I'll be calling in a few days to see if we can choose a convenient time to get together.

Sincerely,

You may adapt this letter to any one of a number of situations merely by changing the opening and closing paragraphs to fit your circumstances. By doing this, you may use the letter as a preapproach, direct mail (with reply card), or a letter to existing clients — in short, an endless list of possibilities. The essential content of the letter will remain the same and the intent is (still) to secure the interview.

It is important to know whether or not the employer you are approaching is a sole proprietor, partner, or part or full owner of a corporation, because this will vary the Section 105 plan requirements. This should be the last question asked after you have obtained the interview; it is important and will save you time in preparing your presentation.

You have achieved your goal of obtaining the appointment and you can now tell your Section 105 story using the following approach.

The Sales Approach

You have now obtained the interview and are sitting in a corporate employer's office preparing to deliver your presentation. Remember, you have promised the employer that you would leave the decision to use insurance up to his discretion. The sales track that follows is set up to:

1. Point out the necessity of establishing a plan, and then,

2. Explain the difference between self-insuring and buying disability coverage from you.

You may adapt this sales track and its ideas to your own words and style, but the concept should stay intact regardless of the business to which you are making the presentation.

Presentation

• Mr. _____, I'm sure that if either you or any of your key people became disabled, you would certainly want to continue a portion of their income for some period of time, is that correct?

[Wait for an answer. It will generally be "yes." If not, you may reply.]

• "It's certainly up to you, Mr. _____, but have you informed your employees of your decision? I happen to have a letter you may wish to use." Show the employer the letter illustrated in Figure 25.6. This should change that "no" to "yes." If not, there is no further way to handle this immediate objection. In answer to the employer's insistence that salary will not be continued to *key* employees, ask, "Does that include you? Do you mean to say that you wouldn't continue your own salary during your disability?" Emphasize again the need for a plan to be in effect to do this. The employer will now, in all likelihood, let you continue your presentation.

Figure 25.6

Dear Employee:

This letter is intended to clarify our position with regard to any extended period of illness or injury you might suffer.

We have decided that it is in everyone's best interest if salary is not continued during any extended illness or injury. Very likely, a replacement would have to be hired and the money will need to be spent there to assure a continued work flow.

Sincerely,

• Mr. _____, have you adopted a tax deductible Section 105 plan that spells out your intention to continue your key employee's salary should he become disabled?"

[Wait for an answer — you can almost always assume "no."]

• You may be interested to know that a Section 105 plan must be established *before* a key employee is disabled. Otherwise, the amount you pay to an employee will not be a deductible business expense to you. Now please understand, the IRS is not saying you can't make payments without a plan ... they are only saying you can't *deduct*, as a business expense, any payment made to a disabled employee unless you have a section 105 plan in place first.

In your opinion, do you feel that having this plan is important to you and your business?

[Wait for answer. It should be "yes." If "no" you may wish to return to the consequences of having payments treated as made without a plan.]

- To avoid all of these potential IRS and/or key employee problems should they become disabled, you can establish a Section 105 plan for the key person(s) you wish to cover. There are really only two things to do to put this plan into effect before disability begins:

  1. Set forth the benefits in writing, and

  2. Communicate the plan to the key person(s) to be covered.

- Once you've performed this simple procedure, Mr. _____, payments made during a disability are a necessary business expense and are tax deductible to you and may be eligible for a sick pay tax credit to your employee.

  As I mentioned when I first talked to you, this idea is yours to use as you see fit, without any cost or obligation. In your opinion, do you believe that, by using this idea, you can save thousands of dollars by installing a plan that is tax deductible rather than making payments that are not?

  [Wait for answer. You should receive a "yes" answer here. If not, you should probe to find out exactly why the employer feels that way. If necessary, take the employer back through the steps of your presentation. There is one final attractive feature about sick pay plans that may persuade the employer if you are still receiving objections. As established, a formal sick pay plan could help cut an employer's employment tax liability. During a key employee's disability, the employer after six months of disability, does not have to pay Social Security taxes on that individual as long as a formal sick pay plan exists. This could save the employer thousands of dollars in the event of just one long term disability among the key employees. This important feature can have a significant impact as you answer your prospect's objections.]

- Mr. _____, now that you have agreed to the need for establishing a plan, I would be remiss if I didn't explain to you how to back up a bona fide Section 105 plan. There are only two ways you can do it.

  First, you can handle it yourself. Of course, this way creates some problems. You do have a liability. When disability occurs, you will be required to make income payments for as long as your plan calls for them — on each disability for each key person you've covered. Remember also, your payments will come at the worst possible time — when your key person is disabled and no longer productive. And budget ... since disability is not something you can adequately plan for, you have no idea when it might occur or how often. And, you must comply with ERISA regulations as well. Some of these requirements are:

A detailed description of the plan, the appointment of a fiduciary and administrator, bonding requirements, detailed claims procedure ...

There is a second alternative, Mr. _____. You can transfer all these potential burdens we've just discussed to us. Let my company bear the liability. By paying us a level premium (only a small percentage of the actual benefit payments you could be responsible for), we will pay the benefits on each disability for each key person. There will be no timing problem. We will be paying the disabled key person, leaving you free to find an active, productive replacement. You can budget for this plan since our premium is level each year. And our company will be the one to handle the compliance with ERISA regulations.

Now, Mr. Employer, these are the only two alternatives to adopt this plan; a plan that you've told me you think is absolutely necessary. In your opinion, which of these alternatives makes more sense?

Congratulations! You have just sold the concept of the Section 105 plan to the employer. There are now several fundamental details to be worked out such as:

1. Employees to be covered

2. Premium-payment arrangement

3. Product to be sold

4. Formal communication to employees covered

5. Plan formally put into writing

These details have already been discussed earlier in this chapter. Simply adapt them to the desires of your prospect.

CONCLUSION

Providing a salary continuation plan for employees is one method of both attracting and retaining key people. As part of a fringe benefit package, it would be difficult for an employee to leave this coverage behind to take employment at a firm that offers little in the way of salary continuation.

One difficulty that may arise in attempting to obtain insurance coverage on a key person is uninsurability. Disability coverage, as has been shown, is not easy to qualify for since many health questions need to be answered before the insurance carrier approves the policy. If unable to obtain coverage, one cannot easily write this individual out of the salary continuation plan. Criteria for who is covered can be altered and this may accomplish the elimination of the uninsurable person for long term coverage. If this is not adequately done, the best solution is to try to find some type of coverage that will help to offset the employer's liability.

This is an outstanding market to work, not only for its endless prospects but also for the relative ease in which a plan can be formally established. More importantly, it is a true necessity for the employer who can now make specific arrangements for salary continuation and save thousands of dollars in the process.

CHAPTER NOTES

1. "Solving Corporate Problems with Disability Income", by Thomas C. Eusebio, RHU, FLMI, *Insurance Sales*, September, 1988.

2. Resolution and sample letters are samples utilized by Sadler Disability Services, Inc.

3. "Companies Face New Accounting of Benefit Costs", *Wall Street Journal*, November 13, 1992, p. B-1.

4. "FAS 112 and Disability Benefits", *Disability Newsletter*, September, 1993, p. 3.

■ *Chapter 26*

THE PAYROLL DEDUCTION SALE

The salary continuation plan sales track outlined in the previous chapter is designed to generate a substantial amount of new premium sales for you. Long term sick pay is not a liability that companies should shoulder in full. Still, the most likely candidates for individual disability income products will be the key people singled-out by the employer through the available criteria. The sizable liability generated by this sick pay commitment can easily be transferred to the insurer.

But what about the rank and file employees? Many of the gray and blue collar workers in a large firm receive a small amount of sick pay for only a matter of days or (on occasion) weeks. What happens to a disabled person after the sick pay benefits expire?

Depending on the type of salary continuation plan established, you may have an excellent opportunity to talk with each of the firm's employees — on company time and on a very favorable basis. Each employee expects to be covered while out on disability unless told something to the contrary. Your assistance in communicating the employer's intent to the employees with regard to the length of sick pay is a valuable service.

Defining what sick pay is can put the employer in an awkward position initially. By limiting sick pay to a few days or, a couple of weeks, or maybe even a month or two, the employer is telling the employees that they are on their own after that period of time. This is where you come in. In your initial preparation, you've noted the length of time the employer has committed to paying sick pay for the average employee. You can now propose to the employer that while instructing employees as to the financial responsibility of the firm during an employee's disability, a representative of the insurance company (you as agent) will be discussing their options of continuing coverage on their own at a very reasonable cost once the company-provided benefits end.

That's all! You'll have the opportunity to meet with everyone, one on one, to discuss disability income benefits. This is the payroll deduction sale! The employer agrees to deduct the premium for disability income from the employee's payroll check. Not everyone will want to do something about the disability exposure, but many will — and you will achieve a large number of disability income sales.

TAKING THE EASY METHOD

The quickest way to limit employer liability is to recommend a short-term sick pay plan for all employees. For example, the employer agrees to provide sick pay coverage for 90 days and utilizes a short-term group disability income plan to fund this commitment. (See Chapter 29, Combining Group And Individual Disability, for more details about using group disability income.) This agreement to cover everyone for 90 days is in writing and all employees are notified that the business will cover them for injury or sickness during the first 90 days in accordance with the definitions and conditions as laid out in the group disability policy.

While restricting the amount of financial burden to the employer, the natural question asked is, "What happens after 90 days?"

You'll want to show the employee that he can take over the disability income responsibility when the company's sick pay plan reaches the 90 day point by purchasing a disability income policy with a 90 day elimination period (or if an insurer will allow, a 60 day elimination period since benefits are paid in arrears) on a payroll deduction basis.

This clearly transfers the accountability from the employer to the employee by noting that the first 90 days is courtesy of the employer and coverage beyond that can be purchased through the employer's payroll deduction system. Thus, as the agent, you have:

1. Established the sick pay plan which was necessary for the employer to deduct payments made to a disabled employee, and

2. Created a favorable atmosphere in which to pursue the sale of individual disability income insurance beyond the employer's liability.

Not a bad morning's work, is it?

HOW TO PROCEED

The first task at hand is to put the sick pay plan in writing and create a letter to be distributed to all employees informing them of the formalized program. This satisfies the necessary Internal Revenue Service requirements.

Convincing the employer that an employee meeting (or meetings) will be needed to introduce the plan (both the short-term group disability and the opportunity for additional coverage) should not be difficult. It will enable the employer to outline yet another fringe benefit provided by the firm.

Establishing the meeting date is easy. If the firm is a sizable one, there may be more than one meeting spread out over more than one day. Working in smaller groups is more advantageous in effectively communicating the program.

In addition to the meeting date, ask the employer to give you the opportunity to meet with every employee on site. There should be little difficulty in obtaining this permission as you are assisting the employer by helping to furnish benefits beyond the scope of the sick pay plan.

Preparing for meetings with individual employees is critical because the amount of time you may have during the actual sales interview may be limited. It is important to secure some basic employee information in advance of any meeting to enable you to prepare some policy information about benefits and premiums.

The essential information to obtain is:

- date of birth

- gender

- income

- occupation and duties

- date of employment (not always necessary unless there is a years of service requirement under the sick pay plan).

The payroll department of the firm usually has this information and it can often be obtained by generating a report from the computer. An example of this is reproduced in Figure 26.1.

Figure 26.1

BIRTHDAY	SEX	ANNUAL SAL	TITLE DESCRIPTION
11/13/02	M	3489.36	LIBRARY AIDE
07/12/20	F	2325.35	AIDE III ESE K/12
08/11/20	M	6596.43	BUS DRIVER - 9 MONTHS - HOURLY
09/10/20	F	1937.79	AIDE III REGULAR K/3
10/04/20	F	8260.73	AIDE III FOLLOW THRU
01/22/21	F	8504.00	BUS DRIVER - 9 MONTHS - HOURLY
02/27/21	M	7436.00	DIST. HOURLY CUSTODIAN
04/15/21	F	16944.00	REPRODUCTION CLERK
05/09/21	M	43340.00	SPECIALIST - NON INSTRUCTIONAL
06/14/21	F	8984.00	VO-TECH FOOD LAB
07/01/21	M	16080.00	SCHL CUSTODIANS FULL TIME II 12
08/17/21	M	5310.00	BUS DRIVER/STAND BY 9 MONTH
11/02/21	F	6479.00	LUNCHROOM WORKER - 189 DAYS
11/28/21	F	34546.00	TEACHER, TMH

Figure 26.1 (continued)

BIRTHDAY	SEX	ANNUAL SAL	TITLE DESCRIPTION
12/08/21	M	8004.00	BUS DRIVER - 9 MONTHS - HOURLY
03/03/22	M	4413.20	BUS DRIVER/STAND BY 9 MONTH
05/09/22	F	19860.00	SCHOOL SECRETARY - 12 MONTH
05/16/22	F	7493.00	LUNCHROOM WORKER - 189 DAYS
06/12/22	F	34546.00	TEACHER, THIRD GRADE
09/27/22	M	6433.00	BUS DRIVER - 9 MONTHS - HOURLY
09/30/22	F	5995.08	LUNCHROOM WORKER - 189 DAYS
09/30/22	M	31762.00	TEACHER, INDUSTRIAL EDUC - VOT
11/29/22	F	8503.83	BUS DRIVER - 9 MONTHS - HOURLY
12/28/22	M	5469.75	BUS DRIVER - 9 MONTHS - HOURLY
04/08/23	F	19860.00	CONFIDENTIAL SCHOOL SECRETARY
05/03/23	M	51750.00	PROGRAM DIRECTOR - NOW INSTR

If this type of report is not available, you can provide a census form which can elicit the same information as shown in Figure 26.2.

Figure 26.2

Employees: Last Name First	S E X	Birth Date Mo. Day Yr.	Employment Date Mo. Day Yr.	Salary or Earned Income	Salary Code 0-Annual 1-Monthly 2-Weekly 3-Hourly	Occ./ Duties

With this data, you can prepare some preliminary numbers as to how much monthly benefit can be purchased and at what price.

PAYROLL DEDUCTION SLOT

The employer need not be involved any further once the sick pay plan is introduced, other than to sign an agreement with the insurance carrier to deduct the premiums for the employees and remit them with a billing statement to the carrier.

Many of these types of agreements are similar from company to company and one is reproduced in Figure 26.3.[1]

Figure 26.3

**EMPLOYER'S ACCEPTANCE OF
PAYROLL DEDUCTION PLAN**

To: _____ Insurance Company

Until further advised, we are prepared to handle your Payroll Deduction Plan for the benefit of our employees. The Payroll Department has been instructed to honor Payroll Deduction Plan Authorizations signed by our employees on account of insurance issued to them by _____ Life Insurance Company and to forward to you monthly such premium as shall be included in your monthly billings to us and for which deductions have been made at the request of our employees.

The plan shall become effective only if it includes at least _____ lives insured.

It is our understanding that we may, upon reasonable notice to you and to our employees terminate this Payroll Deduction Plan as a whole, in which event the payment of premiums will be a matter of accounting directly between each such employee and _____ _____ Life Insurance Company. Also, that any employee may voluntarily discontinue the Payroll Deduction Plan upon advice that deduction shall no longer be made from his or her pay.

This plan may be terminated by _____ Life Insurance Company when fewer than five persons or less than $100 of monthly premium shall compose this Payroll Deduction Plan.

Name of Company or Firm _____

Address (Street and No.) _____

City _____ State _____

Signed by _____ Title _____

Soliciting Agent _____

This type of form should be signed in duplicate by the employer or an individual designated by the employer. One copy should be kept by the firm, the other forwarded to the insurance company.

In addition, payroll-type information also gives the insurance carrier some important information necessary to prepare billing statements as shown in Figure 26.4.

In advance of the employee meeting, try to arrange a schedule of individual appointments for yourself — four to six employees per hour to whom you will make your sales presentation. Agents differ on how this should be approached. I prefer the individual appointment to best explain your story and to help complete the application accurately and completely.

Figure 26.4

Company Number:	Company Name:		
Address	No. and Street:	City and State	
Zip Code:	Telephone No.:	Area Code:	
Person in charge of payroll deduction		Title:	
Total Number of Employees:	Circle How Employees are Paid: Monthly / Semi-Monthly / Bi-Weekly / Weekly		

If Employees are paid Monthly or Semi-Monthly, circle which day or days paid on: 1-2-3-4-5-6-7-8-9-10-11-12-13-14-15-16-17-18-19-20-21-22-23-24-25-26-27-28-29-30-31			

If Employees are paid Bi-Weekly or Weekly, circle which day paid on:	Date of Last Paid Day		
Sunday / Monday / Tuesday / Wednesday / Thursday / Friday / Saturday	Month	Date	Year

Head of Firm
Other Information:

Others like to have the application process completed as a group to save time. The sales presentation is given to everyone at one time, applications are completed and the individual time is spent covering only individual specifics about amount of coverage and price.

If you use my method of solicitation, you will need to streamline your disability needs presentation. I have a brochure I use which I can follow that presents the need, leaves a place to fill in specifics, and I can leave it with the employee after the application is completed. This brochure appears in Figure 26.5.[2]

Figure 26.5

> What if you became disabled and couldn't work for a long period of time? The facts show that 1 out of every 3 people over age 35 will be disabled for three months or longer before they reach age 65. The average long term disability lasts about 2 years.*
>
> What would happen to your paycheck? Could your family make the monthly rent or house payment? Could they pay for food?
>
> You might answer, I'll qualify for Social Security benefits. But are you aware of the definition of total disability required to be considered eligible? It requires that you be
>
> *(Continued)*

Figure 26.5

so severely disabled, mentally or physically, that you cannot perform any substantial gainful work and that the disability be expected to last a minimum of 12 months or to result in earlier death. Even if you do qualify, could your family live on the amount that would be available? And, what would you do for the 5 month (or longer) waiting period required before benefits are payable?

How long would your savings last if you had to use them for food, shelter and everyday expenses? One severe injury or sickness could wipe out these savings in short order.

This sales story asks a number of questions. Give the employee an opprotunity to answer them.

This presentation takes an average of three to five minutes to present.

INDIVIDUAL DISABILITY INCOME...
the solution.
CAN I AFFORD IT?

Disability income insurance can provide the dollars you need to buy the things most basic to life: food, clothing, shelter, utilities. You will have to make a decision as to whether you should buy this coverage. But, if you need an income to fulfill these basic needs, can you really afford not to buy this valuable protection?

*Source: 1980 revised Commissioner's Disability Table

A PROPOSAL FOR:

_____

❑ If you are totally disabled for _____ days, you
(30, 60, 90, 180, 365)

will receive a monthly benefit of $_____
payable for up to _____ years.
(1, 2, 5)

❑ If you return to work on a part-time basis, you will receive a monthly benefit of _____ for up to 3 months.

❑ If you suffer a catastrophic loss (loss of sight or speech or hearing or use of two limbs), the waiting period will be waived and $_____ in monthly benefits will be paid for up to _____ years.
(1, 2, 5)

Guaranteed Renewable To Age 65, Policy provisions cannot be changed by the Company. Premium rates can be changed on a class basis. Written notice of such change will be given 30 days prior to the policy anniversary

I often complete this section in advance based on the employee census data I receive. If a 30 day sick pay (50% of total) plan has been established, I use a 30 day elimination period and the longest benefit period available. I base monthly benefits on the insurance carrier's individual issue limit tables. I will find out during the presentation if other coverage exists.

This section takes two to three minutes to explain.

NOTE: This is a proposal from _____ Life Insurance Company. Specific wording of the actual policy benefits are detailed in the policy.

In addition to the application form, a payroll deduction authorization is necessary and requires the proposed insured's signature. This instructs the payroll department to make a deduction for a specific amount for the purpose of purchasing disability income coverage. A sample form is illustrated in Figure 26.6.

Figure 26.6

PAYROLL DEDUCTION AUTHORIZATION

Name of Employee	Monthly Payment
(Last)　　　　(First)　　　　(Middle)	
Name of Policyholder	Policy Number
Name of Firm or Employer	Group Number

You are hereby requested and authorized to deduct the monthly payments herein indicated from my salary and to transmit the amount deducted to the _____ Life Insurance Company. Such deductions shall cease: (1) upon termination of my employment, or (2) upon the date when the number of employees for whom life insurance premiums are so deducted and transmitted becomes less than the minimum required, or (3) upon the completion of the premium-paying period as provided in the policy, or (4) upon written notice by me of the cancellation of this order at any time, stating when thereafter such cancellation shall be effective.

It is understood and agreed that premiums may be paid in monthly installments only so long as such premiums are deducted from my salary and remitted by employer and that if such deductions cease as provided above, the premiums thereafter due will be paid direct to the _____ Life Insurance Company in the manner provided by this policy.

First Payment Due

X _____
　　　　　Signature of Employee

If the employee does not want the coverage, have the employee sign a waiver form. This is to protect both you and the employer from liability in the event the employee has a disability. A copy of one utilized for solicitation during a guaranteed issue program is shown in Figure 26.7.

Figure 26.7

(Print Name of Employee)

This acknowledges that a Disability program underwritten by _____ Life Insurance Company through a payroll deduction plan sponsored by my employer has been offered to me. After seriously considering the benefits, I have decided not to apply for coverage. I understand that this coverage is available to me on a guaranteed issue basis provided I am actively at work on the effective date of the plan. All that would have been necessary was the completion of an abbreviated application.

If at a later date, after declining this initial enrollment, my situation changes and I decide to apply for insurance, I understand that coverage will be based on satisfactory evidence of insurability. I further understand that if a health problem does exist, coverage could be permanently denied.

_____   _____
Signature   Date

After the forms are complete, you're ready for the next employee.

As you can see, the potential for sales is tremendous. You have a long list of qualified prospects who will need updating of coverage and who, perhaps, have additional insurance needs. It is at no cost to the employer; in fact, establishing a sick pay plan in writing saved money. Your expenses are low, being in one location and making sales presentations.

Check with your insurance carrier to see if it has a market for this type of solicitation. Be sure to identify the types of businesses that will *not* be eligible for this type of coverage. Using the sick pay plan approach outlined in Chapter 24, Target Marketing In Disability Income, you will be on your way to an outstanding sales year.

CHAPTER NOTES

1. The Employer's Acceptance Form in Figure 26.3 is provided by 20th Century Life Insurance Company.

2. See also "Guaranteed Issue Disability Through Payroll Deduction," by Robert G. Price, *Broker World*, March, 1986 and "Salary Deduction DI," by Paul G. Winn, CLU and Robert J. Broome, *Insurance Sales*, July, 1986.

■ *Chapter 27*

SECTION 125 — THE CAFETERIA PLAN MARKET

When the regulations governing Internal Revenue Code section 125 were finally proposed in 1984, it helped take the payroll deduction sale one step further.

The payroll deduction opportunity was created by the agent's offering to transfer the liability of a long term disability claim from the employer to the employee. By establishing a sick pay plan with finite limits, the employer was defining the financial obligation it was willing to assume in the event of an employee's disability.

Further, the employer introduced the agent to all the employees, advising them that this individual could potentially solve the remainder of their disability problem by giving them the chance to purchase disability income coverage on their own.

The only cost to the employer was the creation of a payroll deduction slot to accommodate any employee who purchased disability and wanted the premium for it withheld from his paycheck. The employees absorbed the premium cost of the disability income coverage.

EMPLOYER CONTRIBUTION

Prior to the availability of a Section 125 cafeteria plan, the agent could suggest, in discussions with the employer, that it contribute some amount toward any purchase by an employee of a disability income plan.

In the example in Chapter 26, The Payroll Deduction Sale, the employer defined sick pay as continuing the salary for 90 days for each employee. The agent was meeting with each employee to discuss how income would be replaced for disabilities extending beyond 90 days.

After further review, the employer agrees to contribute $15 a month for any employee who wishes to purchase disability income coverage. Obviously, this is incentive for the employee to buy the product and the agent should always work towards securing an employer contribution, no matter how small, toward the disability income purchase. Experience has shown that more employees buy when the employer is helping to pay, even if the amount is only a small percentage of the premium.

Thus, in addition to creating the sales opportunity, in most cases the agent must also create the availability of dollars to help purchase the protection.

CREATING MORE DOLLARS

Section 125 of the Internal Revenue Code permits certain types of expenditures for health coverages to be paid for with *before-tax* dollars if offered through a vehicle called a cafeteria or flexible benefit plan. The result of this is the answer to the problem of creating dollars to buy the disability income coverage available for sale.

How does it work? Let's look at a typical employee, age 35, who earns $2,000 a month and is covered under the company comprehensive major medical program. He has a family that he covers under the company medical plan at a cost to him of $150 per month.

His pay check looks like this[1]:

Gross Salary	$2,000.00
Income Tax (15%)	300.00
Social Security Tax (7.65%)	153.00
Adjusted Gross Salary	1,547.00
Dep. Med. Premium	150.00
Net Take Home Pay	1,397.00

Now, his company adopts a Section 125 flexible benefit cafeteria plan. This next illustration shows how the ability to pay for his dependent medical premium with before-tax dollars affects his take home pay.

	No Cafeteria Plan	Cafeteria Plan
Gross Salary	$2,000.00	$2,000.00
Wage Reduction for Cafeteria Plan	- 0 -	150.00
New Gross Salary	2,000.00	1,850.00
Income Tax (15%)	300.00	277.50
Soc. Sec. Tax (7.65%)	153.00	141.53
Adj. Gross Salary	1,547.00	1,430.97
Dep. Med. Premium	150.00	- 0 -
Net Take Home Pay	1,397.00	1,430.97

The result is a monthly saving of $33.97 that can be used to purchase a $1,300 a month disability income policy (using a Social Security offset rider) with a 90 day elimination period and a five year benefit period.

This means the insured will still take home $1,397 but also own a valuable disability income policy.

And the saving is not confined to the employee only. The employer, matching the Social Security contribution of the employee, now would contribute $141.53 instead of $153. Adopting a cafeteria plan not only does not cost the employer any money, it can save thousands of dollars depending upon the number of employees making cafeteria plan contributions.

How can you as the agent take advantage of the outstanding sales opportunity a cafeteria plan offers?

THE SECTION 125 MARKET

The cafeteria plan concept has been around officially since 1978, but until the 1984 clarifications to Internal Revenue Code Section 125 were issued, very little marketing of this exciting employee benefit approach was done. There have been some alterations made legislatively since 1984, but none have really diminished the value of this concept in saving money for both the employee *and the employer*. In times of rising benefit costs, any idea which can reduce expenditures for the employer is one that can put the agent in front of a benefits decision-maker.[2]

The essential thrust of Section 125 was to recognize that no two people are alike in so far as their personal employee benefit needs are concerned. Traditionally, the employer selected the coverages for the employees, paid for their portion of the benefits and offered them a payroll deduction slot for their dependent coverage cost if desired. It was of little consequence that these benefits went largely unappreciated by those who had the same type of coverage under a spouse's plan with another firm. As things progressed, the costs for coverage (usually medical) skyrocketed and employers bemoaned the fact that they were paying a substantial amount for benefits that held only moderate interest for some employees. Further, some employees grumbled that they would rather take home the money that was spent on them for benefits they did not either need or want.

Section 125 solves this dilemma by allowing an employer to offer a "menu" of benefit choices and a specified dollar amount the employees can spend on the benefits of *their* choosing. Further, any dollars spent by the employees (for dependent medical coverage or disability income, for example) over the specified amount are taken out of pay on a pre-tax, rather than an after-tax, basis. This reduces salaries which, in turn, reduces the federal income and FICA taxes the individual has to pay. In addition, the reduced wage base lowers the employer's obligations on FICA and federal unemployment contributions and, in some states, for workers compensation and state unemployment, creating a substantial savings.[3]

What employer would ignore a golden opportunity to save money on employee benefits and satisfy the employees' needs as well?

Depending on what the employer wishes to accomplish with the cafeteria plan, this program can include any or all of the following:

- cash
- AD & D
- dental insurance
- dependent care
- disability income (short and long-term)
- group term life
- medical insurance
- unreimbursed medical expenses
- 401(k) savings contributions

Any contributions made for these benefits (other than cash) can be paid for with before-tax dollars, an example of which was shown above. However, if disability income is bought with before-tax dollars under a cafeteria plan, the disability income benefit is taxable when, and if, it is paid.

WORKING IN THE SECTION 125 MARKET

The key to being successful in this market is having excellent administrative back-up in installing these plans. This is critical. Like a pension plan, a cafeteria plan involves a number of IRS requirements and discrimination tests. In addition, the agent needs to have someone who can work with an employer's payroll department in setting up the cafeteria plan contributions in the payroll system.

Some insurance carriers will administer Sections 125 plans if the agent sells that company's insurance products. There are many independent third party administrators who will work with any agent and insurance product. They will charge an administration fee, but this fee is easily absorbed by the employer and/or the employee with the tax savings created by implementation of the cafeteria plan.

PROSPECTING IN THIS MARKET

There are several desirable characteristics to watch for in your prospecting. You will do best with businesses that have:

- a concentration of full-time, permanent employees;

- employees paying for part of their health plan, or for the cost of dependent health coverage;

- some young parents, with children in day care; and

- stability of employment.

Sole proprietors, partnerships, S corporations and C corporations are all prospects. While the sole proprietor, partner or S corporation stockholder cannot personally participate in the Section 125 plan, their *employees* can, potentially helping the company bottom line.

Some of your lead-in questions can be:

"Mr. Corporate Officer, would you like to reduce your payroll taxes, without eliminating any employees? What if we could improve benefits for you and your employees at the same time, at no cost to your business?"

"Ms. Sole Proprietor, I can reduce your payroll taxes by 15 percent to 20 percent and offer your permanent employees a valuable retirement plan at no out-of-pocket cost to you or them. How soon can we get together to discuss this?"

"Partner A and Partner B, have you considered buying that buy-sell plan we discussed? What if I can find the dollars to pay for it by cutting your payroll taxes? We'll even throw in a no-cost retirement plan that your employees will love."

Cafeteria plan prospecting can lead you into not only disability income sales but also into financial planning for many of the owners and key employees of the firm. In addition, as in payroll deduction sales, you can work further with employees beyond the benefits available through the cafeteria plan.

While there is no set minimum number of employees that indicates the potential success of a cafeteria plan, the higher the number (at least 25 employees or more) the better. There are nondiscrimination requirements to be wary of since they involve the highly compensated individuals.

Preplanning Survey

To review whether the business consists of the elements that would make a cafeteria plan work in terms of tangible savings to the employer and the employee, the agent should distribute a preliminary worksheet for the employees to complete and return. Shown in Figure 27.1 is a sample of such a survey.

Figure 27.1

EMPLOYEE BENEFIT CENSUS

Please complete the following questions to the best of your knowledge and detach and return the form to your plan representative. The numbers you provide will be computed to arrive at a projection of your tax savings through participation in a CAFETERIA PLAN. You will then be given the opportunity to review the projection and discuss your personal situation with the plan representative so that you can determine which benefits best fit your individual needs.

Name _____ Marital Status _____

Company _____

Group Insurance   **Circle One**

1) Do you currently pay an insurance premium for
   one of the following through a payroll deduction?

   Health   Yes   No
   Life Insurance   Yes   No
   Disability Insurance   Yes   No

2) If so, approximately how much are these premiums $_____
   annually?

Medical Expenses

1) Do you or a member of your family incur medical
   expenses which are not reimbursed by insurance?   Yes   No

2) If so, approximately how much are these expenses $_____
   annually, including your insurance deductible?

3) Does your spouse pay for group health insurance   Yes   No
   premiums through his/her employer?

4) If so, approximately how much are these premiums $_____
   annually?

Dependent Care

1) If you are married, does your spouse work or   Yes   No   N/A
   attend school on a full-time basis?

2) If you are not married, do you have a child or   Yes   No   N/A
   other dependent living in your home?

3) If the answer to numbers 1 or 2 above is yes,   Yes   No
   do you have a child (under age 15) or other
   dependent (spouse or other family member) living
   in your home who requires day care or other
   similar expenses? (day care center, babysitter,
   and housekeeper)

4) If the answer to number 3 is yes, approximately $_____
   how much are these expenses annually?

A large number of employees with high current after-tax contributions for medical and dependent care expenses render a firm a prime candidate for substantial tax savings through Section 125.

Disability Income Coverage

The agent's objective, of course, is to sell disability income policies. This is a benefit that is not ordinarily part of existing employee benefit plans. Four out of five businesses have no disability income coverage and, of the ones that do, short term group disability is the predominant vehicle.

Disability income policies can be purchased by using the tax savings to both the employer and the employee that can come from adopting a cafeteria plan. The agent has created the funds needed to buy the product. One of the objections to adding disability income plans to the employee benefit package is the cost of the policies. This objection has now been answered and the products can be funded by the employer (using FICA savings), the employee (with income tax and FICA savings), or by a combination of the two.

The agent's presentation will differ from the payroll deduction sale in that an explanation of the cafeteria plan mechanics will be critical to the employee's overall understanding of the plan. Effective communication is important and as much information as can be released in simple, easy-to-read form prior to any employee meeting and individual appointment is vital to a successful enrollment.

This chapter is intended only to make the agent aware of the potential of the cafeteria plan sale and not to be a complete, how-to package for design and installation of this plan.

CONCLUSION

An employer would want to get involved in a flexible benefit cafeteria plan for the following reasons:

First, flexible benefit plans, regardless of their tax status, work to the advantage of employers and employees alike, in that they permit choice in the use of benefit dollars to meet more closely the needs of each individual employee.

Second, the IRS has provided rules and proposed regulations that contain considerable opportunities for flexibility and, in particular, options to support health cost management programs, while still retaining the tax advantages of traditional benefits.

Third, a plan sponsor's analysis of the worth of flexible benefits will prove to be extremely valuable in determining if benefits are cost effective and appropriate in this era of changing work force makeup.

Fourth, a flexible benefit plan will help a firm and its employees to develop an understanding of how employee benefit plans function.

There are numerous reasons to pursue this market as many are doing today. The Congress may or may not change the tax laws to eliminate, or lessen the value of, the cafeteria plan. The most recent effort was wrapped inside President Clinton's massive health care reform bill which, among other items, called for an elimination of the payment of health insurance premiums inside the Section 125 plan. This bill, of course, never made it to the floor vote. To date, heavy resistance from large employer-lobbyists has kept the hounds at bay.

From personal experience, I have found that disability income is the product that works best here. It can act as a conduit for a large number of sales for the agent as well as provide income protection for working employees that may not be secured otherwise.

CHAPTER NOTES

1. The Social Security percentages are 1995 figures.

2. "No Fuss, No Muss Markets for Disability Income Sales", *Life Association News*, February 15, 1992, p. 58.

3. "How Section 125 Works", *Health Insurance Matters*, November, 1994, p. 2.

∎ *Chapter 28*

THE EXECUTIVE BONUS SALES

An individual who personally owns a disability income policy pays the premium with after-tax dollars out of his own pocket. Benefits, if and when received, are free from federal income taxation.

Under salary continuation plans (see Chapter 25, The Salary Continuation Plan Sale), the business purchases the policy for the employee, who is the owner and beneficiary, and deducts the premium paid for the contract as a business expense. Benefits, if and when received by the employee, are taxed as ordinary income.

The best of these two methods can be blended to create an almost ideal arrangement of providing disability income coverage to key employees: the employer gets a tax deduction and the employee receives benefits federal income tax-free.

Sound too good to be true? Read on!

IRC SECTION 162

Section 162 of the Internal Revenue Code (IRC) allows deductions by a business for the ordinary and necessary expenses paid or incurred during the firm's tax year in the course of conducting business. One of these is reasonable compensation for employees, including salaries and bonuses.

An employer can deduct a bonus paid to any employee as long as it (plus other compensation) is reasonable payment for services performed. "Reasonable" does not have any specific number attached to it, but depends upon the facts and circumstances of each situation. If an individual earns $24,000 year, a $2,000 bonus will probably be considered reasonable while a $12,000 bonus might be considered excessive unless a substantial amount of evidence is available to justify it.[1]

DISABILITY INCOME PLANS

What does this have to do with purchasing disability income policies? Assume you have convinced an employer of the need for disability income coverage for the key employees of the firm. The business wants to purchase the coverage on these individuals and pay for (and deduct) the premiums. The employer is discouraged to hear that benefits will be taxed at the time the employee receives the claim dollars. It is still a valuable perk, but is there any way to avoid the back-end taxation of the policy proceeds?

The answer is to pay a bonus in the amount of the premium to each key employee and let him pay for his own coverage.

The plan would work as follows:

1. The bonus must be reasonable compensation to an employee. Usually, the cost of disability income coverage is a small percentage of actual gross pay, making it relatively easy to meet the "reasonableness" requirement for the employer to deduct the bonus under IRC Section 162. The business deducts the bonus as a business expense.

2. The amount of the bonus will be taxed to the employee as ordinary income each year that it is paid. However, it is easier to pay tax on a $1,500 annual bonus when working than to pay tax on $3,000 per month of benefits when unable to work due to injury or sickness. Note that $36,000 a year in taxable benefits would cost $10,080 in a 28 percent marginal tax bracket.

3. An amount equal to the tax on the bonus could be added to the bonus provided it stays within the framework of reasonable compensation for services performed. For $1,500 annual premium, the tax is $420 in a 28 percent marginal bracket.

4. The policy is then paid for by the employee with the bonus money — after-tax dollars so that any benefits received are exempt from federal income taxation.

Because the employer takes the deduction for the bonus paid, this plan is commonly called a "Section 162" plan.

ESTABLISHING A SECTION 162 PLAN

There are no specific requirements for a Section 162 Plan, but it is always wise to have a written plan that clearly defines the plan and the employees who will participate. Some of the same procedures involved in setting up a salary continuation plan can be followed here.

• The corporate minutes of the corporation can be written to reflect the fact that the business has adopted a Section 162 bonus arrangement and list the key employees to be covered by this program. (As a general rule, partners and sole proprietors cannot take the deduction for the bonus payment to themselves, thus the value of this type of funding is minimal for them; however, they can take the deduction for payment to their employees.)

- Notify the specific employee that he will receive a bonus to pay the premium for the policy.

- The employee can take the bonus annually and pay the premium directly to the insurance company or a payroll deduction arrangement can be made where the employer is billed and remits the premium that has been deducted from the employee's check.

The end result is a benefit to the key employees that can further tie them to the company and help the business avoid costly turnover in important positions. It is the only method available that allows the employer to take a deduction for the amount of premium and the employee to receive the benefits income tax-free.

CHAPTER NOTES

1. "The Tax Reform Act of 1986 and the Selling of Disability Income," Larry D. Patterson, *The Health Underwriter*, April, 1987.

■ *Chapter 29*

COMBINING GROUP AND INDIVIDUAL DISABILITY INCOME

The importance of blending group and individual disability income products together has been elevated significantly in the recent past. With the reduction in individual issue limits for the professional market, the utilization of group disability income will increase in importance.[1]

For the last several years, major disability insurers have been fine-tuning their marketing programs involving the installment of a combination program where both group and individual policies are sold together to achieve the greatest amount of coverage at the lowest possible cost. Group disability is written as a base and then individual policies, primarily for the higher income earners, are added.

Three factors are at work here:

1. the previously mentioned lower individual issue limits for professional risks which force the agent to use other products to achieve the total coverage objectives for the client;

2. the necessity to keep employee benefit costs as low as possible; and

3. the proliferation of multi-life practices, especially among professionals.

Let's examine these issues specifically.

Lower Issue Limits

Professional risks such as physicians and attorneys are used to being able to purchase large amounts of disability income benefits. In the past, it was not uncommon to see a $25,000/month policy being issued on a regular basis to cover personal needs. With limits effectively cut back to $15,000/ month by most companies, many professionals will need to look elsewhere for additional coverage and newer prospects will have to settle for far less in monthly benefits than their older colleagues. Conversely, the corporate executive has tackled the disability income issue in reverse. More than two million of the top five percent of the country's corporate wage earners have bought only group long term disability (LTD) to cover their disability needs. If one of these individuals leaves his present position for any reason, his disability insurance coverage stays behind.

In both of these instances, a combination group/individual sale would be beneficial. For the professional with a large amount of individual coverage and no further place to expand, group disability presents an alternative way to add monthly benefits at a fraction of the cost of an individual policy. The executive risk who may not have as much monthly benefit as he needs under his group LTD policy can add an individual policy which will provide both the necessary benefits and a program that can accompany the executive should he leave his place of employment.

Lowering Employee Benefit Costs

Consider this: Public and private employers spent $629 billion on non-cash benefits in 1992, nearly 18 percent of total compensation. Health care costs, which actually dropped overall for large employers in 1994, still represent a substantial portion of these expenditures.[2]

A disability income plan is important. Every employer needs to address the issue of salary continuation to ensure that the payments made to an employee while he is out with an injury or illness will be tax-deductible. (See Chapter 25, The Salary Continuation Plan Sale.) Once the plan parameters are set, the size of the liability assumed by the employer will dictate whether or not funding assistance should be sought through a disability income insurance program. Generally, this funding will be necessary for the higher wage earners who, as key employees, will warrant a sizable salary continuation amount.

Insuring this large payment can be handled cost efficiently by using a combination group/individual plan. A $10,000/month individual disability policy may run up to $6,000 per year in premium for a 50 year old, but a $4,000/month individual policy when written in conjunction with a $6,000 maximum monthly group LTD plan could cut the total premium in half or more. The more employees there are to cover, the more sense this combination approach makes.

Increased Number of Multi-Life Practices

The nature of group LTD is to cover several employees with one master policy. The preferred target market for disability income has been professionals. With overhead costs escalating, these professionals have begun banding together in group practices to share costs and revenue. In the health care field, this is especially true. Today 96 percent of all doctors are in a multi-life practice. This is today's reality. Costs to providers have increased as a result of the requirement that they check with an insurance company, third party administrator or the government before delivering medical care. Preferred provider networks and physician hospital organizations, under which a large group of doctors band together to provide medical services for an enrolled group of consumers, have formed to compete with health maintenance organizations. These factors and others have driven the sole practitioner into partnership with others.

Doctors are not the only ones affected. Eighty-six percent of all lawyers are in multi-life practices, too. This type of business entity is an attractive setting for a combination group/individual disability sale. Large amounts of coverage at a reasonable price are just what the doctor (and lawyer) ordered today.

The purpose of this chapter is to demonstrate how group and individual coverage can be packaged together to achieve the objectives of maximizing monthly benefit amounts while keeping the total cost down.[3] The chart in Figure 29.1 shows the advantages of using both group and individual plans on a combination basis.

Figure 29.1

Plan Advantages By Policy Type			
Feature	Individual DI	Group LTD	Combination Approach
Coverage for *all* employees	No	Yes	Yes
No medical underwriting	No	Yes	Yes
Affordable premiums	No	Yes	Yes
Individually-tailored programs for key employees	Yes	No	Yes
Portable coverage	Yes	No	Yes
Liberal, flexible policy definitions	Yes	No	Yes

INDIVIDUAL VS. GROUP

There are distinct differences in these two types of disability income protection. Each carries its own set of advantages. When blended together into a combination sale, these positive features are all utilized.[4] The combination approach offers cost savings, reduced underwriting, flexibility in plan design and some portability of coverage.

Individual policies have long set the standards in coverage excellence in the disability income market. Drawbacks of individual policies, however, include affordability, tight medical and financial underwriting and the inability to insure all types of employees. Low wage earners and those in hazardous occupations often slip through the cracks of the individual disability income market. And with poor claims experience, these problems have been magnified.

Group LTD has been around longer than its individual counterpart, but has suffered in comparison as the traditional methods of judging disability programs — policy definitions and large benefit amounts — almost exclusively favored the individual policy. However, the evolution of the group LTD market has seen improved definitions to accompany its unique advantages such as low costs and no underwriting.

Rather than debate the positives and negatives of each, the value of the combination approach is to accent the best features of each program. Higher amounts of coverage can be written in combination than on a stand-alone basis. The price of a combination plan is more than the group plan, but far less than the individual policy. Under the combination approach, there is some policy flexibility and an employee will always be able to take a portion of the coverage along when leaving the firm.

For the agent, the combination approach provides increased flexibility in working with small and large employer groups. In addition, it offers an alternative to assisting the professional client in the wake of the individual industry's recent retrenchment. The combination plan allows coverage on all employees while doing a better job of covering high income wage earners than either group or individual can accomplish alone.

Executives have long faced the problem of reverse discrimination with group LTD.[5] Due to maximum limits, the more an employee makes, the lower the percentage of coverage will be achieved. For example, a group LTD plan with a maximum coverage limit of 60 percent up to $5,000 will produce the following results:

Monthly Income Amount	Monthly Benefit	% Covered
$3,000	$1,800	60%
4,000	2,400	60%
7,000	4,200	60%
10,000	5,000	50%
12,000	5,000	41%
15,000	5,000	33%

The employee earning $15,000 a month has only a 33 percent coverage rate versus the $3,000 a month income earner who enjoys benefits at 60 percent of gross pay.

Adding an individual policy in combination with this group LTD plan can give the higher compensated employees a higher percentage of coverage. For example, the $15,000 a month wage earner can qualify for an additional $5-6,000 a month in individual benefits, bringing total coverage up to $10-11,000 or 66-73 percent of coverage. This coverage is higher than the coverage provided by a group policy alone. When using both coverages, the agent can propose a higher amount of benefit than could normally be written alone on either a group or individual basis.

There are several things to remember. First, the group LTD benefit has some offsets to it (such as Social Security and workers compensation) so this could reduce the LTD benefit amount. The individual plan, written in conjunction with the group, usually carries no such offsets. Second, the group LTD plan often covers only salary while the individual plan will include pension contributions, deferred compensation and other fringe benefits in arriving at a total compensation amount for determining issue limits. Third, if the agent uses the same insurance carrier for both the group and individual sales there may be extra advantages such as discounts off the individual policy and an increased amount of income percentage coverage, sometimes as high as 80 percent.

EXAMPLE

The following is an example of a proposal utilizing the combination approach to provide disability benefits to a large employer. The same company is underwriting both the individual and group policies. The group plan furnishes 66⅔ percent coverage of salary up to $10,000 a month in benefits with a 90 day elimination period. The individual plans carry a 90 day elimination period, a to-age-65 benefit period and are discounted based on the volume of more than 150 employees. A sampling of compensation, group coverage alone and the effects of adding individual policies to the mix are shown in the illustrations that follow in Figures 29.2, 29.3 and 29.4.

Figure 29.2

		Total Compensation			
Age	Base Salary	Deferred Compensation	Car Allowance	Bonus	Total Income
50	$248,572	$37,285	$7,200	$39,653	$332,710
50	124,693	12,469	4,800	16,388	158,350
48	138,083	13,808	4,800	21,018	177,409
43	144,676	14,467	4,800	17,216	181,159
38	151,410	15,141	4,800	19,913	191,264
47	78,108	-0-	-0-	3,905	82,013
42	86,008	-0-	-0-	10,751	96,759
38	82,889	-0-	-0-	4,144	87,033
49	65,100	-0-	-0-	3,255	68,355
45	75,112	-0-	-0-	1,126	76,238
44	79,785	-0-	-0-	3,989	83,774
38	75,541	-0-	-0-	3,777	79,318
35	64,932	-0-	-0-	1,298	66,230
30	73,393	-0-	-0-	3,669	77,062
30	70,975	-0-	-0-	2,129	73,104

Figure 29.3

		Group Disability Coverage	
Total Annual Income	Monthly Income	Monthly LTD Benefit	% of Income Covered
$332,710	$27,726	$10,000	36%
158,350	13,196	6,297	52%
177,709	14,809	7,671	52%
181,159	15,097	8,037	53%
191,264	15,938	8,411	53%
82,013	6,834	4,339	63%
96,759	8,063	4,778	59%
87,033	7,253	4,604	63%
68,355	5,696	3,616	63%
76,238	6,353	4,172	66%
83,774	6,981	4,432	63%
79,318	6,610	4,196	63%
66,320	5,526	3,607	65%
77,062	6,421	4,077	63%
73,104	6,092	3,943	65%

Figure 29.4

Monthly Income	Group LTD Benefit	Individual Benefit	Total Benefit	% of Income Covered
$27,726	$10,000	$10,400	$20,400	74%
13,196	6,927	3,630	10,557	80%
14,809	7,671	4,177	11,847	80%
15,097	8,037	4,041	12,077	80%
15,938	8,411	4,340	12,751	80%
6,834	4,339	1,129	5,468	80%
8,063	4,778	1,673	6,451	80%
7,253	4,604	1,198	5,802	80%
5,696	3,616	941	4,557	80%
6,353	4,172	910	5,083	80%
6,981	4,432	1,153	5,585	80%
6,610	4,196	1,092	5,288	80%
5,526	3,607	808	4,415	80%
6,421	4,077	1,060	5,137	80%

In Figure 29.2, you can see the various compensation levels this firm carries. The presence of deferred compensation, automobile allowance and a bonus indicates that the group LTD will not cover at the 66⅔ coverage level as stated in the master policy due to the exclusions of this kind of compensation in calculating the benefit level. These calculations are shown in Figure 29.3 and illustrate that the group LTD can provide a sizable amount of coverage even though it may not reach the level where an employee feels confident about maintaining his own standard of living.

Figure 29.4 gives you a complete look at the combination plan benefit levels, achieving, with one notable exception, an 80 percent coverage rate by using both programs. For a time, companies were also waiving their underwriting requirements on the individual policy, too, but this is not as prevalent today after several years of losses. However, this chart shows what can be accomplished by taking a combination approach to selling disability income.

You do not have to write the group and individual policies with the same insurance company. You can package products from two companies into one marketing effort and be successful. The employer will have two bills to track instead of one, a minor inconvenience in exchange for a high standard of coverage at the lowest cost.

The combination group/individual sale can be a ticket to multiple life sales of a substantial size.[6] There are a number of large companies who have not yet seen this type of program and would be excellent prospects for a sales call.

CHAPTER NOTES

1. "Group and Individual D.I. Work Better As A Team", *Life Association News*, October, 1994, p. 108.

2. "Employee Benefit Costs Continue to Rise", *Life Association News*, October, 1994.

3. "Group and Individual D.I. Work Better As A Team", *Life Association News*, October, 1994, p. 108.

4. "The Combo Plan", *Onward*, May, 1994, p. 12-13.

5. "Eliminate Reverse Discrimination in Group LTD", *Life Association News*, August, 1992, p. 129.

6. "Jump Start Your D.I. Sales With Managed Disability", *Life Association News*, July, 1994, p. 103.

GLOSSARY

A

ACCIDENT: Accidental bodily injury for which benefits under a disability policy are paid.

ACCIDENTAL DEATH & DISMEMBERMENT (AD&D): Coverage, often provided as an optional benefit to a disability policy, which pays scheduled amounts in the event of an accidental death or dismemberment.

ACQUIRED IMMUNE DEFICIENCY SYNDROME (AIDS): An illness which effectively shuts down an individual's immune systems. This disease has precipitated widespread blood testing for disability income cases with monthly benefits of $2,000 to $3,000 and higher.

ATTENDING PHYSICIAN STATEMENT: A report, completed by the proposed insured's (or, in a claim situation, the insured's) physician which documents current and prior health history used in the evaluation process of approving an application (or a claim).

AUTOMATIC INCREASE BENEFIT: A policy provision that increases, annually, the policy monthly benefit by either a stated percentage or the latest Consumer Price Index measure, without evidence of either medical or financial insurability.

AVOCATION: Extracurricular activity engaged in by the proposed insured, such as hang gliding or scuba diving, which may affect the insurability of the individual due to increased risk exposure.

B

BENEFIT PERIOD: The length of time for which disability income benefits will be payable under a policy. Examples: two years, to age 65.

BLOOD PROFILE: A test which is required on applications with benefit levels of $2,000 to $3,000 and above, that provides the underwriter with a number of clinical values.

BUSINESS OVERHEAD EXPENSE: A policy that reimburses the insured business owner, during a disability for covered business expenses that are incurred in the day to day operation of the business.

BUY-SELL (OR BUY-OUT): A policy that pays to a corporation or co-owner either a lump-sum or installment payments on disability of an insured owner to provide the necessary funds to buy-out the business interest of the disabled owner.

C

CAFETERIA PLAN: An employee benefit arrangement under Internal Revenue Code Section 125 whereby an individual is allowed to select among certain employee benefits on a pretax rather than an after-tax basis. Disability income is one of those employee benefits.

CARRY-OVER ACCOUNT: In a Business Overhead Expense policy, this is the fund that accumulates unused benefits to be paid out to the insured at a later date.

CASH SICKNESS BENEFITS: A state disability income program in New York, New Jersey, Rhode Island, California, and Hawaii that provides a small benefit on a short-term basis to help replace lost earnings for a worker's "off the job" disability.

CASH VALUE RIDER: Also called Equity Builder, this form of a return of premium begins building values equal to an ever-increasing percentage of premiums paid for a disability policy. Initial values usually appear in the third policy year and build to 100 percent at age 65, which can be returned to the insured at that time, less any claims.

CONDITIONALLY RENEWABLE: Under this policy provision, an insurance company agrees to renewal of a disability income policy providing the insured meets certain qualifications, such as full-time employment.

CONTINGENT WORKFORCE: This is a growing portion of the labor market consisting of part-time, temporary, and leased employees, the self-employed and independent contractors. These individuals do not conform to the traditional employer-employee relationship.

CONVERSION: A policy feature common in Business Overhead Expense and Disability Buy-Out plans that provides that the insured can convert to an individual disability policy if the need to have the business disability policy changes.

COST OF LIVING RIDER: An optional benefit that increases the disability benefit by a percentage or the latest Consumer Price Index measure.

COVERED EXPENSES: In a Business Overhead Expense policy, a listing of typical business expenses that are eligible to be reimbursed during an insured's disability. Examples: rent or mortgage payments, electricity, employee salaries.

CROSS-PURCHASE AGREEMENT: In a disability buy-sell situation, this arrangement has the owners themselves as owner and beneficiary of the policy proceeds. Generally used only where two owners are involved.

D

DISABILITY INCOME: A monthly benefit paid to an individual in the event of an accident or sickness, to help replace earnings lost.

E

ELECTROCARDIOGRAM (ECG, EKG): A test that measures the changes in electric potential produced by the contractions of the heart, it is often requested by underwriters for larger monthly benefit amounts or to acquire more medical information in evaluating an application for approval.

ELIMINATION PERIOD: The policy deductible, usually the number of days from the onset of disability for which no benefits are payable. Examples: 30 days, 180 days.

EMPLOYER-PAID LIMITS: A table used by an underwriter and agent to determine the maximum amount of monthly benefit the insured can purchase when the employer is paying the premium. This limit is higher than the ordinary issue limit because of the taxation on benefits when received due to the employer's deducting the premium paid as an ordinary business expense.

ENTITY PURCHASE AGREEMENT: In a disability buy-sell situation, this arrangement has the corporation as owner and beneficiary of the policy proceeds. Generally used in situations where there are more than two owners.

EXCLUSIONS: A policy provision that indicates what will not be covered under the disability income policy. Example: disability as a result of war or an act of war, declared or not.

EXCLUSION RIDER: Attached to and made a part of the policy, this document, which the insured generally must sign, indicates a condition(s) which is specifically not going to be covered under this insured's policy. Example: any disease or disorder of the lungs. This rider is placed as a result of the individual evaluation of the insured's history.

EXECUTIVE BONUS: A premium paying arrangement for which a deduction is allowable under Section 162 of the Internal Revenue Code for a salary bonus to the insured with which to pay the disability policy premium.

F

FIELD UNDERWRITING: The process by which an agent conducts his own evaluation of the prospect through the thorough completion of an application for insurance on the prospect's behalf.

FINANCIAL UNDERWRITING: A method of evaluating data relevant to earned income, unearned income, net worth, fringe benefits and other components of compensation to determine the proper amount of monthly benefit for which the insured qualifies.

FLEXIBLE BENEFITS: Under a Cafeteria Plan, these are the qualifying selected benefits that the insured may choose among on a pretax basis. Disability income is a qualifying flexible benefit.

G

GAINFUL WORK: As defined under Total Disability, any job for which the insured is reasonably qualified to perform in accordance with education, training and experience and usually with due regard to prior income.

GROSS EARNINGS: Income, before business expenses are deducted and taxes are applied.

GROUP LTD: Disability income coverage issued as a master policy to an employer to provide benefits for employees in the event of a long-term disability. The minimum Elimination Period is usually 90 days with benefits often paid until age 70.

GUARANTEE OF INSURABILITY: An optional benefit in a disability income policy that allows the insured future increases to the policy monthly benefit at specified dates, with a requirement of only financial (and not medical) insurability.

GUARANTEED RENEWABLE: Under this policy provision, insurance company agrees to renewal for as long as premiums are paid on a timely basis by the insured. Premiums may be increased with prior notification, but policy provisions can never be changed.

I

INSPECTION REPORT: Information, ordered by the underwriter, that provides a summary description of the insured's employment, health history, and habits as a result of a direct interview and interviews with business and personal associates.

INSTALLMENT OPTION: In a Disability Buy-Sell policy, this policy provision offers an alternative payout to a lump-sum settlement by having the insurance company pay out a level benefit in monthly installments for a specified period of time.

K

KEY PERSON POLICY: A product designed to reimburse the business for financial loss during the key person's disability until recovery or a suitable replacement can be found.

L

LIMITED CONDITION RIDERS: Utilized by the Underwriter, a modification of the full exclusion rider is meant to provide some coverage for a medical condition. Example: The policy will not cover any disease or disorder of the right shoulder for the first 90 days of disability.

LIVING BENEFIT RIDER: An optional benefit available to be added to life insurance policies that pays out a portion of the death proceeds in advance due to the insured's catastrophic and/or terminal illness.

LUMP-SUM PAYMENT: In a Disability Buy-Sell policy, benefits are usually payable in a lump-sum at the trigger (or effective) date of the buy-sell. The trigger date is the day following expiration of the Elimination Period.

M

MEDICAL UNDERWRITING: The process of evaluating a disability income application for approval by reviewing the potential insured's individual health history.

MINIMUM RESIDUAL BENEFIT: During the first six months of a claim under the Residual Disability provision, this benefit stipulates that the minimum benefit payable to the insured will be no less than 50 percent of the total disability benefit. Note: Some carriers are applying this benefit for longer than the first six months.

N

NET WORTH: The total nonbusiness related assets of an insured used in the financial evaluation of the disability insurance application. For disability buy-sell policies, net worth is that of the business and is used in the calculation of the value of the owner's interest.

NONCANCELABLE: The renewal provision of the policy which states that the insurance company cannot change any policy provisions or increase premiums after the policy has been issued as long as the insured makes timely payments of premium.

NONMEDICAL LIMITS: The amount of monthly benefit, at or under which no medical exam is routinely required to apply for disability income coverage. In these circumstances, the proposed insured would answer only the medical questions on the application.

O

OCCUPATION CLASS: A category of insured based on specific job duties that dictates the premium and contractual grouping under which the insured would be placed.

OPTIONAL BENEFIT: Coverage in addition to the basic policy, this extra protection assists in the individual design of a disability income program to meet the insured's needs. Examples: Cost of Living Rider, Guarantee of Insurability benefit.

OUTLINE OF COVERAGE: A simplified benefit summary of a disability policy provided by the insurance company and required by law in many states to be delivered to the individual insured either at the time of the sales presentation or policy delivery.

OVERHEAD MAXIMUM: The total possible benefit payout under the Business Overhead Expense policy, this amount is calculated by multiplying the monthly benefit by the number of months in the selected benefit period. Example: $3,000 monthly benefit, 18 month benefit period would provide an Overhead Maximum of $54,000 ($3,000 x 18).

OWN OCCUPATION: A term that defines the most liberal wording of the total disability contractual provision, it applies only one test, that of the ability to perform the duties of one's own occupation, in determining disability for purposes of paying a policy benefit.

P

PARTIAL DISABILITY: A short-term version of residual disability benefits, this policy provision, which also could be available as a rider, pays a specified percentage of the total disability benefit (usually 50 percent) if the insured is unable to perform one or more of the duties of his own occupation.

PERSONNEL REPLACEMENT EXPENSE: An optional benefit that may be added to a Key Person Disability policy, this rider reimburses the business for the costs of searching for and hiring a replacement for the disabled key person.

PHYSICIAN CARE REQUIREMENT: This policy provision states one of the eligibility requirements for disability benefits, requiring that the insured be under the regular care and attendance of a physician. Many companies waive this requirement if it can be shown that future treatment would be of no benefit to the insured.

POLICY SCHEDULE PAGE: Found in the early pages of a disability income policy, this sheet details all the specific individual policy data such as name, policy number, monthly benefit, and premium.

PREDISABILITY EARNINGS: A policy provision under the Residual Disability Benefit, it defines what constitutes prior income for purposes of calculating the Residual Benefit. Example: the average monthly earnings for the 12 consecutive months immediately prior to disability.

PREEXISTING CONDITION: This policy provision is intended to define certain illnesses or injuries that occurred or manifested themselves prior to the policy effective date for which benefits are usually not payable. Generally, conditions disclosed on the application are not considered to be preexisting.

PREMIUM MODE: The particular method of premium payment selected by the insured. The policy can be paid for annually, semi-annually, quarterly or monthly. The choice elected will be indicated in the policy schedule page.

PRESUMPTIVE TOTAL DISABILITY: A policy provision that waives the normal total disability eligibility requirements in the event of a catastrophic-type disability such as the loss of sight, hearing, speech or use of two limbs.

PROGRAMMING: The process of determining how much disability income coverage an individual needs and the sources that will make up this coverage.

Q

QUALIFICATION PERIOD: Under the Residual Disability Benefit, the number of days at the start of a disability that the insured must be totally disabled before becoming eligible for Residual Benefits.

R

RATING: An underwriting decision to approve disability income coverage but at a higher than normal premium due to an increased risk which is usually associated with adverse medical history. An extra premium of anywhere from 15 to 100 percent or more can be applied.

RECURRENT DISABILITY: A policy provision that defines when an injury or illness will be considered continuous if there has been a recovery for a short period (usually six months) and then a recurrence of the same or related cause. A condition considered recurrent will not necessitate new satisfaction of the Elimination Period.

REHABILITATION: A policy provision under which the insurance company agrees to assist in the expenses associated with a rehabilitation program that the insured enters following disability.

RELATION OF EARNINGS TO INSURANCE: A policy provision stipulating that money received from all income sources, including insurance, will not be greater than 100% of the insured's prior earnings.

RENEWABILITY: The policy provision that details the conditions upon which the insurance company agrees to continue to insure the disability income policy. Examples: Noncancelable, Guaranteed Renewable, Conditionally Renewable.

RESIDUAL DISABILITY BENEFIT: A policy provision or an optional benefit that promises to pay the insured a portion of the total disability benefit after a return to work based on the percentage of income loss suffered due to the disability. This benefit is usually effective until insured's age 65.

RETURN OF PREMIUM: This optional benefit provides a refund of a specified percentage of policy premium at specified dates less any claims that have been paid during the specified time period. Example: 80 percent return of premium less claims paid after the policy has been in force for 10 years.

RETURN TO WORK BENEFIT: A provision under the Residual Disability benefit that waives some of the eligibility requirements for Residual Benefits and bases the claim upon earnings loss only. This provision operates for a short specific period of time, usually 3 to 6 months.

S

SALARY CONTINUATION PLAN: A program, also called a Section 105 plan, under which the employer makes deductible wage payments, in part or in full, to an individual unable to work due to illness or injury.

SHORT-TERM DISABILITY: Usually associated with group insurance, this program pays a monthly benefit for total disability after a minimum Elimination Period for up to 13, 26, 39 or 52 weeks.

SICKNESS: A policy provision defined as illness or disease which first makes itself known to the insured following the policy effective date. Sickness covers both physical and mental illness unless otherwise specified.

SIGNIFICANT EARNINGS LOSS: A provision under the Residual Disability Benefit that promises the full total disability benefit if the insured is back to work and suffers a substantial loss of income, usually 75 to 80 percent.

SOCIAL SECURITY: A federal program which provides benefits to all working Americans in the form of disability, retirement or survivor benefits. Disability is strictly and narrowly defined and benefits begin in the sixth month of a disability that has an expectation of lasting at least 12 months or will result in the individual's death.

SOCIAL SECURITY OFFSET RIDER: An optional benefit that co-ordinates benefits with any benefits received through Social Security disability (and, often, other public programs) to avoid either underinsurance or overinsurance.

STEP-RATE: A method of premium payment under which the insured pays for the disability income policy with a low initial price that increases after a set number of years (usually five) to a higher, level premium.

SUBSTITUTE SALARY EXPENSE: An optional benefit available under the Business Overhead Expense policy, it reimburses the insured for expenses incurred in paying a replacement during the insured's disability.

SUPPLEMENTAL HEALTH STATEMENT: A form that is a direct communication from the underwriter to the proposed insured that asks for more details about a specified medical condition(s).

SUPPLEMENTAL MONTHLY BENEFIT: This part of the programming puzzle in calculating disability income coverage for the insured is a non-offset payment of additional monthly benefits for the insured with the same Elimination Period as the base policy and a short benefit period of six to twelve months. Also called Additional Monthly Benefit, among other terms.

T

TOTAL DISABILITY: Often the key policy provision in the disability income policy, this feature defines the eligibility requirements necessary for an individual to qualify for full monthly benefits. Usually, an inability to perform work is the major requirement in the definition.

TRANSPLANT DONOR BENEFIT: A policy provision that considers an insured to be disabled under the sickness provision if donating a body organ.

TREATMENT OF INJURIES: A policy provision or an optional benefit, it pays for expenses incurred during treatment by a physician of an injury, and is paid in lieu of any other policy benefits.

TRIAL APPLICATION: A documented request from an individual to an underwriter to review an extensive and/or serious medical history for the purposes of making a conditional offer under which disability income coverage may be written.

U

UNDERWRITING: The confidential process of reviewing and evaluating personal, financial and medical data regarding an individual for the purpose of approving or disapproving the applicant for disability income coverage.

UNEARNED INCOME: Money that will be available to an individual whether or not he is disabled, it affects the amount of disability coverage that may be purchased based on earned income.

W

WAIVER FORM: Utilized in the solicitation of disability income insurance, an individual signs this paper documenting that coverage was proposed but not accepted by the insured.

WAIVER OF PREMIUM: A policy provision that specifies the exemption of the insured from making premium payments following a specified number of days of disability, until the insured recovers. In many cases, any premium paid during the initial days following disability is refunded.

WORKERS COMPENSATION: A system administered by each individual state that provides benefits if a worker is hurt or contracts an illness on the job.

INDEX

Need Additional Copies?

Use this handy postage-paid form to order additional copies of *Disability Income: The Sale, The Product, The Market,* 2nd Edition, by Jeff Sadler or **call 1-800-543-0874** and ask for **Operator PG** or **FAX** this form to **1-800-874-1916.**

Single copy $19.95	25 copies, ea. $16.25	250 copies, ea. $14.50
5 copies, ea. 18.50	50 copies, ea. 15.50	500 copies, ea. 13.95
10 copies, ea. 17.25	100 copies, ea. 14.95	1,000 copies, ea. 12.95

PAYMENT INFORMATION

*Add shipping & handling charges to all orders as indicated. If your order exceeds total amount listed in chart, call 1-800-543-0874 for shipping & handling charge. Any order of 10 or more or over $250.00 will be billed for shipping by actual weight, plus a handling fee. Unconditional 30 day guarantee.

Shipping & Handling (Additional)	
Order Total	Shipping & Handling
$10.00 - $19.99	$5.00
20.00 - 39.99	6.00
40.00 - 59.99	7.00
60.00 - 79.99	9.00
80.00 - 109.99	10.00
110.00 - 149.99	12.00
150.00 - 199.99	13.00
200.00 - 249.99	15.50

SALES TAX (Additional)

Sales tax is required for residents of the following states: CA, DC, FL, GA, IL, NJ, NY, OH, PA.

NATIONAL UNDERWRITER

The National Underwriter Co.
Customer Service Dept #2-PG
505 Gest Street
Cincinnati, OH 45203-1716

2-PG

Please send me_____copies of *Disability Income: The Sale, The Producct, The Market,* 2nd Edition, by Jeff Sadler (#203)

❑ Check enclosed*   ❑ Charge my VISA/MC/AmEx (circle one)   ❑ Bill me

Card #_____Exp. Date_____

Signature_____

Name_____ Title_____

Company_____

Street Address_____

City_____State _____Zip+4_____

Business Phone (_____)_____

*Make check payable to The National Underwriter Company. Please include the appropriate shipping & handling charges and any applicable sales tax.

Offer expires 12/31/96

NATIONAL UNDERWRITER

The National Underwriter Co.
Customer Service Dept #2-PG
505 Gest Street
Cincinnati, OH 45203-1716

2-PG

Please send me_____copies of *Disability Income: The Sale, The Producct, The Market,* 2nd Edition, by Jeff Sadler (#203)

❑ Check enclosed*   ❑ Charge my VISA/MC/AmEx (circle one)   ❑ Bill me

Card #_____Exp. Date_____

Signature_____

Name_____ Title_____

Company_____

Street Address_____

City_____State _____Zip+4_____

Business Phone (_____)_____

*Make check payable to The National Underwriter Company. Please include the appropriate shipping & handling charges and any applicable sales tax.

Offer expires 12/31/96

NO POSTAGE
NECESSARY
IF MAILED
IN THE
UNITED STATES

BUSINESS REPLY MAIL

FIRST CLASS MAIL   PERMIT NO. 68   CINCINNATI, OH

POSTAGE WILL BE PAID BY ADDRESSEE

The National Underwriter Co.
Customer Service Dept. #2-PG
505 Gest Street
Cincinnati, OH 45203-9928

NO POSTAGE
NECESSARY
IF MAILED
IN THE
UNITED STATES

BUSINESS REPLY MAIL

FIRST CLASS MAIL   PERMIT NO. 68   CINCINNATI, OH

POSTAGE WILL BE PAID BY ADDRESSEE

The National Underwriter Co.
Customer Service Dept. #2-PG
505 Gest Street
Cincinnati, OH 45203-9928